Safe for Democracy

SAFE FOR DEMOCRACY
A HISTORY OF AMERICA, 1914-1945

JOSEPH M. SIRACUSA

Reader in History
University of Queensland

REGINA BOOKS
Claremont, California

Library of Congress Cataloging-in-Publication Data

Siracusa, Joseph M.
    Safe for democracy : a history of America, 1914-1945 / Joseph M.
Siracusa
    p. cm.
    Includes bibliographical references.
    ISBN 0-941690-49-0 : $26.95. -- ISBN 0-941690-50-4 (pbk.) : $12.95
1. United States--History--1913-1921. 2. United States-History--1919-1933.
3. United States--History--1913-1945. 4. World War, 1914-1918--United
States. 5. World War, 1939-1945--United States. I. Title.
E766.S58 1993   93-18839
973.91--dc20   CIP

Regina Books
Post Office Box 280
Claremont, California 91711

Manufactured in the United States of America.

CONTENTS

for the only woman in my life

PREFACE

I have attempted in the following pages to write a brief, narrative history of the United States between the two world wars, from 1914 to 1945. Organizing my chapters around the various presidential administrations, I have sought to focus on American behavior at home and abroad. Within this context two major interrelated themes emerge. Domestically, American society continued the process of industrialization and urbanization that had begun in the late nineteenth century. Industry, and agriculture to a lesser degree, increasingly developed into big business absorbing vast amounts of capital and controlled by a corporate elite only theoretically answerable to stockholders. "Organizational" or corporate capitalism largely supplanted the earlier more individualistic type; in a very real sense, then, corporate capitalism nationalized American industry and finance. Urban growth accompanied industrialism and, as more Americans lived in the cities, posed vast new social problems of employment, housing, education, health and recreation. Rural habits and traditions gradually gave way to social modes and thought more suitable to urban life, though the transition often was disturbing and painful.

Government also had to adjust and expand its functions beyond its traditional scope. In 1914 the federal government was still comparatively a small enterprise; challenges of the next three decades transformed it almost beyond belief until it touched almost every aspect of American life. Before the New Deal the majority of Americans did not expect government to do anything for them; they did not think that government could or should do anything for them. By 1945, and against the great weight of tradition, Americans had finally become persuaded to look to Washington for help. In this sense, the New Deal was a political revolution.

The second theme of this work relates to foreign affairs. Because of its industrial growth and vast wealth, and consequent interest in foreign markets, the United States became one of the foremost great world powers whose very existence necessarily affected the international balance of power. American actions as a nation, whether as positive attempts to mold events abroad or as negative efforts to enjoy material abundance in political isolation, probably could not help but affect the course of world history. Here, too, Americans found it difficult to adjust to changing conditions. Despite involvement in World War I, which should have made it plain that the United States could not insulate itself from world distress and conflict, many Americans clung to traditional foreign policy attitudes and refused to allow the nation to play the kind of constructive political role that its own enlightened interests demanded in the Twenties and Thirties. Yet economic and educational forces, and the sheer exigency of events, culminating in the nation's participation in World War II, gradually broke down the isolationist psychology and prepared the nation for the American diplomatic revolution that accompanied the defeat of Nazi Germany and the rise of Stalinist Russia.

St. Lucia, Queensland   Joseph M. Siracusa
February 2, 1993

Chapter 1

THE GREAT DEPARTURE

In remote Sarajevo on June 28, 1914, an assassination ignited a crisis that culminated in a major world war. Gavrilo Princip, an ardent Serbian nationalist and member of a terrorist group, the Black Hand, mortally wounded Archduke Franz Ferdinand, heir to the Austro-Hungarian throne, and his beloved wife Sophia. Blaming Serbian authorities for the political murder, the Austrian government decided to crush or humiliate Serbia and end its constant threat to the stability of the multi-national Hapsburg empire. When Belgrade failed to comply fully with its ultimatum, Austria-Hungary declared war against Serbia on July 28. Because of Europe's rival alliances and age-old ambitions and passions, the war could not be localized. Within a few bewildering days, the principal powers found themselves engulfed in war. Germany joined her ally Austria (the Central Powers) against Russia, France, and Great Britain (the Entente or Allied Powers) in a titanic struggle for mastery of the continent. Germany violated Belgium's neutrality in an attempt to eliminate France from the war, Japan came in as Britain's ally in the Far East, and Italy joined the Entente in 1915. Eventually Turkey, Bulgaria, Rumania, and Greece also became immersed in the great struggle.

To most Americans it seemed incredible that the most civilized powers of Europe should plunge the world into war. Thoughtful if optimistic people had ignored previous crises threatening a large armed conflict in Europe, confident that the world had outgrown such madness. After recovering from the initial shock, Americans rejoiced that their country stood apart from the folly of the Old World, saved by its geography and by its policy of abstention from foreign alliances and entanglements. They applauded President Woodrow Wilson when he proclaimed official neutrality and urged his fellow citizens to impartiality of thought as well as speech. One newspaper editor summed up the prevailing sentiment: "Peace-loving citizens...will now rise up and tender a hearty vote of thanks to Columbus for having discovered America."

PROPAGANDA CAMPAIGNS

Impartiality of sentiment proved to be an impossible goal. The major ethnic groups in America's melting pot understandably sympathized with the countries of their origin. In 1914 approximately one-third of the American population of nearly ninety-two million people were "hyphenated Americans," either foreign born or with one or both parents immigrants. Eight million German-Americans sympathized with the cause of the Central Powers, joined by many of the four million Irish-Americans embittered by centuries of English rule of Ireland, and by many of the Russian-hating American Jewry. Old-stock Americans, on the other hand, tended to align with the Entente Powers, reflecting cultural and economic bonds with England and the traditional Franco-American friendship. Moreover, German-American relations had been slowly deteriorating for several decades as a result of economic competition, rivalry over Samoa, and misunderstandings over the Philippines during the Spanish-American War. By 1914 many Americans regarded imperial Germany and its blustering Kaiser Wilhelm II as the very incarnation of militarism and autocracy.

Both the Entente and the Central Powers undertook propaganda campaigns designed to win popular approval for their causes in America. German spokesmen depicted their country as fighting a war imposed on it by Russian imperialism and French desires to revenge their defeat in the 1870 Franco-Prussian conflict. A secret and effectively organized British propaganda machine, known as Wellington House, came under the direction of Charles Masterman. It had a special branch for America directed by Sir Gilbert Parker, aided by the young historian Arnold Toynbee among others. Utilizing such guides as *Who's Who*, Parker's staff compiled a carefully selected mailing list of influential Americans, who ultimately received a stream of propaganda pamphlets, books, and other materials. Weekly surveys of the American press facilitated the shaping of propaganda to appeal to ethnic, religious, and social groups. British propagandists depicted the Entente as fighting a defensive war against a ruthless and inhumane enemy who had cruelly violated Belgian neutrality (a "scrap of paper") and emphasized the necessity of upholding democracy and decency against German autocracy and militarism. German propagandists found it difficult to portray the Central Powers as waging a defensive war when their troops stood on Belgian and French soil. Moreover, Germany introduced new weapons and tactics that seemed barbarous: poison gas, dirigible aerial bombardments of cities, and submarine attacks against noncombatant enemy passenger and merchant vessels. Because Britain controlled the seas and the trans-Atlantic cables, German propagandists also had much difficulty in getting direct news from Germany into the United States. The majority of major American newspapers and magazines, such as the *New York Times*, tended to adopt a pro-Allied line in editorials and coverage of the war.

Although few historians now attribute United States intervention in the war to the effects of propaganda, the more intensive British campaign undoubtedly had a cumulative impact on the American public. British propagandists effectively utilized blunders such as the German execution in 1915 of Nurse Edith Cavell, a British nurse caught as a spy in occupied Belgium, and the alleged German atrocities and war crimes related in the famed Lord Bryce Report in 1915 to portray Germany's rulers as barbarous and utterly ruthless. The Bryce Report, endorsed by eminent British historians and journalists, contained exaggerated or unproven stories of deliberate German massacres, rapes, and destruction supposedly inflicted upon occupied Belgium and France. The famous affair of Dr. Albert's briefcase followed closely on the heels of the first submarine crisis and the release of the Bryce Report. Dr. Heinrich Albert, one of the German officials in America responsible for propaganda, somehow lost his briefcase on a New York city elevated train; American agents following him quickly picked it up. Its contents, published in the American press, revealed German propaganda activities and touched off a major spy scare that discredited the German effort. Of course, a majority of Americans had been at least mildly pro-Ally when the war began, before British propaganda and German blunders had any real effect. Yet British efforts strengthened that favorable predisposition and probably helps explain why the United States accepted Allied maritime war measures more readily than it did those of Germany. British propaganda probably also made it easier for the United States eventually to enter the struggle against Germany. Nevertheless, the majority of Americans during 1915 and 1916 agreed with President Wilson that the United States should remain neutral.

THE GERMAN "MENACE"

An influential "realistic" minority in the United States viewed the European war as deeply significant for the security and economic interests of the American nation. For some years a number of Americans had observed Germany with distrust, suspecting the Kaiser's government of seeking coaling stations, naval bases, and perhaps even colonies in the Caribbean and in South America. These fears reflected the fact that both the United States and Germany, industrially progressive and dynamic nations, emerged nearly simultaneously as great powers on the world scene. Army War College and Navy General Board planners saw Germany as the one major power most likely to challenge American hegemony in the Western Hemisphere. Theodore Roosevelt, Admiral Alfred T. Mahan, Henry Cabot Lodge, journalist Walter Lippmann, and academicians George Louis Beer and Amos S. Hershey, to name a few, at one time or another held that Germany was a potential menace and valued British sea power as protecting the Western Hemisphere.

In an article in *The Independent* in 1909, Amos S. Hershey, Professor of Political Science at Indiana University, illustrated these fears. He described Germany as a threat to American interests and to world peace, and he urged an Anglo-American alliance to meet the danger. Hershey predicted that "the people of the United States could hardly remain neutral in a war between

Germany and Great Britain which might possibly end in German naval supremacy." An English observer, the well-known journalist Sydney Brooks, concluded in 1909 that an influential minority of Americans perceived that Germany was America's problem as well as Britain's. Brooks foresaw that in case of an Anglo-German war the United States would practice a benevolent neutrality toward England. If Germany should threaten American trade in foodstuffs with the British Isles, he concluded, the United States might enter the war on Britain's side.

When the European conflict began in 1914, a number of thoughtful Americans concluded that America's own interests—national security, economics, and the preservation of democratic institutions—required an Entente victory. They feared that a German triumph would replace British with German sea power and would dangerously isolate the United States in the Atlantic and Pacific Oceans. These Americans, of course, were not simply "realists"; underlying their concepts of endangered national interests lay a strong conviction that democracy was threatened by German militarism and statism. "Prussian autocracy" soon became the stereotype to symbolize that ideological threat as well as the security danger. Whether primarily realistic or idealistic, this body of opinion made it easier for the United States eventually to enter the war against Germany.

A number of high administration officials and advisers held similar views, particularly the influential Colonel Edward M. House and Robert Lansing. House, an able and wealthy politician from Texas, attached himself to Wilson during the 1912 elections. With an acute understanding of Wilson's psychology, the Colonel astutely mixed flattery with an apparently selfless interest and quickly became the new President's most intimate adviser. In his "gray eminence" role as a power behind the throne House became an important factor in shaping Wilson's policies. Lansing, the son-in-law of a former Secretary of State, John Watson Foster, and uncle of a later Secretary, John Foster Dulles, entered the State Department as Counselor or second-in-command in 1914 with an extensive background in international law and arbitration. Formal, precise, and with a keenly analytical mind, Lansing also exerted much influence in framing neutrality policies. Wilson and

Secretary of State William Jennings Bryan depended heavily upon
Lansing's knowledge and experience in international relations,
particularly during the early months of neutrality.

Colonial House made several wartime trips to Europe on
special missions for President Wilson. These persuaded him that
Germany represented unrestrained militarism dangerous to the
peace of the world. He commented on one occasion, late in 1915,
that the Allies should know that "we considered their cause our
cause, and that we had no intention of permitting a military
autocracy [to] dominate the world if our strength would prevent it."
Yet for a long time House thought that the preferable outcome of
the war would be not total defeat for Germany but a limited Allied
victory to curb Germany but still leave her powerful enough to
restrain the expansionist tendencies of Czarist Russia.

Lansing essentially agreed with the Colonel, but he thought
German power should be completely shattered. A German victory
or even a stalemate in the war would be harmful to the security and
economic interests of America. Moreover, in his view, democratic
principles and institutions necessitated the defeat of German
autocracy and militarism. In a private memorandum, in July of
1915, Lansing wrote: "I have come to the conclusion that the
German Government is utterly hostile to all nations with
democratic institutions because...[its leaders] see in democracy a
menace to absolutism and the defeat of the German ambitions for
world domination." Therefore the United States should do no more
than mildly protest against Allied acts while holding Germany
fully accountable for her violations of neutral rights. He also hoped
to reduce or eliminate German influence and intrigue in Latin
America, especially in Mexico, and to enhance American security
by purchase of the Danish West Indies (which he obtained in 1916
for $25 million).

President Wilson initially reacted to the outbreak of the
European war with sympathy for Great Britain and France as
fighting defensively against the aggressive Central Powers. He
soon achieved a more balanced and less emotional view that the
causes of the conflict were more complex and responsibility more
diffuse than he had thought. Yet, because of his deep admiration of
the British government and its traditions, he had a greater trust in

the Allied than in the German leaders. The British government appeared to Wilson, at least until 1916, to be seeking more reasonable war goals than its opponents. Wilson apparently agreed with House that a German victory was undesirable and its threat might necessitate American intervention. On one occasion, he agreed with the Colonel's remark that "if Germany won it would change the course of our civilization and make the United States a military nation." Nevertheless, the President did not think of Germany as an immediate menace to the vital interest of the United States. He earnestly believed in the wisdom of the continued neutrality and he made great efforts to keep the nation out of the conflict.

THE PERILS OF NEUTRALITY

Shielding the nation from the material effects of the war proved as impossible as achieving genuine impartiality of thought and speech. The war disrupted the flow of trade to Europe and worsened an economic recession already underway in the United States. Shortages developed in certain materials normally imported from Europe. For example, the United States had imported dyes from Germany before the war, but now, cut off from such imports by the Allied blockade, Americans had little choice but to develop their own dye industry. Finer grades of optical glass could no longer be obtained from Germany, and some American astronomers had to delay the completion of planned telescopes until after the war. Entente orders for food, raw materials, and munitions soon began to flow in, however, and the American economy quickly recovered from the slump and went on to a booming prosperity destined to last until the end of the war. Yet the war boom had its penalty, for Allied purchases caused shortages of some materials for home consumption and triggered rising prices. In accordance with its traditional policy and with international practice, the United States opened its markets to all the contending powers and freely permitted private citizens to sell munitions and war materials to the belligerents. Although theoretically even-handed, the trade benefitted the Entente countries because of their control of the seas. American exports to Europe vastly increased. Trade with the Allies by 1917 rose to 184 per cent above peacetime levels. Vast quantities of food, fiber, and metals, and over $1 billion worth of munitions flowed across the Atlantic to the Allies.

The one-sided war trade in effect made the United States an integral part of the Entente war effort. Disillusioned postwar critics later charged that these economic forces eventually pulled the United States into the war against Germany. Although the trade produced much bitterness in Germany, the evidence does not support that interpretation. The majority of Americans welcomed the war boom, and the administration naturally defended the commerce as neutral and desirable for the economy, but it never considered entering the struggle merely to ensure continued prosperity. Moreover, most Americans, officials and private citizens, assumed that the Allies would win a war of attrition. Germany's unrestricted use of submarine warfare in 1917 aimed at not only disrupting the war trade with America but cutting off all commerce and starving England into submission.

The burgeoning war trade also brought financial bonds with the Entente Powers. At first the administration, upon Secretary Bryan's recommendation in August 1914 frowned upon private loans to the warring powers as inconsistent with "the true spirit of neutrality." Wilson and his advisers, however, soon perceived that the so-called loan ban conflicted with the country's interest in the expanding war trade. If the Allies could not obtain sufficient credit and loans to finance their purchases, war orders would dry up and prosperity disappear. Consequently the administration in October 1914 decided to permit credit arrangements, and it abandoned the rest of the ban in the fall of 1915. As Lansing wrote the President, retention of the ban would mean "restriction of outputs, industrial depression, idle capital, financial demoralization, and general unrest and suffering among the laboring classes" of America. By early 1917, American bankers and private investors had lent the Allies nearly $2.33 billion, largely guaranteed against an Allied defeat by securities and other collateral.

American neutrality, though not planned that way, clearly operated in favor of the Allied cause. It was almost inevitable, granted Allied control of access to the American market. Obviously, the United States, whether passive or active in world affairs, could not help but exert a significant influence in the international arena.

At the beginning of the war Americans argued with the British rather than the Germans over neutral rights on the high seas. As in the Napoleonic Wars, Britain used her vast naval power to strangle her opponents by imposing drastic restrictions on neutral commerce with Europe. She greatly expanded contraband lists of goods subject to seizure and effectively prevented direct trade with Germany even in non-military materials. The Royal Navy halted American ships and often seized cargoes consigned to neutral European countries, presumably destined for overland re-exportation to Germany and Austria. In alleged retaliation to the German submarine campaign, the British government in March 1915 proclaimed a blockade of the Central Powers and nearby neutrals.

The State Department began a long campaign of protests against these Allied interferences as contrary to international law and the rights of neutrals. Although its notes did not lack sharpness, the State Department never pressed controversies to the point of a possible diplomatic rupture. For example, the long American note to Britain of October 21, 1915, one of its strongest to the Allies, denied the legality of the blockade and condemned interferences with neutral cargoes, but it ended with a mild expression of hope that future British action would be guided by law rather than expediency. Most American trade went to the Allies anyhow, and it would have been economically self-destructive to permit disputes over neutral rights to disrupt it. Moreover, Wilson and House trusted and admired English leaders such as Sir Edward Grey, the Foreign Secretary. In fact Grey at first managed relations with America with a large degree of understanding, and he made some concessions thereby strengthening the moral as well as economic ties between the two countries. For example, when Britain deemed it necessary to treat cotton as contraband, it softened the effects upon the American South by purchasing surplus cotton. In the State Department, Lansing labored to prevent diplomatic controversies with Great Britain from becoming too acrimonious. In his view, American interests dictated the avoidance of a break, and he was aware of the precedents created by the Union Navy during the Civil War in interfering with neutral commerce. Therefore, in his words, "Everything was submerged in verbosity."

Washington reacted less tolerantly to Germany's submarine warfare. German navalists, their surface fleet virtually bottled up in the North sea by the British, turned eagerly to the underseas weapon as a means of challenging enemy control of the seas and carrying the war home to Great Britain. On February 4, 1915, allegedly retaliating for Allied mining of the North Sea, the German Foreign Office proclaimed that belligerent shipping in a zone around the British Isles would be subject to destruction even though it would not always be possible to save crews and passengers. Germany cautioned neutral vessels to avoid the area, claiming that Allied use of neutral flags and the ramming of U-boats on the surface made it impossible always to observe the customary procedure of "visit and search." Accidental attacks on neutral ships therefore sometimes could not be avoided. Wilson refused to accept these justifications and in a note sent on February 10 expressed "grave concern" at the Berlin proclamation. Rejecting the legality of the German position, he warned that if violations of American rights occurred it would be necessary "to hold the Imperial German Government to a strict accountability for such acts...and to take any steps it might be necessary to take to safeguard American lives and property...on the high seas."

The strict accountability note clearly opposed what Germany regarded as the most efficient use of the submarine. In the American view, neutral citizens and ships had the right freely to use the high seas subject only to visit and search by belligerent warships to intercept war contraband goods. Apparently President Wilson and Lansing adopted the strict accountability policy primarily to defend the nation's honor and rights and to protect its economic interests against what they deemed an illegal and inhumane method of warfare. They did not consider possible alternatives, such as requesting American ships and citizens to avoid the submarine zone.

On May 7, 1915, the German *U-20* was off the Irish coast heading for home port when it unexpectedly sighted the pride of the British trans-Atlantic fleet, the *Lusitania,* in its periscope. The captain of the *Lusitania*, nearing the end of an uneventful voyage from the United States, failed to take the normal defensive measure of zigzagging and had reduced speed preparatory to the final run into port. The *U-20* stalked its prey and at 2:10p.m. fired one torpedo into the starboard side of the great passenger ship. The Cunard liner came to a stop and began to list to starboard; it sank within eighteen minutes with the loss of 1198 passengers and crew, including 128 American citizens. A feeling of indescribable horror and outrage swept across the United States at news of the sinking.

Fearing the imminence of war, Secretary Bryan throughout the crisis pled with the President for a mild course. He argued that citizens voluntarily entering the war zone aboard Allied passenger or merchant vessels contributed to their own deaths by negligence and must not be permitted to embroil the nation in controversies likely to lead to hostilities. The government should not seem to argue that the mere presence of an American aboard a belligerent ship immunized it from German attack, for that would amount to a condemnation of U-boat warfare in general. Moreover, he pointed out, the German public already felt embittered at the one-sided American war trade with the Allies. The American government, therefore, ought to make every effort to avoid the appearance of official partiality toward the Allies and inflexibility toward Germany. Bryan was also disturbed by the presence of contraband goods, including cartridges and shrapnel, in the cargo of the *Lusitania*: "A ship carrying contraband should not rely upon passengers to protect her from attack—it would be like putting women and children in front of an army."

President Wilson agreed with Lansing rather than Bryan. Strict accountability applied not only to Americans aboard American ships but also to citizens travelling on Allied passenger vessels. He viewed the attack on the *Lusitania* and the destruction of noncombatant and neutral lives as an indefensible and immoral act contrary to international law and neutral rights. Nevertheless, the President refused to be swept by emotion into belligerency; he remarked at Philadelphia on May 10 that "There is such a thing as a man too proud to fight,...a nation being so right that it does not need to convince others by force that it is right." Therefore he adopted a firm course condemning ruthless underseas warfare and demanding that Germany comply with his interpretation of international law. The first *Lusitania* note sent to Berlin on May 13 vigorously upheld American rights and expressed confidence that the German government would disavow its illegal acts and make reparation.

The German government failed to comply with the American demands. It claimed that the *Lusitania* had carried troops and hidden armaments, thus becoming in effect a warship subject to destruction. The evidence failed to substantiate those charges, although the Lusitania had carried some munitions. Unable to persuade the President to postpone the issue for postwar settlement, Bryan resigned on June 9, to be succeeded as Secretary by Robert Lansing. Apparently Bryan hoped to mobilize peace sentiment against the administration's policies. He had little success, for the majority of the press while sharply criticizing him for abandoning his post at a crucial time also endorsed Wilson's cautious but firm handling of the crisis. The second American note went to Berlin on the same day as Bryan's resignation, reiterating previous demands. Again Germany failed to give a satisfactory response, although it offered a pledge of safety for American passenger vessels; the mere presence of neutral citizens on a belligerent vessel, Berlin declared, could not be permitted to immunize it from attack. The German government obviously hoped to avoid war, but it was unwilling to abandon use of the submarine. Wilson also wanted to prevent a diplomatic rupture if at all possible. The third American note, on July 21, rejected the German defense as unsatisfactory but only warned that any repetition involving American lives would be viewed as "deliberately unfriendly."

A period of quiet negotiation followed Wilson's third note, as both governments sought to avoid direct confrontation. Wilson had retreated from his initial general condemnation of submarine warfare and in effect accepted use of the U-boat as long as American rights were not violated. Yet the President had committed American prestige and honor to holding Germany fully and immediately accountable for the loss of American lives through undersea warfare. Other alternatives had been ruled out and the policy of the United States toward the issue henceforth was comparatively inflexible.

The torpedoing of another British passenger liner, the *Arabic*, on August 19, ended the brief lull. Two American lives were lost in the attack. Although House and Lansing advised stern measures, the President again sought to defend the nation's rights and still preserve peace. He was aware of the deep cleavage between those Americans who demanded more vigorous measures against Germany and the vast majority of citizens who wanted national rights to be upheld but peace also to be preserved. House recorded in his diary, "I am surprised at the attitude he [Wilson] takes. He evidently will go to great lengths to avoid war." The President directed Lansing to enter into negotiations with the German Ambassador, Count Johann von Bernstorff.

The German Chancellor, Theobald von Bethmann-Hollweg, feared that war with the United States would have disastrous results for Germany. He recognized that the United States would bring almost unlimited financial strength, industrial resources, and fresh manpower into the struggle. Although under pressure within Germany for fuller use of the submarine, the Chancellor temporarily obtained the support of the military leaders, who were apprehensive about increasing the country's enemies. Consequently, he found it possible to make sufficient concessions to the United States to avoid a break while not entirely renouncing use of the U-boat. The *Arabic* controversy ended with a German pledge not to sink passenger liners without warning and without provisions for the safety of those on board. Significantly, the pledge applied only to passenger liners and not to all merchant vessels. Only a truce had been achieved; the larger issue remained unresolved.

POLITICS AND THE WAR

As German-American relations worsened, more and more Americans, alarmed at their nation's comparative military weakness, urged a program of preparedness upon the President and the Congress. Patriotic groups such as the National Security League and the American Defense Society called for more money for the navy and especially the army. General Leonard Wood initiated what became known as the "Plattsburg Idea," a semi-military training of civilian volunteers in special summer camps. Colleges and universities also began to place greater emphasis upon military science courses and R.O.T.C. programs for their students. Ex-president Theodore Roosevelt quickly became one of the leading spokesmen for preparedness. As editor of *The Outlook*, Roosevelt at first had supported neutrality, but soon he advocated a more aggressive course. He raged at Wilson's apparently interminable exchanges of notes with the belligerents as dishonourable and unworthy of a great nation. Morality as well as the national interest required that the country should enter the war on the Allied side, he believed: "it is well to remember that there are things worse than war."

Many progressives and peace advocates, however, strongly resisted the call for military preparedness. Their solution to diplomatic problems lay in ending the war, not preparing to enter it. War, in their view, resulted from selfish economic pressures and competition for markets and resources. Moreover, military preparations and war might well kill the domestic reform movement and erode or destroy democratic rights and liberties at home. They demonstrated their earnestness, if not their practicality, when a group of pacifists persuaded industrialist Henry Ford to charter the ship *Oscar II* for a special peace mission to Europe in December 1915 to attend what its planners called a continuous "peace conference" at The Hague. Unfortunately for the cause of such pacifists as Rosika Schwimmer, who had sold Ford on the plan, the automobile tycoon had only the vaguest concept of the conference, and he was vulnerable to cranks who quickly joined his venture. Ford aroused ridicule when he proclaimed his intention to "get the boys out of the trenches by Christmas." Most of the well-known peace advocates thereupon wisely decided to stay home. Needless to say, Ford's naive gesture failed.

The crisis with Germany in the first half of 1915 and the growing popular appeal of the preparedness movement finally persuaded the President. In the fall of 1915 the administration presented a plan for heavy outlays for defensive purposes. The naval program called for construction of ten battleships, six battle cruisers, ten cruisers, and numerous other craft within five years, with parity with the British to be achieved by 1925. The plan also proposed that the regular army be substantially enlarged and the National Guard in effect replaced by a Continental Army reserve of 400,000 men.

Wilson's recommendations ignited a furious political debate and split progressive ranks. While many progressives could agree with Wilson on preparedness, others fearful of doing anything that might encourage war joined the pacifists. A group of peace leaders, including Oswald Garrison Villard and Jane Addams of Hull House, formed the League to Limit Armaments, while Miss Addams also joined other feminist advocates in creating the Women's Peace Party. At least thirty Democratic members of Congress, mostly from the South and West, including Claude Kitchin of North Carolina, the majority leader in the House, openly rebelled against the President's leadership. Wilson appealed to the Republicans for support in Congress and early in 1916 undertook a speaking tour in the midwestern states where he defended preparedness as necessary to safeguard the Western Hemisphere. America, he declared, "must play her part in keeping this conflagration from spreading on this side of the sea." Although compelled to accept a number of compromises, Wilson obtained the approval of Congress for doubling the size of the army (to about 220,000 men), greater federal authority over the National Guard, and a vastly accelerated construction program for the navy. Congress created a Council of National Defense to advise the President and authorized a federal Shipping Board to own and operate merchant ships and to regulate the merchant marine.

On March 24, 1916, a German U-boat torpedoed the *Sussex*, an unarmed French channel steamer. Although no American lives were lost and the vessel did not sink, the attack clearly violated the *Arabic* pledge. Lansing advised immediate severance of relations with Germany, but Wilson again resorted to diplomacy. On April 18, the President solemnly warned the German government that he would sever diplomatic relations unless ruthless U-boat warfare against belligerent merchant and passenger ships immediately ceased.

Despite mounting demands within Germany for increased use of the submarine, Chancellor Bethmann-Hollweg again managed to persuade the Kaiser and his military chiefs to avoid a rupture. In the *Sussex* pledge of May 4 Germany promised that unresisting belligerent merchant and passenger vessels would not be attacked without warning and without provisions for the safety of those aboard. Ominously, however, the pledge reserved freedom of action if the American government should fail to obtain Allied agreement to "freedom of the seas" for neutrals to trade with either side in the war.

A marked deterioration in Anglo-American relations followed the *Sussex* crisis and apparently increased Wilson's conviction that America must preserve its neutrality. Faced with a desperate war with Germany, the British government felt compelled to tighten its blockade to increase controls over neutral countries. The British subjected neutral mails to censorship and publicly blacklisted neutral firms and individuals suspected of trading with Germany. It released a list of 85 American businesses and citizens to be denied use of all British owned insurance, supplies, and other facilities. Such blatant defiance of American sensibilities caused President Wilson to seek and obtain retaliatory legislation from Congress. An act authorized the executive to withhold clearances and port facilities from foreign ships refusing to transport American goods, but Wilson did not use it for the simple reason that it would interfere with exports to the Allies and thereby endanger America's warborn prosperity.

The popularity of the peace issue in the election of 1916 further strengthened Wilson's neutrality. Since Theodore Roosevelt had returned to the fold and the Progressive Party had collapsed, the Republicans seemed to be in a good position to regain the White House. Charles Evans Hughes resigned from the Supreme Court to accept the presidential nomination on the Republican ticket. Hughes spoke of "straight Americanism" and greater executive firmness in foreign policy but played for the pro-German vote, conferring with German-American and Irish-American leaders and indicating a course of strict neutrality toward the European war. Unfortunately he could not escape the more bellicose support of Theodore Roosevelt, which enabled the Democrats to portray Hughes and the Republicans as pro-war. Moreover, party factional strife between conservative and progressive elements hurt his campaign, especially in California, where he unintentionally snubbed Governor Hiram Johnson, and in other western states.

Wilson appealed to progressive sentiment by supporting a series of reform measures of the type he had earlier opposed as class legislation or infringement of states' rights. He appointed to the Supreme Court the liberal Jewish lawyer, Louis Brandeis, despite furious conservative resistance; he obtained approval from Congress for a system of federal farm loan banks to make long-term farm loans, a federal workmen's compensation act, the Keating-Owen child labor act that prohibited goods in interstate commerce made by children under fourteen years of age, and the Adamson Act imposing an eight-hour work day on the railroads. In contrast to the more conservative tone of the Republicans, the Democrats successfully identified their party with the interests of labor and social justice. Into Wilson's coalition came the more advanced wing to the progressive movement, many disillusioned former supporters of Roosevelt, and organized labor, especially the leaders of the American Federation of Labor. After the dramatic response at the Democratic Convention to the slogan that Wilson had "kept us out of the war," the President capitalized on the obvious peace sentiment of most citizens by charging that the election of Hughes would mean war. As a Democratic newspaper advertisement phrased the issue of the people:

You are Working—Not Fighting!

Alive and Happy—Not Cannon Fodder!

Wilson and Peace with Honor?

or

Hughes with Roosevelt and War?

The effort of certain Irish-American spokesmen to attack Wilson's allegedly pro-British attitude failed to divert many Irish voters from their traditional Democratic loyalties. When Jeremiah O'Leary of the "American Truth Society," an anti-British and pro-German propaganda organization, sent the President a telegram charging pro-British policies. Wilson replied publicly. "I would feel deeply mortified to have you or anybody like you vote for me. Since you have access to many disloyal Americans and I have not, I will ask you to convey this message to them." This was an effective rejoinder, especially when the Democrats charged a German and Irish-American plot to defeat Wilson by backing the Republican nominee and it became known that Hughes had conferred with O'Leary and other known pro-German spokesmen.

The early election returns indicated a Republican triumph. The Democratic "victory" dinner at the Biltmore Hotel in New York City was described as "a morgue-like entertainment" rather than a celebration. Wilson retired early that evening, resigned to his defeat. Banner headlines in some newspapers hailed Hughes as the victor and next chief executive. Later reports from the western states, however, revealed that Wilson had edged his opponent by an extremely close margin, receiving 277 electoral votes to 254 for Hughes. In popular votes Wilson got 9,129,606 to Hughes' 8,538,221. It was a victory for progressivism and peace, but the congressional results foreshadowed great difficulties for Wilson. The election pared the Democratic margin in the Senate to eight and control of the House of Representatives rested in the hands of a small number of progressives and independents.

THE END OF NEUTRALITY

Wilson always had been interested in serving as a mediator in the war. In late 1915 Colonel House had worked out with the President and Sir Edward Grey a scheme for mediation-intervention. The resultant House-Grey Memorandum of January 1916 had provided that the United States, at a time deemed propitious by the Allies, would propose a conference of the belligerents to end the war; if Germany declined or subsequently rejected reasonable terms, the United States would probably enter the war on the Allied side. Apparently House had intervention primarily in mind, but Wilson saw the plan only in terms of mediation. It failed because Allied governments opposed a negotiated peace as long as any hope remained of victory.

After the 1916 election Wilson made two direct peace moves on his own. On December 18, despite the embarrassment of a German bid for a negotiated peace on December 12, he requested a statement of war aims from all the belligerents. Neither side responded as positively as he anticipated. Undeterred, on January 22, 1917, he addressed the Senate and publicly appealed for a compromise "peace without victory" based on justice and reason, a lasting "peace among equals." His efforts failed. Both sides had expended too much blood and money, and passions were too deeply aroused, for either to accept a mere restoration of peace without extensive gains. Moreover, neither belligerent camp favored an active role for Wilson in the eventual negotiations.

The failure of these peace efforts was ominous for American neutrality. Events within Germany finally forced the Chancellor to capitulate to the navalists. Field Marshal Paul von Hindenburg and his guiding genius General Erich Ludendorff in effect had become the wartime dictators of Germany. The navalists persuaded Hindenburg and Ludendorff that unrestricted submarine warfare offered the best remaining hope for circumventing the stalemated land war and winning a decisive victory by starving Britain into submission. The navalists argued that the United States was already fully aiding the Allies, therefore its entry into the war would be a mere formality. The Kaiser concurred. Chancellor Bethmann-Hollweg and a few other officials, still dreading war with America, had no realistic option but to acquiesce. The decisive conference came at Pless on January 7. Bethmann-Hollweg, seeing that further resistance would be futile, described the decision as the "last card." "But if the military authorities consider the U-boat war essential, I am not in a position to contradict them." Hindenburg replied confidently, "We are ready to meet all eventualities." On January 31, 1917, Germany notified the United States that after February 1 all ships, belligerent and neutral, would be destroyed—presumably without warning and without safety provisions—in the waters around the British Isles.

In view of his past warnings, President Wilson had no option but to break diplomatic relations with Germany, which he did on February 3. Still reluctant to take the nation into the struggle, however, he clung to a faint hope that Germany might yet curb its submarine campaign; more than ever, it seemed to him, continued American neutrality offered the only hope to the world for a just and stable peace. Wilson apparently contemplated alternative courses short of full belligerency: the arming of American merchant vessels in defense against the U-boat (when a congressional filibuster in the Senate, led by Senator Robert La

Follette of Wisconsin and others, blocked passage of a bill for arming, Wilson armed the vessels on his own authority), or a limited naval war in which the navy would convoy American ships. These options seemed unsatisfactory, having all the disadvantages of war without its sense of national purpose and goals. The destruction of three American ships in mid-March (*Illinois, City of Memphis* and *Vigilencia*), plus the earlier sinking of the British liner *Laconia*, indicated that Germany meant to carry out its threats. The British-intercepted Zimmermann telegram also revealed Germany's hostile intentions. Arthur Zimmermann, the German Foreign Secretary, had proposed to Mexico the conclusion of an alliance against the United States in case of an American-German war—Japan also would be invited to join—and tried to tempt Mexico with the prospect of recovering former territory lost during the Mexican War in 1846-48. The British in late February turned a copy of the decoded telegram over to the State Department which released it to the American press. An aroused American public was fully convinced of German duplicity and hostility.

Wilson addressed Congress on April 2 and recommended that it formally accept the status of a belligerent, forced upon it by Germany's actions. After reviewing his efforts for peace and Germany's repeated violations of American rights, he declared that neutrality was no longer possible. The President then proclaimed the lofty goals for which America should fight:

> The world must be made safe for democracy. Its peace must be planted upon the tested foundations of political liberty. We have no selfish ends to serve. We desire no conquest, no dominion ... We are but one of the champions of the rights of mankind. We shall be satisfied when those rights have been made as secure as the faith and the freedom of nations can make them...It is a fearful thing to lead this great peaceful people into war...But the right is more precious than peace, and we shall fight for the things which we have always carried nearest our hearts—for democracy, for the right of those who submit to authority to have a voice in their own governments, for the rights and liberties of small nations, for a universal dominion of right by such a concert of free peoples as shall bring peace and safety to all nations and make the world itself at last free.

Congress and the galleries cheered and waved flags in wild abandon as the President finished speaking. Republican Senator Henry Cabot Lodge congratulated Wilson for expressing American sentiment "in the loftiest manner." Paeans of praise poured into the White House from the press and in private letters. Opposition to war of course remained within the country and in Congress, but it could not resist the tide successfully. Senator La Follette led the rear guard resistance in the Senate and Claude Kitchin in the House. They were thwarted. Congress adopted the war resolution by a vote of 82 to 6 in the Senate and 373 to 50 in the House. Most of the opposition came from certain midwestern areas where large numbers of German-Americans or Scandinavian-Americans lived, and where a type of parochial agrarian progressivism was strongest. The mood in Congress and the nation as a whole was one of reluctant acceptance of a struggle imposed by Germany. The President formally proclaimed a state of war on April 6, 1917.

In the disillusioned aftermath of the war, it became fashionable to argue that intervention had been unnecessary and unwise. Some "revisionist" writers and historians charged that the country had been duped into the struggle by British propaganda and powerful economic and financial forces interested in profits through an Allied victory. They dismissed the submarine issue as merely an excuse, or asserted that at most its unrestricted use by Germany had been caused by American lack of neutrality. Defenders of intervention, on the other hand, replied that the United States had tried to remain neutral but had been forced into the war because of Germany's illegal and aggressive acts. In recent years, a few writers have even argued that the United States fought not for any of these reasons but to defend its security against the threat of a German victory.

There can be little doubt that, despite the official position of impartiality, the United States followed a course in 1914-1917 of benevolent neutrality toward the Allies, while adopting by and large an uncompromising attitude toward Germany. This reflected strong bonds of sentiment and trade between the United States and the Allied Powers, especially Great Britain. It would be unsound to attribute the eventual entry into the war solely to the submarine issue, therefore, for other options existed beside the policy of strict accountability. Yet the U-boat provided the indisputable point of contact and hence of conflict between the two powers. The United States finally opposed ruthless submarine warfare because it endangered its legitimate economic interests, violated its neutral rights, and affronted its national honor. Moreover, by 1917 President Wilson viewed Germany as a major threat not merely to the rights and interests of the United States but to the peace and progress of the entire world. American involvement therefore seemed necessary not only to safeguard American rights and interests but to eliminate German militarism and provide the basis for an enduring peace of justice and reason. A majority of Wilson's fellow citizens agreed that Germany's actions left no other real choice. Time revealed, however, that they were much less committed to the President's vision of an ideal peace and new world order.

SUGGESTED READINGS

Bailey, Thomas A., and Paul B. Ryan. *The Lusitania Disaster* (1975).

Birnbaum, Karl E. *Peace Moves and U-Boat Warfare* (1958).

Chatfield, Charles. *For Peace and Justice: Pacifism in America, 1914-1921* (1971).

Cohen, Warren I. *The American Revisionists* (1967).

Coogan, John W. *The End of Neutrality: The United States, Britain, and Maritime Rights, 1899-1915* (1981).

Cooper, John M., Jr. *The Vanity of Power: American Isolation and the First World War, 1914-1917* (1979).

Devlin, Patrick. *Too Proud to Fight: Woodrow Wilson's Neutrality* (1975).

Gregory, Ross. *The Origins of American Intervention in the First World War* (1971).

____.*Walter Hines Page: Ambassador to the Court of St. James* (1970).

Hagedorn, Hermann. *The Bugle That Woke America* (1940).

Lansing, Robert. *War Memoirs of Robert Lansing* (1935).

Link, Arthur S. *Wilson: Confusion and Crises, 1915-1916* (1964).

__. *Wilson the Diplomatist* (1957).

__. *Wilson: The Struggle for Neutrality, 1914-1915* (1960).

__. *Woodrow Wilson: War, Revolution, and Peace* (1979).

May, Ernest. *The World War and American Isolation, 1914-1917* (1959).

Millis, Walter. *The Road to War* (1935).

Peterson, H.C. *Propaganda for War* (1939).

Smith, Daniel M. *The Great Departure: The United States and World War I, 1914-1920* (1965.)

Tansill, Charles C. *America Goes to War* (1938).

Chapter Two

WAR AND PEACE

Most Americans in early 1917, confident that the Allies were winning the war, assumed that the United States would need to send only token forces to Europe while providing economic and financial support to Germany's opponents. Even the administration shared that view. That illusion was quickly shattered when the Allies made known their desperate needs for troops as well as war materials. Arthur J. Balfour led a British war mission to the United States, rapidly followed by French, Italian, Belgian, Russian, Serbian and other groups. Received with pomp and ceremony, these visitors not only helped develop the indispensable machinery for a coalition war effort but also stimulated the enthusiasm of the American public for the great struggle. Subsequently Britain sent over Lord Northcliffe, the press tycoon, and France sent André Tardieu to head permanent commissions in America to manage war purchases. Treasury Secretary William McAdoo developed procedures to certify needs and establish priorities as well as financing, while Colonel House led a special mission to Europe in late 1917 to advance inter-Allied coordination of economic, financial, shipping, and military activities. The Allies established a joint purchasing agency in the United States and an Interallied Council on War Purchases and Finance in Paris. In these ways a large measure of order and efficiency began to be brought to the incredibly complex problems of waging a coalition war. Wilson agreed to the establishment of a Supreme War Council in Paris to concert strategy, but he balked when the Allied governments tried to broaden its function to include political decisions. The President thereby made clear his determination to retain diplomatic freedom to formulate liberal peace goals and to prevent the Allies from imposing the terms of the eventual peace settlement.

The great crusade against autocracy required the United States to convert itself into a nation at arms, mobilizing and directing its economy and manpower to the supreme goal of military victory. Reversing gears from its prewar concern with preserving competition, the administration shifted toward a planned and regulated economy. As one government official informed representatives of the steel industry: "This is a crisis and commercialism, gentlemen, must be absolutely sidetracked." The Council of National Defense had been established in 1916 to advise the President on broad questions including war production and procurement.

After the entry into the war, Wilson created a General Munitions Board to supervise the placing of war orders, but owing to difficulties with the military he replaced it with a new agency in July 1917, the War Industries Board. The WIB floundered under its first two directors, until the President overhauled and strengthened the agency in the spring of 1918 and placed it under the direction of Bernard Baruch, a wealthy Wall Street stock speculator and investor. Baruch's agency had the authority to create new facilities for production, convert existing plants to war purposes, set priorities in production and transportation, and allocate scarce materials. It curtailed nonessential civilian production, such as automobiles, and obtained a type of price-fixing on certain basic materials through pressure on industry. Relying largely on persuasion and advice, the WIB encouraged increased efficiency and productivity through standardization of styles and products, lessons that industry remembered in the postwar years. The WIB placed war contracts on a cost plus basis, leading to charges of war profiteering but providing stimulation for the construction or conversion of industrial plants for war purposes.

Armed with authority from Congress, Wilson created a number of war agencies to mobilize the economy. The Food Administration, directed by Herbert Hoover, vastly increased the production of foodstuffs to feed both the American and Allied peoples, setting high minimum prices for government purchases of wheat and pork and curbing civilian consumption by voluntary rationing and "wheatless" and "meatless" days. Wheat acreage increased from 45 million acres in 1917 to 75 million in 1919. Exports of breadstuffs to Europe rose from about 3,320,000 tons before the war to over ten million tons by 1918-1919; the export of meats, fats, and sugar also increased proportionately. The Fuel Administration increased coal production, essential for heat and industry.

The railroads posed a special problem. For a decade and a half prior to the war, labor and physical costs had risen, yet the Interstate Commerce Commission had been slow to authorize rate increases. The sudden burdens of moving military manpower and supplies to the east coast resulted in a gigantic traffic snarl in late 1917. Railroad unions demanded sharp wage hikes and unhappy shippers favored federal operation of the lines, a solution that many rail executives also privately welcomed. The administration's decision to place the railroads under federal control, operated by the Railroad Administration directed by McAdoo, reflected not only wartime needs for an efficiently integrated system but also progressive views that it was a good opportunity to demonstrate the role of government in promoting the public interest.

Shipping posed a related difficulty. For years America had depended for cargo facilities largely on British vessels, but in 1917 German U-boats were sending a phenomenal number of these ships to the bottom of the sea. Even before the war entry, Congress had authorized the Shipping Board to build or acquire merchant craft. Although an ambitious construction program at new shipyards, such as Hog Island near Philadelphia, failed to complete much tonnage prior to the Armistice, the Shipping Board acquired the necessary shipping through purchases, commandeering of vessels under construction in private shipyards, and seizure of interned German ships and of Dutch vessels in American ports. The War Trade Board regulated foreign trade, and the National War Labor Board and the War Labor Policies Board sought to protect labor's interests and to avoid disputes or strikes hampering production.

Mobilization not only increased productivity but resulted in real advances for labor. The eight-hour day spread widely, at least in principle, wages rose and working conditions improved, a US

Employment Service helped bring together workers and jobs, and the AFL grew from two million to over three million members by 1920. Large numbers of women found employment, and many blacks began to migrate from the southern states, attracted by jobs in northern cities. A number of business leaders accepted patriotic service in government agencies as "dollar-a-year men," and many intellectuals from the academic and literary worlds for the first time entered the federal service as expert advisers, technicians, and administrators. Among the less desirable side effects of the mobilization of civilians and soldiers, an influenza epidemic struck America in the autumn of 1918 and caused thousands of deaths. Housing shortages, rising rents, and some racial frictions and clashes in northern cities also resulted from the impact of the war.

Politics, behind a facade of patriotic unity, continued as usual during the war years. Both major political parties maneuvered for advantage. Democrats relied upon President Wilson's great prestige as a war leader to help them retain political power in the forthcoming 1918 mid-term elections, while Republicans seized advantage of real or alleged failures in the mobilization program to attack their opponents. The election of 1916 had given no clear mandate to either party in Congress, especially in the lower house where a handful of independents held the balance between the two factions. Divided, confused, and ill-equipped to manage its own affairs efficiently, Congress nevertheless was inclined to challenge the executive's direction of the war effort.

Theodore Roosevelt, remembering his heroic exploits in 1898, eagerly proposed to raise and lead a division of volunteers to France. Although his plan aroused great enthusiasm across the country and in Congress—and even France favored it as a morale booster in quickly bringing some American troops into action—the administration refused to approve it. Secretary of War Newton D. Baker rejected TR's project as an unwise diversion of arms and supplies; politics may also have played a part. Roosevelt called upon his hated enemy in the White House to plead in a rare display of humility for his scheme. He accepted defeat with very poor grace, and the continued maneuverings of his supporters in Congress cost him much popular support.

Although Wilson generally tried to balance Democratic and Republican appointees to the various war agencies, he encountered sharp criticism for playing politics with the war. Coal shortages, railroad tangles, lagging armaments production, and alleged administration favoring of southern cotton growers versus western wheat farmers provided ample grist for the Republican mill. Aircraft production threatened to become a major scandal until defused by Wilson. The administration had promised overoptimistically to manufacture 100,000 warplanes to sweep the Germans from the sky and thereby save countless soldier lives. Despite the expenditure of $840 million, reports revealed that little had been achieved. Wilson effectively countered critics by ordering an investigation headed by the respected Charles Evans Hughes and reorganized the Aircraft Production Board.

Wilson stoutly resisted all demands by Republican critics for a coalition war cabinet or a Civil War type of joint committee of Congress to oversee the Overman Act of 1918 which authorized the president to reorganize, abolish, or establish war agencies and to transfer funds as needed. Though the act was criticized for making the chief executive a war dictator, Wilson used his new powers sparingly.

The wartime government, which not only regulated the economy but managed it for the purposes of victory, signified a willingness to accept a more regulated economy. Many progressives welcomed the war as an opportunity to modernize the political economy. The results, temporary though they seemed to most citizens, did not all disappear with the coming of peace.

Benefitting from the Allied example and the American Civil War experience, the administration decided to rely upon conscription rather than volunteers to raise manpower of the armed services. There was to be no hiring of substitutes or purchases of exemption as during the Civil War, nor, as in the Roosevelt controversy, did the War Department want to be encumbered with "political generals" raising volunteer outfits. Many citizens, both liberals and conservatives, opposed conscription as un-American, dishonorable, and a violation of personal liberties. Several administration lieutenants, such as House Speaker Champ Clark, deserted Wilson on this issue. Some southerners also feared dire consequences would result from drafting and arming blacks.

The administration finally persuaded Congress that conscription would be more democratic and efficient than any other method. The 1917 act required all males between 21 and 30 years of age, later extended from 18 to 45, to register with their local draft boards. Draft officials assigned each district a quota and drew numbers from a lottery in Washington to determine the order of induction. The law exempted men with dependents or in vital employment; conscientious objectors on religious grounds were usually given non-combatant duties. The government, however, dealt harshly with political objectors, many of whom received heavy prison sentences. An estimated one-third of a million draft dodgers evaded registration or refused to comply with induction notices. Even so, there was far less resistance to the draft than many, recalling Civil War anti-draft riots, had feared.

Ultimately the draft conscripted nearly three million men, which combined with the National Guard and volunteers increased the armed forces to close to five million. The military hastily erected training camps to receive this flood of manpower. Life in the jerry-built camps came as a great shock to most of the trainees, as farmers, immigrants, blacks, and urban middleclass youth drawn from every section of the country, were thrown together in a new type of melting pot. The War Department found an appallingly high percentage of the men it called for examination and induction deficient in health and education. The army adopted standardized psychological testing to discern various abilities useful to the military, a technique thereafter to be utilized increasingly in civilian life—another example of the thrust of an industrial corporate society toward greater rationalization. Despite the novel and disrupting experience of military life, morale remained high. Various church organizations, the Red Cross, the Salvation Army, and the Young Men's Christian Association provided entertainment and comforts for the "boys in service." Soldiers and civilians alike sang popular war songs, such as "Over There" and "Oh! How I Hate to Get Up in the Morning."

General John J. Pershing commanded the American Expeditionary Force to France. At first only a trickle of men could be trained, equipped, and shipped to Europe, but these few raised the morale of the war-weary Allies. In the early summer of 1917 the American 1st Division paraded through the streets of Paris to a tumultuous welcome. American soldiers found life in France confusing and often complained of dirty villages and greedy merchants. The AEF's newspaper, "Stars and Strips," and improved mail services and supplies helped ease the "doughboy's" adjustment.

Pershing's AEF increased rapidly after the early spring of 1918, numbering about two million men by the time of the Armistice. At the War Department's and his insistence, the American forces were kept together as a unit rather than being dispersed among the Allied Armies. Pershing was convinced that Allied morale had so deteriorated that victory would depend primarily upon the fresh and less daunted American troops. The AEF fought courageously and well at Chateau-Thierry, Belleau Woods, St. Mihiel, and the Meuse-Argonne. It helped stem the last great German drive in 1918 and took a prominent part in Allied Generalissimo Ferdinand Foch's counter-offensive that smashed the Hindenburg Line and set the stage for the German request for peace. Although no American-built aircraft saw combat duty, the Army Air Service fought in Allied-provided craft. By the fall of 1918, Pershing commanded nearly one million troops in the battle zones and held nearly a fourth of the entire Western Front. Although the Americans suffered far smaller battle losses than the Allies (50,000 men killed to 1,700,000 Russian, 1,385,000 French, and 900,000 British troops), the addition of fresh American manpower swung the balance against the German armies and played a decisive part in the defeat of Germany. The navy convoyed supply and troop ships to Europe and engaged in anti-submarine warfare, with some battleships stationed with the British Grand Fleet to watch the German High Seas Fleet in its lair across the North Sea.

The war cost the United States approximately $33.5 billion by 1920. The Treasury raised about two-thirds of this vast sum through the sale of Liberty and Victory bonds and the remainder by taxation. A great furore ensued in Congress and the public over the wisest method of raising taxes. Conservatives favored reliance primarily upon consumption or excise taxes, while many progressives advocated shifting the burden to the wealthier citizens by steeply increasing the income tax and levying taxes on so-called excess profits or "blood money" from war production. The 1917 War Revenue Act, a compromise, increased the rate sharply on the upper income brackets and on excess profits, but also dropped the minimum level to annual incomes as low as $1000. Dissatisfied progressives denounced it as a betrayal of the average man and some called for confiscation of all incomes above $100,000 a year. Such criticism, together with mounting war expenditures, caused the rates on upper incomes to be raised even more in the 1918 and 1919 revenue acts, to 77 per cent on the highest income levels and to 65 per cent on excess profits. Despite charges of "profit-bloated" manufacturers and financiers, those acts shifted much of the taxation burden to those more able to bear it while farmers and laborers made very substantial gains in income.

Public opinion, by no means universally enthusiastic about the war in 1917, also seemed to require mobilization. A Committee on Public Information, directed by the colorful journalist George Creel, undertook to "sell" the war to the American people. Patriotic "four minute men" speakers, often well known entertainment or sports personalities, helped sell the four great Liberty Bond and the one post-armistice Victory Bond drives. Lurid movies, such as "The Beast of Berlin" and "The Prussian Cur," and war posters aroused the emotions of the American people. One poster depicted an American's reaction to German atrocities with the words, "Tell That to the Marines!" Various groups—the super-patriots, conservatives eager to counter radicalism, and ordinary citizens—demanded drastic measures to suppress opponents or critics of the war. Elihu Root, a former Secretary of State, told a cheering New York City audience in mid-1917 that "there are men walking about the streets of this city tonight who ought to be taken out at sunrise tomorrow and shot for treason." Theodore Roosevelt called for vigorous repression to cope with the opponents of war, whom he described as pacifist, socialist, IWWs (International Workers of the World, a radical syndicalist union), and "a whole raft of sexless creatures."

To deal with "disloyalty", Congress enacted the Espionage Act in 1917 and the Sabotage and Sedition Acts in 1918. These harsh laws provided heavy fines and imprisonment for anyone obstructing the draft, inciting rebellion, or aiding the enemy; denied use of the mails to disloyal publications; made sabotage a federal offense; and punished utterances deemed abusive to the American government, flag or uniform and language intended to obstruct the war effort. The Wilson administration requested from Congress formal censorship powers; however, it was rejected by the legislative branch.

President Wilson warned in his Flag Day Address in 1917, "Woe to the man or group of men that seeks to stand in our way in this day of high resolution...." The government used its legal powers to suppress pacifist and radical dissent. The post-office banned a number of pacifist and socialist books, magazines, and newspapers from the mails. The Justice Department arrested a number of critics of the war who were sentenced to long terms in prison. Eugene Debs of the Socialist Party received a sentence of ten years imprisonment for an anti-war speech. Robert Goldstein drew ten years in prison for making a movie, "The Spirit of '76," that was viewed as anti-British and pro-German propaganda.

Many "patriotic" organizations such as the American Defense Society, the National Security League, the American Anti-Anarchy Association, and the American Protective League, staged witch-hunts for individuals (especially German-Americans) suspected of being less than 100 per cent loyal supporters of the war. State and municipal councils of defense and safety also flourished, and the Justice Department encouraged these organizations to investigate disloyalty. Ostracism, boycotts, threats, whippings, and worse occurred. The madness even descended to the level of repudiating German music and culture, and the renaming of such foods as sauerkraut and hamburger ("liberty cabbage" and "liberty sausage"). Wilson made little effort to counter the hysteria, apparently because of his desire to promote national unity and his faith that sanity would be restored eventually. Perhaps too he was not displeased at the silencing of the more radical critics of his war policies. Even after the Armistice, Wilson refused to release Debs and others imprisoned for opposition to the war. Debs was freed in 1921, after Wilson was out of office, but it was not until 1923 that the last of the political offenders left prison.

While many Americans succumbed to the war hysteria, others gave serious thought to the nature of the postwar world. Many earnest peace advocates concluded that alliances and balances of power, the obvious culprits in 1914, must be supplanted by a world court and law or by an international concert of power to achieve peace and promote disarmament. The secret diplomacy of the past must be abolished and the war ended on the basis of an enlightened peace and universal democracy to lay the basis for the new world order. The League to Enforce Peace came into existence in the United States in 1915 to work for these goals—William Howard Taft, among others, joined—and a similar society existed in Great Britain.

By May of 1916, Wilson had clearly identified himself with the liberal peace program. Like most Americans, Wilson long had believed that the United States represented a new Zion among nations, freed of the militarism, autocracy, and reaction of the Old World. Its liberal values—political democracy, social mobility, private property, and economic freedoms—clearly represented the wave of the future. America had an historic mission, a sacred duty, to encourage the spread of these liberal political and economic doctrines and institutions to all mankind. He and his advisers saw World War I as the opportunity to achieve an "open-door" world that would be safe both from Prussian autocracy or old-fashioned imperialism and from the social revolutions promulgated by radical socialists such as the Russian Bolsheviks. Such a world view merged both American interests and its ideals.

Wilson concentrated on a collective security organization as the key to an equitable and enduring peace. A universal organization of states by a mutual guarantee of integrity would be able to prevent any war begun contrary to treaty obligations or enlightened world opinion. Hopefully also it could remove barriers to international trade, with the major industrial powers cooperating in developing backward areas. As the foremost economic state in the world, such an order would benefit America greatly but also presumably everyone else. In his peace move in late 1916 and early 1917, and in his war message, Wilson clearly stated America's interests in a just peace and an international concert of power to ensure its preservation. After America became a belligerent, he began to develop his thoughts into a more definite program.

Wilson recognized that the Allied governments did not share his concept of an ideal peace. In a series of secret treaties and agreements, the Allied Powers had planned a postwar division of territorial spoils, the inevitable though not necessarily evil results of a coalition war. The American government knew most of the details of these arrangements by the time of the peace conference in 1919 but did not officially recognize them. Wilson confidently expected that by the end of the war the Allies would be so dependent upon American economic and financial power that he could impose his own views of a just peace. As part of his strategy of preserving his diplomatic freedom, the United States did not enter into any formal alliances or ties with the Allies. Even in referring to the coalition, Wilson adopted the phrase the "Allied and Associated Powers," with the United States in the latter category. Although some scholars have criticized Wilson's failure to challenge directly the secret treaties, it should be noted that a coalition war presented special difficulties; any other position by the President might well have lowered Allied morale and surely would have led to disruptive arguments with the Allied governments.

In a series of speeches, President Wilson mobilized American and world opinion in support of his concept of a just peace. He and his aides articulated fully the concept of a world-wide authoritarian menace to political democracy and liberal capitalism. Most of the American intellectual community, as the writings of John Dewey and Walter Lippmann, among others, attested, shared the President's views. These officials and private citizens at first defined authoritarianism or statism principally in terms of Prussian or German autocracy. Thus Wilson in his Flag Day Address, June 14, 1917, attacked "the military masters of Germany" whose plots and aggressive actions had driven the United States into the war. Germany's rulers must be crushed or no nation could be safe from their aggressive designs. Secretary of State Lansing more intemperately described Germany as a "wild beast" led by "assassins and butchers" lusting for world domination.

If Wilson and Lansing were bad historians in these versions of German imperialism and the causes of the war, they at least reflected widely-held opinions in America and helped work up popular support for the war. At Mount Vernon, on July 4, 1917, the President flailed the Central Powers for imposing statist controls over every aspect of the lives of their own and subjected peoples, "making every choice for them and disposing of their lives and fortunes as they will." Wilson thereby sought to drive a wedge between enemy rulers and their subjects and to dampen extreme anti-Germanism in America by focusing animosity upon the Kaiser and his clique. He repeated that distinction when he rejected Pope Benedict XV's appeal for a negotiated peace in August 1917. There could be no peace, he declared, until the world had been freed "from the menace and the actual power of a vast military establishment controlled by an irresponsible government which...planned to dominate the world." Eventually the concept of authoritarianism came to include militarist Japan, which American officials privately viewed as the "Prussia of the Far East," and even more the undemocratic regime of Bolshevik Russia which after 1918 called for class war and world revolution. By 1919 Wilson and Lansing publicly described Soviet Russia as in fact as brutal, autocratic, and statist as the Kaiser's Germany, despite its professed noble aim of liberating mankind.

Wilson began preparations for peace by establishing the Inquiry, a group of scholars under the direction of Colonel House, to study war goals and to draft reports on the problems expected to arise at the eventual peace conference. Indicating progressivism's faith in experts and social planning, the President hoped these scholars would give him a "guaranteed position" for the peace negotiations—that is, a sound preparation for the independent role he intended to play. Enlisting the services of about 150 experts, the Inquiry undertook detailed geographical, economic, political and historical studies of problem areas. Most of the scholars used turned out to be specialists in American or European history, geography, and archaeology; few experts could be found in African, Middle Eastern, and Asian studies. The Inquiry labored diligently, compiling large numbers of maps and nearly 2,000 reports, ranging from the useful to the trivial. When the American peace commission sailed to Europe after the Armistice, it took many of these reports and a number of the experts to guide its work at the Paris Peace Conference.

Wilson delivered the most famous of his wartime utterances, the Fourteen Points address, to Congress on January 8, 1918. He hoped to liberalize Allied war aims, to bind the "liberal" and the "left" in Europe and America to his cause, and to woo the Russian masses away from the Bolsheviks. Listing the essential provisions of a lasting peace, Wilson stated that the enemy must evacuate all Allied territory and return Alsace-Lorraine to France; an independent Poland should be created with access to the sea; and autonomous development should be given to peoples of the Austrian and Turkish empires. He postulated certain general principles to guide the writing of the peace: open diplomacy (no more secret treaties); freedom of the seas in war and in peace; reduction of armaments to a level sufficient for national security; and the adjustment of colonial claims with consideration of the interests of the colonial peoples as well as the claimant powers. Wilson viewed his fourteenth point as the key to the peace: "A general association of nations must be formed under specific covenants for the purpose of affording mutual guarantees of political independence and territorial integrity to great and small states alike."

In subsequent addresses, Wilson added other points to his prescription for a lasting and liberal peace. Peoples and territories must not be treated as mere pawns to be allocated by the great powers, and due consideration should be accorded to the aspirations for self-government of previously oppressed nationalities. More than any other single leader in modern world history Wilson succeeded in touching the conscience and the imagination of mankind. His inspired language and exalted vision rallied liberal opinion to his cause and eventually had some effect in encouraging popular discontent within the Central Powers. The leaders of the Allied states, despite their lack of enthusiasm for the President's noble prescription for peace, dared not openly object or criticize. Wilson clearly had become the chief, if self-appointed, spokesman for the Allied and Associated States.

In essence, Wilsonian goals projected a global reform, envisioning the spread of democracy and the encouragement of freer trade throughout the world. German militarism would be destroyed and the democratized nation absorbed into a universal system characterized by political democracy, liberal capitalism, and great power cooperation within a League of Nations for peace and progress. Evolutionary change would supplant both reaction and revolution. Although most Americans thought their country alone was without selfish goals—it had no need or desire for territory or spoils—obviously Wilson's world order promised the kind of world in which the United States could be secure and flourish.

"Self-determination" of peoples became one of the most popular slogans of the war. It would be incorrect, however, to attribute the emergence of the new states of Poland, Czechoslovakia, Finland, Latvia, Lithuania, Estonia, and Yugoslavia primarily to Wilson's support. Americans and many Europeans, sharing the old liberal belief in the beneficence of nationalism, of course regarded these independence movements with sympathy, and undoubtedly Wilson's words stimulated nationalist aspirations. But the fact remains that nationalist currents ran strongly in these areas long before the war; the debacle of World War I finally made it possible to translate these hopes into reality.

Russia confronted Wilsonian liberalism with one of its severest tests. Americans had rejoiced when the March Revolution in Russia in 1917 overthrew the czarist regime and began to transform Russia into a democracy. Elihu Root led a special mission to Russia in mid-1917, and the American government extended financial ($325 million) and other aid to the new regime. Unfortunately, both American officials and private citizens failed to appreciate the depths of war-weariness in Russia, the collapse of military morale, the breakdown in transportation and the economy, and the growing influence of radical political doctrines. They too easily assumed that Russia under moderate democratic leadership would remain in the war and would continue to develop in the pattern of western liberal capitalist democracies.

The Bolshevik Revolution in November 1917 thus came as a stunning surprise. Exploiting widespread discontent and chaos, the Russian Communist or Bolshevik party clamped a ruthless dictatorial rule on Russia and promptly began to withdraw from the war against the Central Powers. Britain and France feared that Germany would now be able to shift vast numbers of troops from the Eastern to the Western Front and score a decisive victory. President Wilson felt deeply disturbed by the undemocratic nature of the new regime, while Secretary of State Lansing expressed apprehension about Communist ideology and the effort to export revolution and class warfare. The State Department, therefore, denied the new regime diplomatic recognition. That seemed realistic as well as principled, for the Soviets did not control all Russia and their survival appeared highly unlikely.

The Allies began to besiege President Wilson with pleas for armed intervention against the Bolsheviks and the restoration of an Eastern Front. At first he refused, arguing that the Russian people should be allowed to determine freely their own form of government and the impracticality of the military schemes. He finally gave in after receiving exaggerated reports of deep German penetration of Russia, including the releasing and arming of German and Austrian war prisoners. This German advance apparently endangered thousands of tons of war supplies that had been shipped from America and Europe to Russia and stock-piled at the ports of Murmansk and Archangel. Probably even more decisive to Wilson, between 45,000 and 65,000 Czechoslovak troops, previously allowed by the Russian provisional government to form and fight on the Russian front, found themselves trapped by the Bolshevik withdrawal from the war. While they were evacuating Russia, clashes between the local Soviets and the Czech legion rapidly turned into large scale hostilities.

Capitulating to these alleged military exigencies, the President in mid-1918 agreed to limited armed interventions in Siberia and northern Russia. He insisted that the intervention should not include political activity, but should confine itself to rescuing the Czechs and guarding the war supplies. He hoped, of course, that the presence of Allied and American forces would "stabilize" conditions in Russia and encourage by their mere presence the formation of a non-Bolshevik government. The Allies, however, wanted more; they sought to overthrow the Bolsheviks and restore Russia to the war. Japan increased its forces in Siberia to over 70,000 men, far in excess of the American contingent of 9,000 troops. Obviously Tokyo hoped greatly to extend Japanese influence in the area. Yet while Wilson could not completely restrain the Allies, he managed to prevent a much larger intervention. After the Armistice he refused to broaden the intervention, and he withdrew the American troops from northern Russia in 1919 and from Siberia early in 1920. Though these interventions helped create a legacy of hatred with the Bolshevik government, at least Wilson had helped to avoid a costly and probably futile all-out war.

THE COMING OF VICTORY

The Central Powers began to collapse militarily by the fall of 1918. Turkey, Bulgaria, and Austria-Hungary sued for peace. The last great German offensive on the Western Front had been checked, partly by fresh American manpower, and the Allied armies under Generalissimo Foch launched a successful counter-drive that broke the Hindenburg Line and threatened to invade Germany itself. Faced with a military disaster and a war-weary people at home, Hindenburg and Ludendorff forced the German government to request a peace based on Wilson's Fourteen Points. Although usually depicted as suffering from a temporary loss of nerve, Ludendorff merely overestimated Allied readiness for a new offensive against his weakened armies. Apparently he hoped for generous terms or at least a breathing-spell permitting him to regroup the German armies. Despite fears in Europe and America that he would be duped by the wily Germans, Wilson maneuvered with skill and probably hastened the end of the war by several months and thousands of lives. By the time the German high command decided to continue the fighting rather than accept harsh terms, German morale had shattered and the civilian officials were forced to overrule the army. The government accepted Wilson's terms, Kaiser Wilhelm fled into exile in Holland, and a German republic was formed. The Allied leaders reluctantly agreed to the so-called "Pre-Armistice Agreement" to give Germany a peace based on the Fourteen Points, though they inserted two qualifications dealing with freedom of the seas and damages inflicted upon civilians.

On November 8, Matthias Erzberger led the representatives of defeated Germany to a railway carriage in Compiègne forest where Marshal Foch and his triumphant staff presented them with armistice terms. They were harsh, designed to ensure that Germany could not renew the war. Germany must evacuate occupied territory immediately and surrender vast quantities of guns, ammunition, and other supplies. The new German government had no choice but to sign the Armistice. The guns at last fell silent on the Western Front at eleven o'clock on the morning of November 11, 1918.

TO THE PARIS PEACE CONFERENCE

Politics continued in America during the war despite lip-service to the slogan "politics is adjourned." The Republican leadership, under National Chairman Will Hayes, anticipating a return to power worked energetically to heal the 1912 breach in the party and to capture a favorable position for the 1918 and 1920 elections. Under the guise of "constructive criticism," Republicans hurled charge after charge of mismanagement and waste at Wilson and the war agencies and tried unsuccessfully to drive Secretary Baker from the War Department. Democrats suffered particularly from their failure to adopt a uniform price-fixing policy or to impose controls on scarce raw materials and manufactured goods. The administration had limited price regulations to certain basic commodities, while inflation mounted, the cost of living rose steeply, and profiteering flourished. Wilson failed to see that his war policies had lost support and counted on the electorate sharing his over-riding concern with world affairs.

Anxious to strengthen his position at the forthcoming Peace Conference, Wilson appealed to the voters in the 1918 midterm elections to vote Democratic, for "The return of a Republican majority...would...certainly be interpreted on the other side of the water as a repudiation of my leadership." Although not unprecedented, the President's appeal proved to be a major political blunder. Republicans charged that Wilson had violated his own earlier plea "that politics is adjourned" and that he had impugned the loyalty of Republican members of Congress who had cooperated in the war effort. When the Republicans won control of both houses of Congress, their leaders declared that the President had asked for a popular vote of confidence and had lost. The outcome thus impaired his position at the Peace Conference and, probably more important, made the new Congress resentful of his leadership.

In a far more serious error, the President failed to appoint a prominent Republican or any members of the Senate to the commission to negotiate the peace at Paris. He chose four persons as commissioners who either were closely connected with his administration or who lacked major political stature: Robert Lansing, Colonel House, General Tasker H. Bliss, and Henry White, a diplomat and a minor Republican. Wilson gave his opponents additional ammunition when in an unprecedented move he decided to include himself in the commission and to play a direct part in the negotiations. Critics raged that he had packed the group with yes-men and charged him with having a messiah complex. Humorist Will Rogers quipped, "There was so much argument about who was to go, that Wilson says, 'I tell you what, we will split 50-50—I will go and you fellows [Republicans] can stay.'" Wilson brushed aside prominent Republicans whom he could have selected as commissioners: Senator Lodge as personally unacceptable, and Elihu Root and ex-President William Howard Taft as too conservative. Moreover, the President made no effort to consult powerful senators on the peace terms, despite the obvious fact that any treaty would require approval by the Senate. Apparently Wilson felt so certain of his own rectitude and vision, and so resentful of criticism and opposition, that he ignored the probable consequences of his actions. By so doing he virtually ensured that the Senate would challenge his leadership in foreign affairs and that the peace treaty would become a partisan issue.

The *S.S. George Washington* sailed for Europe on December 4, 1918, bearing the first American President to visit the Old World while in office. Wilson took with him his wife and members of the American delegation, including scholars and experts from the Inquiry. Europeans went wild with joy at the arrival of the

American Prophet. Parisians gave him a tumultuous reception, reportedly unequalled since Napoleon's triumphal entries. Wilson passed under one huge banner proclaiming "Honor to Wilson the Just." He also briefly toured England and Italy. Everywhere the multitudes hailed him as the deliverer of mankind, the hope of the future. Unfortunately, too many of the Allied peoples envisioned justice as crushing Germany into the ground. Equally unfortunately, these wildly enthusiastic receptions apparently strengthened Wilson's conviction that he alone spoke for mankind.

Delegates from 32 governments assembled at Paris for the conference that finally began early in January 1919. Strictly speaking, this was a preliminary meeting of the victors, for the formal Peace Conference began only when the delegates of defeated Germany arrived in May to receive the virtually completed treaty. In theory, plenary sessions of all the attending states, large and small, were to make the decisions at the Conference; but in fact the Big Four directed it: Wilson; David Lloyd George, the British Prime Minister; the French Premier, Georges Clemenceau, the "Tiger" of France; and, to a lesser degree, Premier Vittorio Orlando of Italy. When issues arose involving the Far East, Japan ranked as a fifth great power. The leaders at first operated in the Council of Ten and subsequently in the Council of Four. To the disgust of newspapermen attending the Conference, these smaller governing bodies conducted their affairs in secrecy, despite Wilson's earlier slogan of "open diplomacy." Of course, he had intended that slogan to mean only that treaties and agreements should be fully published *after* negotiations, but the masses had interpreted it to signify full publicity during decision-making—a good example of the dangers of sloganeering.

The unquestioned moral spokesman of the Big Four, Wilson often revealed a more practical and realistic approach than might have been expected. He labored diligently to master the details of the peace-making and impressed many observers with his knowledge and comprehension of complex issues. He tended to isolate himself from his fellow American commissioners, however, except for Colonel House, thereby depriving himself of advice and support that could have been of great benefit to him. Apparently Wilson viewed Lansing, Bliss, and White as tedious encumbrances, and he realized that Lansing disagreed with his plans for a league of nations. Lansing, like most American internationalists, objected to the use of collective force to preserve peace, preferring instead to rely upon arbitration and an international court to settle future world difficulties. Lloyd George, known as a master politician and opportunist, was much less informed than Wilson on the problems that arose at Paris. In general, however, he agreed with the American president in opposing the more selfish schemes of the other powers. He also relied more than Wilson upon his advisers at Paris. Clemenceau, nearly eighty years of age, tirelessly advocated French interests. He was determined to so weaken Germany through heavy reparations and losses of territory that it could never again menace France. The cynical Clemenceau, who once described Wilson as that "Buddha in Washington," frequently was either amused or puzzled by the President's idealism. On one occasion the French Premier reportedly remarked to Colonel House that "talking to Wilson is something like talking to Jesus Christ!" As for the Fourteen Points, "God gave us the Ten Commandments, and we broke them. Wilson gives us the Fourteen Points. We shall see." Orlando, the last of the Big Four, and the only one who did not speak English, generally played a small role at the Conference.

THE DRAFTING OF THE COVENANT

President Wilson saw the most important task of the Peace Conference as the framing of the Covenant of the League of Nations. The American and British delegations generally worked together harmoniously, for basically the Anglo-Americans agreed on many issues at Paris. Unfortunately that collaboration stopped short at the highest levels, because of Wilson's preference for independent action and his distrust of Lloyd George. France tried to mould the league into a military alliance of the great powers but failed. The League Covenant, formulated as a part of the treaty of peace, provided for an assembly composed of all members; a council to consist of the five great powers as permanent members who elected representatives of the smaller states; and a secretariat headed by a Secretary-General for administrative duties. The council, bearing the primary responsibility for preserving or restoring peace, could invoke economic and military sanctions or adopt other substantive measures only by unanimous vote. Article X, the heart of the Covenant, pledged members to respect and uphold the territorial integrity and political independence of all members of the League.

After the Covenant had been drafted and read to the conference, the President left Paris in mid-February for a brief trip to the United States. Various legislative items demanded his attention, and he particularly wanted to explain the Covenant to the American people. Already critics, mostly Republicans, had attacked the new organization as a world superstate that would impair American sovereignty. Colonel House urged the President to strike a conciliatory note, but his fighting blood was up. He landed in Boston, Senator Lodge's stronghold, and in effect denounced critics as narrow and selfish. Subsequently he did invite members of the Senate and House committees on foreign relations to dinner at the White House where he patiently tried to explain the Covenant, to little avail.

Wilson noticeably failed to win over Senator Lodge, a cold, sarcastic, and arrogant but able man who would become chairman of the influential Committee on Foreign Relations in the next Congress. The Massachusetts senator heartily detested Wilson, a sentiment that the President fully reciprocated. According to Lodge, his feelings derived from study of Wilson's public record which he viewed as irresolute and even dishonest. Yet personal factors probably played an even larger role than principles in Lodge's relations with the President. A Harvard-trained historian, Lodge long had been known as the "scholar in politics" until the even more renowned Wilson entered the White House and eclipsed him. By 1919 the Lodge-Wilson relationship while outwardly icily correct had deteriorated beyond repair. Apart from the usual political motives—Lodge as a Republican leader had to guard his party's interests—it is quite clear that the senator hoped to humiliate and defeat the man in the White House. The League issue seemed to offer the opportunity, even though Lodge himself earlier had endorsed the general concept. In fairness, however, it must be noted that Lodge like most other American internationalists favored arbitration and law rather than a coercive international organization.

In a speech two days after the White House conference, Lodge declared that the Covenant should be separated from the main body of the peace treaty, and he warned of the danger of entangling alliances as a departure from America's traditional policy of diplomatic freedom. He expressed alarm that the League might interfere with domestic questions and, via Article X, impair the Monroe Doctrine. Lodge concluded that the Covenant must be substantially changed before the United States could safely join the new organization. The Republican leadership then used delaying tactics to compel Wilson to call a special session of the new Congress elected in 1918, in order to obtain a vantage-point for continuing attacks on Wilson's work at Paris. A Republican "Round Robin," signed by 39 senators or senators-elect, six more than necessary to block approval of a treaty, declared the Covenant in its present form unacceptable.

Swallowing his outrage at what he regarded as unfair or ignorant criticisms, Wilson upon his return to Paris obtained several changes that he hoped would satisfy his critics. These provided that a member could decline a mandate offered by the League (former enemy territories and colonies were to be administered as League mandates or trusteeships); exempted domestic matters from League jurisdiction; and in effect sanctioned the Monroe Doctrine as a regional understanding permissable under the Covenant. Members also could withdraw from the League, after two years' notice. Wilson refused to ask for additional changes, especially in regard to Article X. He felt that he had answered legitimate criticism; the Senate would either have to accept the revised Covenant or reject the entire peace treaty.

A PEACE OF JUSTICE?

In other phases of the peace-making, Wilson tried to steer a middle course between too harsh and too soft a peace. He hoped for a settlement sufficiently moderate to reintegrate Germany into world society, yet he too felt that Germany richly deserved some punishment. Moreover, he faced demands for punitive treatment from his own countrymen as well as from the Allies.

Consequently, he agreed to a harsher peace than he desired. Even so, he stood firmly against extreme demands for humiliating and disabling the defeated enemy. With Lloyd George, he resisted French schemes to dismember Germany by annexing the Saar Valley, bringing the Rhineland under French control as a puppet state, and dissolving the Reich into several independent states. Loss of the Rhineland, together with the rather harsh military terms already agreed upon for Germany—an army of 100,000 men, abolition of the general staff, prohibition of tanks, military aircraft, and poison gas, and a small navy—would have ensured French revenge and power over an impotent Germany. The American and British feared that dismemberment, besides violating the principle of self-determination, would outrage German nationalism and sow the seeds of a future war. The controversy became so heated that Clemenceau accused Wilson of being pro-German and angrily left the conference room. The Peace Conference seemed on the verge of disruption and Wilson threatened to return home rather than accede to French desires.

The Big Three finally worked out a compromise that seemed to provide adequate protection for France without dismantling Germany. France would occupy the Saar Valley, with its valuable coal mines, for a period of fifteen years, followed by a League-supervised plebiscite to determine its future allegiance; and the Rhineland would be demilitarized to a distance of fifty kilometers east of the river, with France and Belgium occupying strategic bridgeheads along the Rhine for as long as fifteen years. As an additional guarantee, intended to function only until the League could become operational, Britain and the United States signed bilateral treaties with France promising military assistance in case Germany should launch an attack against France. When the American Senate subsequently failed to act on the pact, Britain unfortunately decided that her pledge therefore also became inoperative, leaving France without the hoped-for guarantees.

Dealing with the reparations issue also proved difficult for Wilson. The Americans wanted the amount of civilian damages for which Germany was responsible under the Pre-Armistice Agreement to be based on reasonable estimates of Germany's ability to pay over a limited period of time. The Allies, however, sought to shift as much of the entire cost of the war as possible to Germany. Thus during the 1918 elections British voters had been promised by their leaders that Germany would be made to "pay to the last farthing." The Americans managed to rule out imposition of the total war costs; Article 231 of the final treaty held Germany and its allies responsible for all the damages of the war (the "war guilt" clause), but Article 232 limited actual reparations to civilian damages. Wilson, however, gave in to Allied pleas that veterans pensions be included in the category of civilian damages, thereby more than doubling the final bill. Moreover, he also abandoned the effort to fix a specific sum in the treaty and to set a reasonable time for payment. Unfortunately the failure of the United States to ratify the peace treaty prevented it from participation in the Reparations Commission that subsequently assessed German reparations at the astronomical sum of $33 billion, payable over a period of 42 years. Disillusioned liberals in America and Britain attacked these provisions as unwise and a violation of promises to Germany, while Germans reacted with deep bitterness at the apparent injustice. Whether Germany could have paid such an amount is irrelevant, for it was not to be paid in fact.

Wilson made other compromises at the Conference, but in general he stood firmly by his principles. France sought the creation of a large Poland, Czechoslovakia, and Rumania in order to restrain Germany in the future. Although aware of strategic and security factors, Wilson and Lloyd George resisted the more extreme proposals. Poland obtained a corridor across German territory to give it access to the Baltic Sea, but the German-inhabited port of Danzig, instead of being annexed to the new state, became a free city under League supervision. The eastern boundaries of Poland could not be then determined, because of the absence of Russia from the conference. Strategic factors also required inclusion of the Sudeten Germans within the new Czechoslovakia, an arrangement that rankled in Germany and later gave Adolf Hitler a popular grievance to exploit. Italy, although gaining Austrian-inhabited areas in the South Tyrol area and Slavic populations around Trieste on the Adriatic Sea, met defeat in its demands for the port city of Fiume. Fiume had a core population of Italians, surrounded by a Slavic area. The Italian delegation briefly

walked out on the conference when Wilson publicly opposed it on
Fiume which he believed ought to be reserved as a port for the new
Yugoslav state. Wilson scored only a temporary "victory,"
however, for Italy eventually forced Yugoslavia, in 1920 and 1924,
to give way.

The Americans, and the British also, felt deeply concerned at
Paris about the danger of Bolshevik revolutions sweeping across
the defeated countries and penetrating even into the victorious
nations. The Russian question at the peace conference thus
involved more than the existence of a detested Bolshevik regime in
Moscow and a civil war between the reds and the anti-communist
or "White" forces. The war had ended German imperialism, only to
usher in an era of revolution with threats to Wilson's new order by
leftist radicals and rightist reactionaries. A communist regime
under Béla Kun came to power briefly in Hungary in 1919, until it
collapsed before invading Rumanian troops and Allied opposition.
Austria seethed with communist agitation; and in Germany, the
Spartacists led by Karl Liebknecht and Rosa Luxemburg sought a
communist regime. The centrist and moderate Social Democratic
government in Berlin beat off these challenges, crushing both a
communist and rightist uprising in Berlin and a "soviet republic" in
Bavaria. Even Italy, of the victors, experienced turbulence and
uncertainty from socialist and ultranationalist movements.

Within the allied countries and the United States, conservative
influences—the forces of "order"—sought a punitive peace against
Germany and containment or destruction of the Bolshevik virus, in
part out of vengeance and fear, but also to curb or defeat liberal
and socialist reform movements at home. Thus within the United
States the opposition to Wilson's liberal peace plans and the
League Covenant reflected in part conservative desires to blunt the
impetus of progressive reforms and to recapture control of the
national government. In this atmosphere, conservatives and
reactionaries grossly exaggerated the Bolshevik menace and used it
as a weapon in politics and diplomacy.

Wilson and Lloyd George came under great pressure at Paris to
approve open intervention against the Bolsheviks. Clemenceau
hoped to strangle Lenin's regime by an economic blockade and he
viewed sympathetically the scheme advanced by Winston

Churchill, British War Minister, for sending volunteer troops to Russia to aid the Whites. The Anglo-American leaders, aware of liberal opposition within the United States and Britain to an overt anti-Bolshevik crusade, and fearful of deeper involvement and the triumph of reactionary forces in Russia, refused to agree. President Wilson, clearly an anti-communist, still hoped to cope effectively with the problem by diplomacy and economic aid. The Peace Conference tried to end the civil war in Russia and no doubt eventually to undermine the Bolsheviks, by calling for a truce and inviting the Russian factions to meet at Prinkipo Island in the Sea of Marmara. Lenin agreed, but his opponents declined to negotiate with the "Reds." The Americans then proposed an extensive food relief and economic aid program in Russia, attended by a truce. Since the latter clearly would have weakened the Bolsheviks, Lenin rejected it. Finally, Wilson reluctantly agreed to give support to the Omsk regime headed by Admiral Alexander Kolchak, who promised to crush the Reds and extend his rule to the entire country. At Wilson's insistence, Kolchak promised democratic reforms after his movement had vanquished the communists and reunited Russia. Kolchak proved unequal to the task, however, in large part because of the reactionaries, who opposed such reforms, supplied much of his forces. Ultimately he was defeated by the red army directed by Leon Trotsky in early 1920. Yet "containment" had forced communism onto the defensive in Russia and prevented its success in the rest of Europe.

In the Shantung controversy, Wilson met more of an apparent than a real defeat of his principles. Japan in 1914 had seized the German leasehold in the Chinese province of Shantung (along with the German islands in the North Pacific). Subsequently Japan forced the weak Chinese government to recognize that conquest and to yield other concessions in the "Twenty-one Demands" crisis in early 1915. The American government refused to recognize these gains obtained by force and intimidation. Viscount Kikujiro Ishii had led a special mission to Washington in mid-1917, hoping to arrange some kind of bargain recognizing Japan's recent gains. He failed because Wilson was determined to check Japanese pretensions and to eradicate all spheres of influence in China. Lansing, conversely, perceived the relative weakness of American interests and power in China and preferred a "bargain" recognizing Japan's dominant role in exchange for promises of moderation. Probably Lansing's views represented the more realistic course that if followed might well have averted future Japanese-American difficulties. Facing irreconcilable differences but anxious to maintain a facade of harmony, Ishii and Secretary of State Lansing turned to a vague formula capable of such interpretation as each side might choose. The Lansing-Ishii Agreement, signed in November 1917, pledged both powers to observe and uphold the Open Door in China, but it failed to define the meaning of the Open Door or the nature of Japan's "special interests" in China. Subsequently Japan interpreted the agreement to signify recognition of her preeminent position politically as well as economically in all China, while the State Department maintained that it merely had recognized that Japan had special geographical relations to its huge neighbor.

At the Paris Conference Wilson hoped to compel the restoration of the Shantung leasehold to China, only to face Japanese threats to leave the Conference and boycott the League. Fearful that Japan's defection would doom the League—Italy had briefly walked out—Wilson finally consented to a clause in the Treaty transferring the former German holdings to Japan. Few provisions of the Treaty aroused more widespread condemnation in America than the Shantung clause. Yet here Wilson acted realistically, adjusting to a Japanese *fait accompli*. Moreover, the Japanese delegation did give reassurances that political control of the province soon would be returned to China, a promise Japan kept in 1922.

The German representatives arrived in Paris to receive the Treaty of Peace on May 7, 1919. They had only a few days to study the document and propose changes, most of which the victors summarily rejected. Facing the threat of Allied invasion, Germany reluctantly accepted the peace presented to it at the point of a bayonet. On June 28, the fifth anniversary of the assassination at Sarajevo that had ignited the war, the Allies staged the final tableau in the ornate Hall of Mirrors at the Versailles Palace. Before the assembled Allied and American statesmen and crowds of exultant observers, the unhappy German delegates signed the

Treaty of Versailles. Treaties with the lesser Central Powers remained to be concluded, but the most dramatic part of the Conference had ended.

Even before the formal signing, critics denounced the Treaty—some for its being too generous terms, others for its harshness. The British economist John Maynard Keynes (*The Economic Consequences of the Peace, 1920*) flailed the treaty for its punitive provisions saddling Germany with extensive losses of territory and its colonies and overseas investments and imposing heavy reparations. Moreover, he argued that Europe unwisely had been Balkanized or fragmented economically. Self-determination had also been violated by the inclusion of large numbers of German-speaking peoples within Italy and the new states of Poland and Czechoslovakia, and Italian annexation of Slavic lands along the Adriatic Sea. Keynes and other critics concluded that hopes for a liberal peace had been betrayed, primarily because of President Wilson's defects. The clever and unscrupulous Old World politicians, Keynes wrote, had "bamboozled" and deceived the New World prophet, who had turned out to be not a philosopher-king, as many had hoped, but a stubborn and narrow Presbyterian.

Such criticisms were unfair. Wilson had worked tirelessly at Paris and his efforts unquestionably improved the final Treaty. No doubt the Treaty of Versailles with its several harsh provisions fell short of a complete realization of liberal peace goals. But in the nature of human affairs ideals can rarely be entirely achieved. Wilson had met defeat on the reparations issue, Germany alone was disarmed, and a number of departures had been made from boundaries drawn along lines of strict nationality. On the other hand, he had helped oppose French schemes to dismember Germany, created the mandate system to administer former enemy colonies and dependencies under League supervision, and balked at excessive Italian demands for territorial gain. Above all, he had succeeded in establishing the League of Nations. Wilson recognized that the Treaty had defects, but he hoped that in the course of time, as passions cooled, the League would be able to repair them. It was not an unreasonable hope. Given proper support by the United States and the major Allied governments, the

Versailles settlement might well have preserved peace and have evolved into a more progressive world order.

THE DEFEAT OF THE TREATY IN AMERICA

Even as Wilson left Paris for home, many Americans already had begun to lose interest in the League of Nations. Americans traditionally had given little attention to foreign affairs except in times of crisis, and they revealed a marked tendency after the Armistice to concentrate once more on private interests. Oversold on the Great Crusade for democracy and peace, people quickly tired of idealistic exhortations. War-stimulated patriotism also encouraged many citizens to oppose League membership as a threat to American sovereignty and a departure from the solemn advice of Washington's Farewell Address. Some professed to fear that the League would breach the American tariff wall and prevent restriction of immigration. Large numbers of German-Americans, Irish-Americans, Italian-Americans, and others criticized the Versailles Treaty for betraying the hopes or the interests of their former homelands. Finally, many liberals who formerly had supported President Wilson and the war to end all wars felt alienated by the apparent failure to achieve more fully the liberal peace program. Liberal journals, such as the *New Republic* and *The Nation*, denounced the Treaty as vindictive and a guarantee not of enduring peace but of future wars of revenge and rectification.

Despite growing disillusionment and apathy, however, the majority of Americans as indicated by newspaper editorials and polls, speeches, and public meetings, probably still favored membership in the League. Their support lacked intensity, however, and seemed to diminish as the struggle over ratification of the Treaty continued. Most Americans were "mild internationalists" and wanted to move cautiously in assuming world responsibilities. Probably Wilson would have been more successful in arousing public support if he had put the major emphasis upon the practical advantages of League membership for the United States—security, stability, and trade—instead of America's duty to the world.

On July 10, 1919, the President formally presented the bulky 264-page Treaty to the Senate. Observers noted that he was not at his best in the address, rising to a level of eloquence only when he referred to the League of Nations as the best hope of mankind: "The stage is set, the destiny disclosed....We can only go forward, with lifted eyes and freshened spirit, to follow the vision." While the assembled Democrats applauded his remarks, most Republicans listened to the President in ominous silence. The Republicans held a narrow majority (49 to 47) in the Senate that gave them control of the powerful Committee on Foreign Relations. Republican leaders, flushed with their triumph in the 1918 elections and looking toward the White House in 1920, anxiously sought to reap the maximum gain from the Versailles Treaty. They could not allow Wilson and the Democrats to claim sole credit for waging the war and making the peace.

Moreover, not all Republican senators agreed upon the League issue. A small group of "Irreconcilables" adamantly opposed membership in any kind of league. These were about sixteen senators, ranging from genuine arch-isolationist Republicans such as California's Hiram Johnson, Idaho's William E. Borah, and the maverick Democrat from Missouri, James A. Reed, to some who were merely anti-war or were disgusted by the harshness of the Treaty. One of the group, ex-Secretary of State Philander C. Knox, preferred an outright alliance with England and France to what he viewed as the impractical entanglements of the League. Others viewed the League as an intolerable diminution of American sovereignty and insisted that the wisest course would be for America to adhere to its traditional policy of nonentanglement. Republican "Mild Reservationists," on the other hand, favored membership with only a few changes to clarify the Covenant. The "Strong Reservationists," led by Senator Lodge, Chairman of the Foreign Relations Committee, advocated sweeping changes before the League would be safe for American participation. The Monroe Doctrine must be safeguarded, League interference in domestic questions such as the tariff and immigration precluded, and the obligation to defend other states under Article X reduced or eliminated. The power of Congress to declare war, to make peace, or to send troops abroad could not be transferred to a world organization. Most of these fears were groundless, as a careful reading of the Covenant would have revealed. In addition to doubts about the Covenant, many senators of both parties deeply resented the President's ignoring of the Senate during the peace-making; apparently they saw the debate on the Treaty as a legislative versus executive battle for control over foreign policy.

Lodge directed a well-conceived and brilliantly executed strategy. He decided to draft a number of amendments (eventually reservations) to the Treaty that would unify Republican ranks and embarrass the Democrats. If Wilson accepted them, Republicans could claim that they had remedied the defects of the League: if the President rejected them, Republicans could attribute the responsibility for defeat of the Treaty solely to the Democrats who refused to make the League safe for American participation. Lodge clearly expected that Wilson would spurn his reservations and thereby doom the Treaty and the League. When a Republican colleague, Senator James E. Watson of Indiana, expressed fear that Wilson might accept the Treaty with the reservations, Lodge reassured him:

> But, my dear James, you do not take into consideration the hatred that Woodrow Wilson has for me personally. Never under any set of circumstances in this world could he be induced to accept a treaty with Lodge reservations appended to it.

Lodge deliberately stalled for time, taking two weeks to read aloud the entire Treaty before a nearly empty committee room, despite the fact that printed copies were available. He used an additional six weeks in hearings. Secretary of State Lansing, increasingly alienated from his chief and deeply resentful of presidential snubs at the Paris Conference, badly damaged the cause of the Treaty in his testimony. Lansing admitted that he and others at Paris had objected to Wilson's capitulation on Shantung and he revealed that his advice had not been often sought by the President at the Conference. William C. Bullitt, a young and ardently liberal critic of the Peace Conference who had resigned in protest from the American delegation, also appeared before the committee. Bullitt violated personal confidences to relate to the eager Republicans that Lansing privately had criticized the Treaty and Covenant in most unsparing language.

The committee reported the Treaty to the Senate loaded with 45 amendments and four reservations (which were ultimately reduced to fourteen reservations), designed primarily to embarrass the President and curtail his authority. The most important reservation involved Article X of the Covenant: the United States would assume no obligation to defend the integrity of other states or to use its armed fores at the request of the League without the specific approval of Congress. Other reservations specified that the United States would determine the domestic matters to be excluded from the competency of the League and declared the Monroe Doctrine entirely beyond League jurisdiction. The last reservation, a clear reflection of anglophobia, refused to bind the United States to any League decision in which any member had cast more than one vote—the British Empire and Commonwealth had six seats in the League Assembly. Meanwhile, Republican opponents of the League, backed by financial contributions from Henry Clay Frick and Andrew Mellon, among others, established the League for the Preservation of American Independence and sent speakers across the nation to attack Wilson and the Covenant.

While Lodge's strategy unfolded, President Wilson decided to appeal his case directly to the people. His efforts to conciliate and to win support from moderate critics of the League had proved unsuccessful. Wilson would accept mild interpretive reservations provided that they were not a formal part of the act of ratification and therefore would not compel renegotiation of the Treaty. In any case he deemed most of the proposed changes as unnecessary, dishonorable, or ruinous to the League. In September the President began a speaking tour through the mid-western and far-western states. Although warned by his personal physician that his health had been weakened by the toils at Paris, Wilson decided that his duty came first. Despite the late summer heat and the discomforts of railroad travel, he delivered over thirty major addresses in defense of the League before he collapsed at Pueblo, Colorado. Exhausted and suffering blinding headaches, the President reluctantly canceled the remainder of the tour. Probably it had been ill-advised in any case, for even if the Democrats had won all the Senate seats at stake in 1920 as the result of Wilson's campaign, he would still have fallen short of the two-thirds majority required for Senate approval of the Treaty without reservations.

Soon after his return to the White House, Wilson on October 2 suffered a cerebral thrombosis that left him partially paralysed. For days he lay near death and, even when he began to recover, could not perform many of his presidential duties. Despite an obvious disability under the Constitution, Wilson's wife and close advisers refused to request that the Vice President assume the executive duties. Secretary of State Lansing, who called cabinet meetings on his own authority, thought seriously of declaring a disability but gave up when Wilson's private secretary and his physician resisted. Wilson's wife and aides imposed a virtual conspiracy of silence around the President's sickroom, and carefully restricted the official business brought to his attention. Even cabinet members could not see the President and had to rely upon brief notes by Mrs Wilson stating the President's wishes. Yet it would be an exaggeration to accuse her of running the government. In fact, for a period no one was in effective charge and the executive branch functioned largely by inertia.

When the President did begin to recover, he adamantly refused to compromise with Senator Lodge. Wilson's intelligence apparently remained unimpaired by his illness, although he seemed much more rigid, irritable, and suspicious. His aides warned him that the only hope for Senate approval of the Treaty in any form lay in compromise with the Republican leaders. Wilson preferred defeat to what he felt would be a cowardly and hesitant entry into the League under the Lodge Reservations. He still had confidence that the great majority of the people were with him, when in fact signs indicated that a growing number, blaming both Wilson and Lodge for the deadlock, desired a compromise. When the Treaty came to a vote in the Senate on November 19, 1919, and again on March 19, 1920, the President urged loyal Democrats to vote against it with the Lodge Reservations. He thereby ensured its defeat, for the Democrats could not muster enough strength to approve the Treaty without changes. In the final vote on the Treaty in March 1920 the tally for the Treaty with the reservations fell seven short (49 ayes, 35 nayes) of the necessary two-thirds for approval.

THE "SOLEMN REFERENDUM"

The President refused to acknowledge defeat. For a while, with his fondness for the British parliamentary system, he thought of challenging senatorial opponents to resign and stand for reelection; if a majority won, he would name a Republican Secretary of State and, with the cooperation of the Vice President, resign the presidency to that Republican. Legal problems and the probability that most Republican senators would not cooperate caused him to abandon that novel scheme for resolving an executive-legislative deadlock. Wilson then determined to make the 1920 presidential contest a national referendum on the League. Apparently he wanted a third nomination by the Democratic Party, but his loyal friends, fearful for his life, prevented his name from being presented to the convention meeting in San Francisco. Instead the convention nominated James M. Cox, Governor of Ohio, with Franklin D. Roosevelt as his running mate. The Republicans chose Senator Warren G. Harding of Ohio, an impressive looking man but a mediocrity; Governor Calvin Coolidge of Massachusetts received second place on the ticket. Cox and Roosevelt supported membership in the League, though they agreed to accept moderate reservations to the Covenant. Cox would even accept the essentials of the Lodge reservation relating to Article X. Without repudiating Wilson, Cox clearly indicated that if elected he would not continue the existing deadlock with the Senate.

Harding's position on the Treaty and League seemed less clear. His acceptance address expressed satisfaction that Republicans in the Senate had rescued America from a "merged government of the world" and preserved American sovereignty and diplomatic independence. Yet some of his remarks during the early phases of the campaign suggested that he favored membership in the League after some changes; on other occasions he seemed to advocate negotiation of a new and better association of nations. Harding's personal feelings inclined toward isolationism, however, and when the Irreconcilables brought pressure to bear he finally repudiated Wilson's League. The League, he declared, was a "stupendous fraud" and the provisions of Article X endangered America's independence and peace. Even so, Harding continued to refer vaguely to some kind of association of nations and such pro-

League Republicans as Elihu Root, Charles Evans Hughes, and Herbert Hoover argued that Harding would take the country into the League. They hoped not so much to win votes for the Republican ticket—victory seemed assured—but to prevent Harding in office from spurning membership in any kind of a world organization. In view of all these confusing statements by Republican spokesmen, the voter could be pardoned if he remained unclear about the Republican candidate's intentions.

By their very nature, presidential contests are not designed to provide a mandate on any one issue. Too many factors are involved for such an interpretation. In 1920, traditional political loyalties, personalities, and a variety of local and national issues and grievances obscured or eclipsed the question of the League. Administration war-time mobilization policies had alienated many western farmers, northern laborers, and consumers everywhere; German-, Irish-, Italian-Americans, and disillusioned liberals objected strongly to various provisions of the Versailles Treaty; and highly nationalistic and patriotic groups feared loss of sovereignty through League membership. The progressive coalition that had brought Wilson victory in 1916 clearly had disintegrated by 1920. Moreover Harding made an attractive if uninspiring candidate, and many Americans simply desired a change in government and a return to what Harding called "normalcy."

When the election returns came in, Harding had overwhelmed his opponent, polling 16,152,200 votes (61 per cent) to 9,147,353 for Cox or a plurality of over seven million votes. Harding carried the electoral votes of all the states outside the "Solid South" and even won Tennessee. Cox went down to a defeat unequalled by any Democratic candidate since Stephen A. Douglas in 1860. The Republicans also won heavy majorities in both houses of Congress.

Although historians agree that the election was not a mandate on the League or any other single issue, Wilson by his insistence on a "Solemn Referendum" had helped ensure that the Republican victory would be interpreted it as a decisive popular rejection of membership in the League. The Republicans in office treated the issue as dead, and the United States joined Bolshevik Russia, defeated Germany, and lesser states such as Arabia, Tibet, and

Nepal in shunning the League. A variety of factors explain the final defeat of the Treaty: political and personal partisanship, isolationist sentiment, and genuine doubts by many citizens of the wisdom of too rapid an assumption of world obligations. Above all, Wilson by his insistence on all or nothing contributed mightily to the final outcome. The United States in a very real sense thereby betrayed its own ideals and national interests. It had entered the war to defend imperiled interests and rights and yet, after turning the conflict into a struggle for a just peace and a stable post-war world, abandoned the field when victory was in sight. American withdrawal left a badly weakened France and an impaired Britain to uphold the new settlement.

While Wilson and his internationalist supporters had lost, it proved impossible in the 1920s to ignore the legacy of American intervention and victory in World War I or to return fully to the nineteenth century pattern of isolationism. The First World War marked the beginning of a great departure for the United States from the neutrality and isolationism of the past to the global responsibilities of the future. The war also marked a movement toward a larger role for government in regulating and directing the American economy. Wilson's Republican successors could no more ignore that fact than they could the implications of the war for foreign policy. The task of the 1920s lay in defining and improving the new relationship of government and the economy, while developing a new foreign policy to protect American interests.

SUGGESTED READINGS

Bailey, Thomas A. *Woodrow Wilson and the Great Betrayal* (1945).

___. *Woodrow Wilson and the Lost Peace* (1944).

Baker, R. S. *Woodrow Wilson and World Settlement*, 3 vols., (1922).

Birdsall, Paul. *Versailles Twenty Years After* (1941).

Czernin, Ferdinand. *Versailles, 1919* (1964).

Fleming, Denna F. *The United States and the League of Nations* (1932).

Floto, Inga. *Colonel House at Paris* (1980).

Garraty, John A. *Henry Cabot Lodge*. 1953.

Gelfand, Lawrence E. *The Inquiry: American Preparations for Peace, 1917-1919* (1963).

Hoover, Herbert. *The Ordeal of Woodrow Wilson* (1958).

Kennan, George F. *Russia Leaves the War* (1956).

Keynes, John M. *The Economic Consequences of the Peace* (1920).

Levin, N. Gordon, Jr. *Woodrow Wilson and World Politics: America's Response to War and Revolution* (1968).

Mamatey, Victor A. *The United States and East Central Europe, 1914-1918* (1957).

Chapter Three

THE TWENTIES

Until recently, most historians portrayed the Twenties as an interlude between two great reform eras, Progressivism and the New Deal. The national mood was depicted as weary with crusades at home and abroad,, longing to return to the peace and prosperity Harding termed "normalcy." Big business, no longer suspect as in the muckraking era, had gained immense prestige from wartime miracles of production and the service in government of a number of business tycoons as patriotic "dollar-a-year" men. The Republican party seemed the preferred political instrument for a return to the politics of business and the "good old days" of prosperity and contentment. The reactionary and conservative, as well as the bizarre elements in American politics and society during the decade, were unduly emphasized.

Yet many of the people who lived in the 1920s, from businessmen to economists and sociologists, viewed the decade as a hopeful new era characterized by material plenty, the gradual elimination of poverty, and technological and scientific advances. It was disillusioned and alienated intellectuals who fastened a misleading label of crassness and reaction on the era. From the present viewpoint it can be seen that the Twenties witnessed profound economic and social changes almost revolutionary in nature. The movement toward greater order and stability in business and finance, the scientific and managerial rationalization of industry, the growing urbanization, and the transformation of American values and institutions, long underway, continued apace and gave the decade its major significance. Part of the process of transformation and adaptation, which seemed conservative and even reactionary to some older style liberal critics, came from the growing involvement of government in the economy, the closer relationship between business and the federal government. The reform legislation and regulatory bodies of the Progressive Era, supposedly intended to curb big business, in fact often had been sought by the large corporations and operated to stabilize and encourage business activity. World War I especially brought about an intimate relationship between business and government and a continuous involvement of federal authorities in stimulating, directing, and controlling the economy. These economic and political changes and tendencies, not the colorful but superficial image of flappers, gangsters, booze, and reaction, represent the deeper meaning of the Twenties.

THE RATIONALIZATION OF INDUSTRY

Scientific management in industry and business appeared to be triumphant in the 1920s. The prosperity of the decade resulted primarily from enormous increases in productivity, rising 46 percent for all branches in 1929 over the 1920 level, attributable in large part to more efficient management. As early as 1900, Frederick W. Taylor pioneered in scientific study and planning in production, "time and motion" studies, to eliminate waste and inefficiency in the use of time and materials. Industry adopted "Taylorization" and utilized technical research, cost studies, production planning, salesmanship, and market surveys. The Commerce Department also preached the new gospel of efficiency of operation and standardization and simplication of products to businessmen. Greater use of electrical energy also contributed to increased production. Technical advances reduced the cost of electricity, so that while only one-third of industry was electrified in 1914, by 1929 three-fourths used electrical power. Output per worker increased by forty percent in industry from 1919 to 1925. A growing technological unemployment, however, became a socially undesirable by-product of the increased use of machinery; for example, the continuous strip-sheet rolling mill for sheet steel and tin-plating eliminated 40 to 50 workers per mill; cigar machines by 1930 had taken over 47 per cent of what used to be hand labor; and heavy construction was mechanized by use of power shovels, belt conveyors, and concrete mixers doing away with large numbers of unskilled laborers.

Consolidation in business, a trend underway since the late nineteenth century, reflected the desire to promote efficiency and stability, reduce costs, and above all to eliminate cutthroat competition and price wars. During the Twenties, over 6,000 factories and mining companies disappeared, 4,000 utility companies were consolidated into larger units, and there were 1,800 bank mergers. Samuel Insull built a giant utility holding company that operated gas and electric firms in 23 states, while A.P. Giannini of California controlled a chain of 500 banks across that state and became the fourth largest banker in the nation. By 1930 the 200 largest non-financial corporations in America owned nearly half the total national corporate wealth. Four meat packing firms dominated 70 percent of that industry, four tobacco companies manufactured over 90 percent of the cigarettes consumed, and so on.

The larger firms, regarded as "price leaders," in effect set price levels for the lesser members of an industry. Such competition as existed was more in brand advertising than in prices. Expansion and consolidation proceeded swiftly in the automotive, radio, and chemical industries, to name only a few. The DuPont firm, benefitting from wartime production of explosives and confiscation of German dye patents, dominated the chemical industry with its new synthetic fibres such as rayon and cellophane. Newspaper chains began in the late nineteenth century but reached a peak in the Twenties. By the end of the decade about 60 chains owned over 300 daily newspapers. Chain stores thrived in the wholesale and retail grocery and merchandising fields; the Great Atlantic and Pacific Tea Company (A & P) had 17,500 stores across the country by 1928. Other chains, such as Woolworth and Rexall, spread across regions or the entire country. Although these chains drove many small independents out of business and dominated one-fifth or more of the retail field by 1929, they were often highly competitive with one another.

During the Twenties, business and government worked closely together. Herbert Hoover, Secretary of Commerce during the Harding and Coolidge administrations, converted the Commerce

Department from a minor to a major executive agency to encourage greater business productivity and efficiency. The Commerce Department investigated economic problems, distributed technical information and reports on foreign markets, and facilitated greater standardization of sizes and designs in production. For example, it reduced the varieties of paving brick from 66 to four and basic types of hospital beds from 44 to two. An economic nationalist, Hoover saw the world's welfare as dependent upon American prosperity. He sought American control of vital foreign raw material resources and an expansion of Aemrican exports, while at the same time encouraging American economic self-sufficiency. A new era had dawned which was not simply a return to the old order favoring business but one of close government-business cooperation. Hoover envisioned a benevolent government helping business to achieve greater efficiency and productivity, thereby benefitting the nation as a whole. As President Calvin Coolidge was to remark, the business of America was business. Under Hoover's inspiration, the federal government sought not merely to create a favorable climate for business but to aid business to take a more positive approach through persuasion and suggestion.

The prosperity of the Twenties tended to be irregular. Total national income rose from $74.3 billion in 1923 to $89 billion by 1928, and corporate profits increased by 62 percent during the same period. Real wages also rose but more slowly—11 percent from 1923 to 1929—and the average work week declined from 47.3 to 45.7 hours. Yet there was much unemployment, especially in such ailing industries as coal mining and textiles. Coal prices remained depressed, in part because of an over-abundant supply and in part due to the more efficient use of coal by industry. In textiles, except for booming sales in rayon and silk, prices were relatively low although production was high. That situation reflected both sharp competition and style changes as clothing and shoes for women and men became lighter. Layoffs of workers and low wages also resulted from the large-scale movement of textile industry from the north-eastern states to the south, exploiting cheaper labor and lower land costs. For their part, farmers received a disproportionately small share of the general prosperity.

LABOR IN A BUSINESS ERA

Organized labor also retreated during the Twenties. Labor had made considerable progress during the Progressive era, and especially during the war when worker shortages and a government anxious to avoid strikes had created a favorable climate. After the Armistice, labor leaders were determined to preserve and extend these gains and to obtain wage hikes to compensate for inflation. However in addition to employer resistance, the conservative craft-union philosophy of the American Federation of Labor (AFL) unions, presided over by Samuel Gompers' colorless successor William Green (1924), made it difficult to organize mass production industries with their hordes of unskilled and semi-skilled workers. Overseas immigration had been curtailed, but rural migration, nearly 17.5 million between 1920 and 1929, flooded the cities with cheap labor and potential strike breakers. White-collar employees, growing in number, also found unionism unappealing.

Many industrialists had consented with reluctance to the government's wartime labor policies and resolved to end them after the war. Opponents of unionization discouraged national union membership by practising "welfare capitalism" to remove worker grievances through higher wages and improved employer-employee relations. John D. Rockefeller, Jr., deeply shocked by the violence of the 1914 Ludlow Massacre in Colorado, led the way. Even at its best, welfare capitalism was paternalistic and clearly anti-union. Henry Ford, the automotive tycoon, pioneered the "Doctrine of High Wages" in 1914, inaugurating in his non-union plants the "Five Dollar" workday wage scale. In practice, however, Ford granted no general wage increase between 1919 and 1929, and he laid off 60,000 workers without wages for over a year in 1927 as he retooled for a new automobile model. The National Association of Manufacturers and the US Chamber of Commerce endorsed the "American Plan" or open-shop approach against compulsory unionism. As a condition of employment some employers forced workers to sign "yellow-dog" contracts renouncing national union membership. Mine workers in West Virginia had to sign a contract reading: "I am not now a member of the United Mine Workers...and I enter this employment with the understanding that the policy of the company is to operate a non-union mine...and [that it] would not give me employment under any other condition." Employers supported company controlled plant unions and used blacklists of known national union organizers.

In the reactionary postwar climate, Congress and the executive, even under Wilson, tended to favor business in disputes with labor. Wilson called a National Industrial Conference, but it failed to harmonize the interests of employers and workers. A wave of disruptive strikes swept the nation in 1919, involving about four million workers and threatening to plunge the country into economic paralysis. A coal miners' strike pulled 435,000 miners out of the bituminous coal fields, until broken by federal court injunctions. The miners subsequently received a substantial wage increase.

One of the bitterest conflicts occurred in the steel industry. Over half the laborers worked a twelve-hour day for very low wages. Previous attempts, the 1892 Homestead strike and clashes in 1901 and 1910, to unionize these semi- or unskilled workers had failed. Judge Elbert H. Gary served as Chairman of the Board to the giant United States Steel Corporation, which was controlled by Morgan interests. A dignified lawyer and pious Methodist, Gary was determined to defeat unionization and to uphold the non-union or "open shop." In 1918 the AFL established a committee to assault this bastion of anti-unionism with William Z. Foster, a labor radical but not at that time a communist, providing much of the committee's zeal and leadership. Unfortunately, the AFL rejected a single industry-wide union and tried to organize workers under appropriate craft unions. After initial success, the labor committee encountered resistance from the company—Judge Gary refused even to confer with union spokesmen—and a major strike broke out in September, 1919. Although only about half the workers walked out, the strike disrupted a vital national industry. The press in general reacted sharply against the union organizers, depicting the strike as an industrial war led by radicals and revolutionaries. The *New York Times* called it an attempt to bolshevize America, and others agreed that it was a radical conspiracy. Exploiting this theme, US Steel and the other companies charged that the strike was foreign in origin and without appeal to native born workers.

Foster especially became the target of calumny, and he was hauled before a congressional investigating committee. Facing industry intimidation, employment of strikebreakers, and arbitrary arrests by local and state police, the union organizers failed. The strike collapsed by early 1920; not until the 1930s did the steel industry at last capitulate to unionization.

The most shocking postwar labor disturbances took place in Seattle and Boston. James A. Duncan, a radical labor agitator who had outspokenly opposed American intervention in the war and sympathized with the Bolshevik cause in Russia, took advantage of a shipyard dispute to call a general strike of all workers in Seattle early in 1919. This new type of strike which virtually paralyzed Seattle for five days was denounced by Mayor Ole Hanson as a communist plot. Public revulsion caused several of the participating unions to withdraw their support, and the general strike collapsed. In Boston, lowly-paid policemen had formed a union and received AFL endorsement. E.U. Curtis, the stubborn police commissioner, refused to permit police to belong to the union, and when he dismissed nineteen of their union leaders over 1100 of the city's 1544 policemen walked out. Criminals looted stores and robbed citizens on the streets, yet Calvin Coolidge, then Governor of Massachusetts, delayed calling out the state guard for two nights of crime and public panic. By the time he finally acted, Boston's mayor already had largely restored order by use of volunteers and state guardsmen living in the city. The newspapers exaggerated the effects of the strike and assured a horrified public that it was the work of communists and other radicals. President Wilson denounced it as a "crime against civilization." Coolidge received national plaudits for his famed telegram to Samuel Gompers: "There is no right to strike against the public safety by anybody, anywhere, anytime."

There was another coal miners' strike in 1922 when operators declined to renew contracts with the United Mine Workers union and announced sharp wage reductions. After the strike dragged on for months and a bloody clash occurred in southern Illinois between strikers and strike-breakers, President Harding ordered the mines opened and endorsed the use of state troops. The miners returned to work on the basis of the old arrangement and a federal investigation into working conditions, but despite the inquiry's findings of deplorable mine conditions, Congress failed to act. In 1925, when the UMW refused to accept wage cuts as the price of coal fell, the Pittsburgh Coal Company, after thirty years of relations with the union, cut wages and reopened with nonunion labor. Wage cuts, strike-breakers, and violence took their toll, and by 1930 John L. Lewis' once powerful United Mine Workers had declined to a fraction of its former size. A railroad shopmen's strike also took place in 1922, again because of a wage slash. Attorney General Harry M. Daugherty obtained a sweeping federal court injunction against the strikers, and the strike collapsed.

Communist organizers and agitators during the 1920s challenged organized labor with "dual unionism" (separate communist-controlled unions) and exploited labor grievances to promote communism. In 1928 and 1929, in the cotton mills of Tennessee and North and South Carolina, low wages, unsanitary factories, long hours for women and children, and company town abuses spawned unrest and strikes. Communist agitators helped to arouse workers, and there were bloody clashes at Gastonia, North Carolina. Local police, state troopers, and court injunctions smashed the strikes. Union membership in the AFL and unaffiliated unions declined from five million members in 1920 to about 3.5 million by 1929.

THE PLIGHT OF THE BLACKS

After wartime gains, American blacks experienced serious difficulties in the Twenties. In the course of the Great War, blacks had often been discouraged from enlisting in the armed forces; nonetheless, 2,290,525 managed to register under the Selective Service Law and 367,000 were ultimately inducted. Finding the Marine Corps closed to them and obtaining only menial positions in the Navy, blacks served in almost every branch of the Army, in segregated units, and some held commissions. Black soldiers served and fought well, only to return after a "war for democracy" to encounter the worst kinds of discrimination, violence and, on occasion, death, particularly in the South. During the first two decades of the twentieth century, and especially in the war years, hundreds of thousands of Negroes migrated from the countryside to the city—both in the North and the South—attracted by the prospect of employment. The shift was striking and significant. From 1900 to 1920 the black urban population of northern cities increased by 671,292 or 105 percent, while that of southern cities increased by 886,173 or 65 percent. Moreover, 50 percent of the black gains in the period took place in 24 cities already having a black population of no less than 25,000. Pressed in on by the newcomers, middle-class Negroes from established communities pushed out into white neighbourhoods in search of better and safer housing, thereby setting the stage for the conflict that ensued. Overall, blacks as a group suffered intense white resentment over competition for jobs and housing and recreational opportunities. Lynchings increased from 38 in 1917 to 58 in 1918. In July 1917, a serious race riot in East St Louis, Illinois, a manufacturing city on the Mississippi River opposite St Louis, claimed approximately 40 black lives. The immediate background of the conflict lay in the huge influx of black workers from the South into the region— between 10,000 and 12,000 arriving in the period from the autumn of 1916 to the spring of 1917. The outcome witnessed the sentencing of eight whites and eleven Negroes to the state penitentiary and the flight of 6,000 blacks to Missouri—a former slave state. "The causes, social and industrial," urged Theodore Roosevelt among others of the aftermath, "should be fearlessly and thoroughly investigated so that the primitive remedy may be found."

After the Armistice racial tensions heightened as the revitalized Ku Klux Klan and competition for employment precipitated by the brief postwar recession. Seventy blacks, including ten servicemen still in their uniforms, were reportedly lynched in 1919. And a rash of race riots in predominantly urban centers broke out, the worst one taking place in Chicago.

Large numbers of blacks had migrated to Chicago, especially during the war, bringing the black population there to nearly 110,000 by 1920, up from 44,000 in 1910. As many as 50,000 of the newcomers, the majority of whom came directly from the South, poured into the Chicago region within an eighteen-month period after January 1916; most of these, furthermore, joined the already swollen black population concentrated on the city's

southside. Mounting hostility, which included the bombing of 27
Negro dwellings since 1917, prepared the groundwork for a riot
touched off in the summer of 1919 when on a July day whites
threw stones at a young black swimmer who had drifted into a
section of Lake Michigan putatively "reserved" for whites. The
youth drowned and the rumour soon spread throughout the black
neighbourhoods that he had been murdered (his body showed no
signs of stoning). Mobs gathered and fighting occurred between
blacks and whites in several parts of the city. For almost two weeks
racial hatred plunged Chicago into strife and wreckage, finally
ended by the state militia after thirty-eight people had been killed
and over 500 injured. Blacks suffered the most as over 1,000
families, principally black, were left homeless. In the investigation
that followed, the Chicago Commission on Race Relations, which
was composed of six whites and six blacks, found that, above all
else, "insufficiency in amount and quality of housing is an all-
important factor in Chicago's race problem." Not unexpectedly, the
riot was felt only slightly where blacks and whites were most
accustomed to working with each other.

Led by the National Association for the Advancement of
Colored People, Negro organizations sought a federal anti-
lynching law, but while it passed the House of Representatives in
1921 Southerners filibustered it to death in the Senate. The
NAACP published *Thirty Years of Lynching* in 1919 followed by
Walter White's *Rope and Faggot, A Biography of Judge Lynch*
(1929), based on careful investigation into such outrages. The
NAACP also conducted numerous protest meetings against
lynchings during the 1920s. Advocates of Negro rights made
limited progress in legal attacks on the southern white primary
system and in promoting improved racial relations in the South
through education. The majority of Negroes, however, tended to
look with some suspicion upon the NAACP and similar liberal
organizations as upper class black and white movements remote
from their interests.

In this climate of unemployment, low wages and discrimination
in all parts of the country, large numbers of poor and under-
educated Negroes became increasingly attracted to Marcus
Garvey's black nationalist movement. Garvey was born in poverty

in Jamaica, British West Indies, in 1887. Despite the lack of formal educational opportunities, Garvey became a printer's apprentice, a local labor leader, and travelled extensively in Central and South America and Western Europe. After founding in Jamaica in 1914 what subsequently came to be called the Universal Negro Improvement Association (UNIA), based on local industrial and educational self-improvement programs, Garvey determined to travel America to seek financial aid and support, hopefully from the well-known Negro Booker T. Washington who died Garvey's departure. With few prospects he arrived in New York in March 1916. In ten years' time he established the New York Chapter of the UNIA (1917), was arrested on charges of using the mails to defraud (1922), was found guilty and sentenced to Atlanta prison (1925) and was subsequently released and deported as an undesirable alien (1927).

Within these crowded years, Garvey succeeded in arousing the political consciousness of the urban black masses in a manner that they had never been aroused before. His preachments of racial consciousness and pride found a highly receptive audience among Negro migrants from the South and disillusioned blacks in general whose efforts in World War I, they believed, were under-appreciated. In short, writes one of Garvey's biographers, the postwar Negro located in Garveyism "a program that would tend to restore even a measure of their lost dignity and respect."

The principal aim of Garveyism centered on the race redemption of all black peoples throughout the world. Garvey and his followers assumed that a redemption of the world's blacks would only come through a rebuilding of their shattered racial pride and the restoration of a truly black culture. The specific means toward this goal were a reaffirmation of one's blackness and the establishment of a great African nation. Accordingly, Garvey exalted all things black and exhorted his followers to take special pride in their distinctive features and color; to demonstrate his point, he called his merchant marine the Black Star Line, his nurse corps the Black Cross, advertized black dolls in the *Negro World* (the main organ of the UNIA), encouraged black studies, and even promoted a black Virgin and Christ.

Equally significant, Garvey sought to establish a great African nation, reclaiming, by force if necessary, that entire continent from white imperialists. In this regard, it was commonly held that Garveyism constituted, simply, a back-to-Africa movement for the New World blacks. Nothing, it seems, could have been further from Garvey's intention, as he believed that once a strong African nation established, Negroes could then draw racial pride, prestige and protection from it. It was only in this sense, that Garvey was willing to concede that America would always remain a white man's country.

Negro opposition to Garvey came essentially from two sources: the upper classes and the intellectuals. Upper-class blacks considered the Jamaican a presumptuous foreigner whose real aim was to milk the poor; further, they resented his strong emotional appeal to the lower classes. Black intellectuals of the Twenties led by W.E.B. Du Bois, who once referred to Garvey as "the most dangerous enemy of the Negro race in America," disliked Garvey almost as much as he disliked them. Generally, black intellectuals entertained serious reservations about the ability of a newly-arrived immigrant to interpret correctly American race problems and, for the most part, tended to ignore him. In reply, Garvey thought it, in his words, "astonishing how disloyal and selfish is the average Negro intellectual of the passing generation of his race." Garvey saved most of his anger, however, for Du Bois and the NAACP. For, according to Garvey, in pursuing a policy of "social equality," Du Bois and his followers demonstrated beyond doubt "they hate their black blood, and God and man know it." Though he died in relative obscurity in 1940 and the UNIA movement declined, Garvey's ideas were to experience a revival in the 1960s under the auspices of the Black Power movement.

THE CULTURE OF A BUSINESS AGE

In the Twenties boosters bragged that a democratic revolution had occurred in the ownership of stocks in American corporations. The great bull market saw stock-ownership increase from two million people in 1920 to some 17 million by the end of the decade. Office workers, clerks, and laborers joined businessmen in purchasing stocks for investment or speculative purposes. John

Raskob of General Motors suggested that anyone could get rich within twenty years by investing $15 weekly in stocks and letting them grow in value. Hoover voiced the prevailing optimism and "get-rich-quick" urge in 1928: "We seem only to have touched the fringe of our potentialities."

These optimists usually overlooked a darker side to the dispersion of stock ownership. Diffusion of ownership did not mean that large corporations became more responsible to their small stockholders, but only that insiders, owning a minority of the stocks, found it easier to control and even wreck the corporations. Many stocks in fact were non-voting issues; one textile firm issued 2,000 voting shares out of a total of 600,000 shares outstanding. The holding company device, with one holding company pyramided over a number of lesser holding and operating companies, facilitated a ruinous manipulation by the few speculators in control at the top. Small stockholders and the assets of the actual operating companies could be fleeced through overcaptilization, excessive service charges, and other techniques. Samuel Insull erected a holding company on top of holding companies until his system defied analysis; it collapsed in 1932 with an estimated loss to investors of a billion dollars.

Still, businessmen became the popular heroes of the day. No longer under the "robber-baron" onus of the muckraking era, big businessmen often spoke in the Progressive rhetoric of public service and the common good and identified their cause with democracy and progress. Booster clubs, trade associations, and chambers of commerce extolled the new hero and the American "way of life." President Calvin Coolidge commented that "Brains are wealth and wealth is the chief end of man." "The man who builds a factory builds a temple," he proclaimed, and "the man who works there worships there." The parlance of business crept into every facet of American life. An article in *The Independent* praised the business community for providing the "sanest religion" in America, for "any relationship that forces a man to follow the Golden Rule rightfully belongs amid the ceremonials of the church." Bruce Barton, in the best seller *The Man Nobody Knows* (1925), described Jesus Christ as the world's most successful businessman who had recruited twelve disciples "from the bottom ranks of business and forged them into an organization that conquered the world."

Industry transformed American society and life. Probably the automobile had the greatest single impact on the economy and society. At first highly experimental and expensive, by 1910 standard production type automobiles had been developed. Henry Ford, the high-priest of assembly-line production, flooded America with the cheap but durable Model T; his assembly-line technique reduced the time required to produce a car from over 12 hours to less than two hours. Satisfied with a small unit profit on a large volume of sales, Ford reduced the price of a Model T from $950 to $290 by 1924. He owned the majority of stock in the Ford Motor company and zealously guarded his family firm from raids by bankers and financiers.

Ownership of an automobile changed from a symbol of social status that it had been prior to 1914 to a commonplace convenience. Ford became a national hero, rated by a group of college students as the third greatest figure in history, behind only Jesus Christ and Napoleon. His many admirers overlooked his anti-union policies, his peculiar politics, and his anti-semitism. General Motors ranked next in the automotive field, organized by William C. Durant but falling under the control of J.P. Morgan and the DuPonts after the First World War. Ford and General Motors between them shared 60 percent of the automobile market. The increasing sales of General Motors' Chevrolet forced Ford to introduce a new car, the Model A, in 1928. Third among the giants, Chrysler Corporation competed with its Plymouth in the low price field.

The automobile created a whole new industry, involving not only the makers of the product and the suppliers of metals and fabrics for the vehicles but petroleum refineries and innumerable service stations, garages, and highway inns to care for the car and its occupants. The industry consumed annually 90 percent of the country's refined petroleum products, 80 percent of its rubber, 75 percent of the plate glass, and 25 percent of the machine tools. By 1929 Americans drove 26 million vehicles and annual passenger car production reached three million units. Highways vastly increased in mileage, spurred by matching grants to the states inaugurated under the 1916 Federal Highway Act and subsequent legislation. Authorities expended an estimated $1 billion per year during the decade on highways and $400 million on city streets. Trucking and bus transportation also grew steadily, to the corresponding loss of the railroads.

The automobile helped break down rural isolation and made possible the rapid growth of city suburbs and vacation retreats. A fantastic real estate boom in Florida, touted as America's Riviera, reached incredible proportions by the mid-Twenties. Miami grew from 30,000 in 1920 to 75,000 by 1925. Around the city, and indeed over much of the entire state, land values rose exorbitantly and developers launched scores of construction projects for housing, hotels, and resorts. Lots, some bought unseen and subsequently discovered by unwary purchasers to lie under water in swamps or the sea, sold for prices as high as $25,000 to $75,000 each, until that bubble burst in 1926. Among other less desirable effects of the automotive age were highway congestion and a mounting toll of accidents. Moreover, the automobile made crime more mobile and, in the view of many, encouraged juvenile delinquency and sexual immorality.

Aviation, born around the turn of the century with the pioneers Wilbur and Orville Wright, was stimulated greatly by military needs in World War I. The industry made slow progress thereafter, however, until the stimulus of the 1925 Air Mail Act. Thereafter a number of major manufacturing and transportation companies began to emerge, and by 1929 forty-eight commercial airlines provided connections between 355 cities.

Advertising, the quintessence of "boosterism," became a major industry of nearly $2 billion by 1929. It brought with it an emphasis on brands and on psychological obsolescence. To clear that way each year for a new flood of consumer goods and gadgets advertisers persuaded the public that this year's model was incomparably superior to last year's. Large industries also indulged heavily in public relations, hiring publicists to extol their merits and to discredit critics. Much of the increased purchasing resulted from a vast expansion of credit or installment buying, that mixed blessing that permits one (briefly) to live beyond his immediate means. By the end of the decade, 15 percent of all goods sold were on credit, accounting for $5 billion of sales annually by 1929.

Development of the radio and the motion picture industry brought a growing sophistication in taste and manners. From an infant industry in 1920, by 1929 one out of every three households (four out of five by 1940) owned a radio, and broadcasting networks such as the National Broadcasting Company and the Columbia Broadcasting System supplied local stations with entertainment and information. Motion picture cameras and projectors, developed by George Eastman, Thomas A. Edison, and others in the late nineteenth century spawned a new industry by the early 1900s. Prior to World War I, David W. Griffith produced lengthy film stories and Mary Pickford, Charlie Chaplin, and others achieved fame and fortune. After the Armistice, motion picture theaters across America—22,731 by 1931—regaled viewers first with silent and then with sound movies (the first "talkie," in 1927, starred Al Jolson in "The Jazz Singer"). Average weekly attendance at the movies numbered 95 million by 1929, consuming a diet of gangster, western, and boudoir films. The movie idols of the day were personalities such as Clara Bow, the "It" girl, Theda Bara the "Vamp," and Rudolph Valentino the "Sheik."

Increased leisure, as well as affluence, led to a growth in recreational activities; municipal and private golf courses, tennis courts, and swimming pools multiplied. Professional sports— baseball, football, and boxing—provided both entertainment and popular heroes for spectators: Babe Ruth in baseball, boxers Jack Dempsey and Gene Tunney, and the immortal Red Grange, an Illinois fullback, to name only a few. When Dempsey fought George S. Carpentier in 1921 for the heavyweight boxing championship, 91,000 people paid over $1 million to see the American flatten the French challenger. Similar receipts flowed in to promoters later when Tunney finally dethroned Dempsey in two highly advertised encounters. College football became frankly semiprofessional and some schools apparently cut back on academics in order to build huge stadiums and hire expensive coaches. Fads for Mah Jong, crossword puzzles, and flagpole sitting ("Shipwreck" Kelly) swept the nation. The idol of the decade, the "Lone Eagle" Charles A. Lindbergh, crossed the Atlantic in 33 hours in a single-engine airplane in 1927. He landed at Paris to a hero's welcome and, on orders from President Coolidge, returned home in triumph aboard an American warship. No single event of the decade so captured the world's admiration and aroused such hero worship as his flight in the "Spirit of St Louis."

THE REVOLT AGAINST "VICTORIANISM"

The revolution against "Victorian" morals and standards, actually underway during the Progressive Era prior to the First World War, became fully apparent in the 1920s. The urbanization and secularization of American life had eroded the appeal and authority of past traditions and morals. The "new woman," enfranchised by the Nineteenth Amendment and by economic opportunities, and above all by the growth of the city, sought greater freedom. Large numbers of women left the shelter of home for employment in the professions, industry, and as typists and secretaries in the business world. Over 10 million women were employed by 1930. As more women enjoyed release from past restraints, the number of divorces mounted and the size of families declined as the birth rate fell. New moral standards prevailed, at first among upper-class women but eventually affecting to some degree women of the middle and lower classes. Shorter dresses and rolled-down hose, bobbed hair, increased use of cosmetics, dances such as the *Charleston*, drinking from hip flasks and smoking, and more illegitimate births seemed to characterize the new woman. The psychological theories of Dr Sigmund Freud, widely misinterpreted as having sanctioned sexual promiscuity to avoid neurotic inhibitions and complexes, became fashionable. Testifying to the new and open emphasis on sex, an estimated one-fourth of the radio broadcasting time in 1928 conveyed erotic messages with such songs as "Baby Face," "Hot Mamma," "Hot Lips," and "Burning Kisses." One movie producer advertised a film as offering "brilliant men, beautiful jazz babies, champagne baths, midnight revels, petting parties in the purple dawn, all ending in one terrific smashing climax that makes you gasp." Sex themes also abounded in certain types of mass circulation magazines, such as *Snappy Stories* and *True Confessions*, and "petting" and "necking" entered the nation's vocabulary.

Americans seemed more hedonistic than ever before, observing the Sabbath more with golf, movies, or afternoon drives than by church attendance. Alarmed moralists spoke out: the head of the Christian Endeavour Society condemned the *Charleston* as "an offense against womanly purity;" the Young Women's Christian Association launched a national drive for more modest female attire; and several legislatures debated laws on the proper length of dresses. Judge Ben Lindsey of Denver ignited a controversy by suggesting "trial marriages" to reduce divorce and illegitimacy. Yet the moral rebellion should not be exaggerated; millions of American continued to live as before. The cult of youth died out in the early 1930s, because it is the nature of such rebellions to burn out or pall and because of the sobering effects of the Great Depression.

Education scored notable advances during this period, although here too materialistic values seemed to predominate. John Dewey's philosophy of progressive education to adjust the learning process to a changing society was often misinterpreted as permissiveness in teaching and the abandonment of traditional subjects of study such as classics, literature, and languages for more practical courses. Enrollments and expenditures in the public schools, especially on the secondary level, vastly increased. Advances took place in student health through physical examinations and use of school nurses. Since many new students were not academically oriented, high schools instituted vocational training embracing subjects such as the manual arts and secretarial skills. By 1926 one out of every eight American youth attended a college or university. The increases in high school and college enrollments reflected not only prosperity and the traditional belief in the value of education, but the needs of the business world for trained professional people and skilled technicians. Higher education expanded beyond the liberal arts to provide courses in commerce and business, home economics, and applied arts and sciences.

REACTION AND THE GREAT RED SCARE

Changes as sweeping as those of the Twenties inevitably aroused bewilderment and resistance. Much of the reaction—the upsurge of Fundamentalism, prohibition, and the revulsion toward the intellectuals—can be understood as responses to the upheaval of war and rapid economic and social transformations threatening the older ways of life.

Political and social reaction did not, however, begin with the Republican era. Some of Wilson's domestic policies in 1919-1920 were far from liberal and made their own contribution to the postwar climate. The government after the Armistice quickly terminated millions of dollars of war contracts and drastically reduced federal construction projects. The armed forces demobilized servicemen with little effort made to ease the shock of return to civilian life or to cope with the increase in unemployment. The government had efficiently operated the railroads as an integrated system during the war. McAdoo, who had supervised their direction, wanted to continue federal operation for five more years to allow time for further study of the matter, while the Railroad Brotherhoods advocated the Plumb Plan for governmental purchase and management. Conservative opposition blocked these solutions but not without some concessions to progressive sentiment. The Esch-Cummins Transportation Act of 1920 returned the roads to their owners but enlarged the supervisory powers of the Interstate Commerce Commission. The ICC could fix rates based on a "fair return" on the value of the property. A "recapture" clause provided that the government would take one-half of any profits above a rate of six percent, but it proved unworkable in practice due to lack of agreement over how to determine the value of railroad property. A Railway Labor Board was created to hear worker grievances but it lacked the power to enforce solutions.

The Water Power Act of 1920, another progressive achievement, established the Federal Power Commission to control construction of private power-generating facilities on federal lands and navigable streams, but it proved ineffective in practice. With the Jones Merchant Marine Act, Wilson and Congress decided to get government out of the shipping business and to subsidize private shipping by selling government owned vessels at bargain rates, roughly one-eighth of the cost of construction. In 1928, to aid a declining merchant marine, Congress authorized loans and mail subsidies. The 1919 Revenue Act continued to tax large incomes heavily, but in general the government changed rapidly from wartime inflationary policies to deflationary ones of steep taxes and sharply reduced expenditures and thereby contributed to a brief postwar economic recession.

The Great Red Scare of 1919-1920 marked a particularly reprehensible blot on the Wilson administration and the nation. Conservatives had long trembled at the growth of radicalism in America, and the war had provided an opportunity to vent hatreds and suspicions not only on hapless German-Americans but also on radical leaders and movements. Fear of radicalism increased after the Bolshevik Revolution in Russian and the founding in 1919 of the Comintern or Communist International to foment world revolution. Eugene Debs' Socialist Party had been weakened and divided during the war, first by the defection of those members who supported Wilson's war program and then by wartime arrests and repression. The communist wing bolted the Socialist Party in 1919 and two revolutionary Marxist parties were formed, a Communist Party based on some of the foreign language members of the old Socialist Party and other alien radicals and a Communist Labor Party led by native-born Americans such as the young radical poet and writer John Reed, who was to die of typhus in Russia in 1921 and be buried in the Kremlin Wall. These rival communist groups slavishly emulated the Russian model and bolstered their own morale by confidently predicting imminent revolution in the United States. Ordered by Moscow to amalgamate in 1921, the united party failed to make much headway even among laborers and by the end of the decade was thoroughly Stalinized under the nominal leadership of William Z. Foster. Even so, the puny communist movement aroused widespread fear and reaction in America during the last months of the Wilson era. Labor unrest gave middle-class Americans further cause for alarm.

Despite mounting fear of radicalism, the Justice Department under Attorney General A. Mitchell Palmer at first pursued a moderate course. Radicals mailed a number of packaged bombs to high government officials and to such prominent citizens as John D. Rockefeller and J.P. Morgan, timed to arrive on May Day 1919. Postal authorities intercepted most of them though one blew up, shattering the hands of a maid in a US Senator's home. Investigation failed to reveal the perpetrators, but the press and public harbored few doubts in attributing the outrage to the Bolsheviks. On June 2, another bomb shattered both the home and the nerves of the Attorney General. The bomber, who carried anarchist pamphlets, blew up with his own device. Similar attacks also occurred in eight other cities.

Palmer, haboring presidential ambitions, tried to exploit the prevailing hysteria against radicalism. He established a General Intelligence Division under J. Edgar Hoover within the Justice Department to keep radical organizations under close surveillance. Although little if any evidence existed of a serious organized attempt at actual revolution, Justice Department officials succumbed to the panics and fears of the times and further aroused them by exaggerated reports and dire predictions. Palmer considered deporting dangerous radicals as early as June, and he encountered much criticism when he delayed repressive action. Finally, while President Wilson was still seriously ill, he launched the so-called Palmer Raids.

Under the 1917-1918 immigration law, aliens advocating violence or the use of violence against the government could be deported. An estimated 90 percent of the members of the two communist parties and the anarchist groups consisted of foreign-born individuals, hence the agitation for large-scale deportations. The Union of Russian Workers, an apparently peaceful anarchist organization, became the first target of the Palmer Raids. The raiders arrested about 300 men and women, including citizens not members of any radical group, who were caught in the building housing the Union in New York City on November 7, 1919, the second anniversary of the Bolshevik coup in Russia. Authorities subsequently released most of them, quite a few with bloody heads or bruises, but held 39 for deportation. A total of 650 were seized in New York City, and there were arrests without warrants in other cities. Palmer justified these basic violations of legal rights on the basis that the country faced imminent revolution. On December 21, 1919, the *SS Buford*, popularly rechristened the "Red Ark," sailed with 249 alien deportees for Russia. In January of the next year, larger raids swept in between 3,000 and 4,000 suspected alien radicals, again without search warrants. After days or weeks in overcrowded jails and detention centers, most of those arrested subsequently obtained release for lack of evidence.

A anti-radical hysteria seized many otherwise sane Americans. Several state legislatures, continuing the wartime search for subversives, launched investigations and passed laws to curb radical activity. The Industrial Workers of the World (the "Wobblies") had been organized in 1905 as a radical union of skilled and unskilled workers, dedicated to the overthrow of capitalism and the creation of a socialist society. Too revolutionary for most Americans and prone to violence and internecine brawling, the IWW appealed mostly to workers in logging camps and mines in the western states. The IWW opposed American intervention in 1917 in what it called a capitalistic war and the government singled it out for legal attack and repression. A number of states enacted anti-syndicalist laws, while the Justice Department convicted and imprisoned 180 Wobbly leaders under the Sedition and Espionage Acts, blows from which the union never recovered. Still other members fell into the hands of local patriotic groups and suffered "tar and featherings," beatings, and even lynchings. On Armistice Day 1919, three parading American Legionnaires were killed as they marched past the IWW headquarters in Centralia, Washington. Although it seems clear that the Legionnaires had provoked the incident, an irate mob demolished the union hall and the authorities arrested twelve members of the IWW; one was lynched and the others imprisoned for long terms. In the aftermath of Centralia, more state legislatures hastened to pass anti-syndicalist laws.

Illustrating the hysteria of the brief Red Scare, South Carolina's James F. Byrnes called for use of federal forces to suppress an alleged communist-directed Negro rebellion in the southern states. Kenneth McKellar of Tennessee proposed converting the remote island of Guam into an American Devil's Island for dangerous native radicals who could not be deported to Russia. And evangelist Billy Sunday suggested saving space on our ships by executing some of the radical leaders by firing squads. But hysteria subsided in the spring of 1920 as a number of Americans became alarmed at the excesses. The Labor Department, charged with responsibility for aliens and immigration, recoiled from Palmer's indiscriminate zeal and insisted on legal counsel and due process for the accused. Consequently, over one-half of those arrested in 1920 were released; when called before Congress to explain, Labor's Assistant Secretary made an effective case. Finally, Palmer's reputation suffered a severe eclipse when a mass radical uprising predicted for May Day 1920, failed to materialize. Appalled by the wild charges and the violations of civil liberties, thoughtful citizens denounced the scare, and Palmer's presidential aspirations faded as sanity began to return to the nation.

To many liberals then and since, the Sacco-Vanzetti case symbolized the reactionary nature of the postwar era. Police arrested Nicola Sacco and Bartolomeo Vanzetti, Italian aliens and admitted philosophical anarchists, and accused them of murdering a shoe factory paymaster and a guard in South Braintree, Massachusetts, in 1920. Although the evidence seemed unsubstantial to many observers, and the trial judge, Webster Thayer, was obviously highly prejudiced against alien radicals ("those anarchist bastards," he once commented), the two men were convicted in 1921 and sentenced to death in the electric chair. They spent the next six years in prison while their defenders made repeated attempts to save them. Intellectuals and liberals rallied to their cause, along with the radicals and the communists at home and abroad. On the other hand, many conservatives resented all the agitation in behalf of the two aliens and no doubt agreed with the sentiments of evangelist Billy Sunday, "Give 'em the juice." Despite world-wide sympathy and numerous appeals for mercy and justice, Sacco and Vanzetti finally were executed in August 1927. Debate about their guilt or innocence persists to the present, and the case did more than any other single event to fasten the label of reaction on the America of the 1920s.

THE NATIVIST UPSURGE

Influenced by such racist books as Madison Grant's *The Passing of the Great Race* (1916) and the writings of Lothrop Stoddard and William McDougall, a eugenics cult flourished during the decade. It had long been widely believed that the superior "Anglo-Saxon" or Nordic racial strain in America was being swamped by the influx of inferior immigrants from Southern and Eastern Europe. Responding to the supposed peril, 29 states enacted racial integrity laws prohibiting interracial marriages. The Ku Klux Klan, revived in 1915 by William J. Simmons of Georgia, fell into the hands of skilled organizers and salesmen. Under the leadership of its new Imperial Wizard, Texas dentist H.W. Evans, the Klan spread across the South and most of the nation. It carried with its pretentious ritual and elaborate secret hierarchy sinister hatreds of minority groups and foreigners, Catholics, Jews, and Negroes especially.

Although the Klan professed to be a patriotic order, it inspired not only white-sheeted parades and nighttime cross burnings but whippings, mutilations, and lynchings. After reaching a peak membership of between four and five million and achieving political influence in a number of states, northern and southern, the movement eventually subsided under the weight of its own excesses. The Klan, long thought to have been confined largely to Protestant rural and smalltown America, also drew great strength from lower middle-class Protestants in the cities (many only recently from the farm) who resented the influx of blacks from the southern states and Catholic and Jewish aliens from Southern and Eastern Europe. Like fascism in Europe, the Klan represented a troubled Protestant and "native" America frantically seeking a return to a presumed older and simpler past, a "native, white, Protestant America."

In such a fevered nativist climate, Congress passed the Immigration Acts of 1921 and 1924. Immigration had declined during the war but rose in 1920-1921 to over a million and a quarter, of which about two-thirds came from Southern and Eastern Europe. The 1921 emergency immigration act set limits for annual entry of three percent of those nationalities present in the United States based on the census of 1910. Congress designed the

1924 National Origins Act even more clearly to curtail or halt immigration of undesirable or "inferior" aliens, imposing an annual quota to admit no more than two percent of those nationalities present in the United States according to the census of 1890, when heavy immigration from Southern and Eastern Europe first had become noticeable, and prohibiting Asian immigration. Northern Europe, which did not need them, received larger quotas in contrast to Southern and Eastern European areas. In 1929 even smaller quotas were set, based upon the 1920 census. During the Great Depression, President Hoover made still more drastic reductions.

An historic era of free immigration to people America, starting in 1607 and 1620, for all practical purposes had ended. By the early 1930s, the combined effect of the law and the depression reduced annual arrivals to less than those leaving the country. Now at last the melting pot presumably could function to "Americanize," though not entirely eliminate, the foreign language enclaves in the great cities. It should be kept in mind, however, that while immigration restriction reflected racist and nativist sentiments, it also in a sense had progressive overtones. Many progressives had long advocated such curtailment on a planned, scientific basis, which the law seemed to embody.

THE NOBLE EXPERIMENT

The Eighteenth Amendment to the Constitution in 1919 imposed prohibition upon the United States. Implemented by the Volstead Act, the law forbade the manufacture, transportation, or sale of alcoholic beverages containing over one-half of one percent of alcohol. Long sought by reformers who atributed most human ills to alcohol and who viewed prohibition as a panacea for slums, poverty, and crime, the amendment had been hastily pushed through Congress and the states as a patriotic war measure to protect servicemen and to reduce industrial absenteeism. Many progressives also had favored it as a means to disrupt malodorous ties between political machines and the liquor interests. Rural Protestants were particularly dedicated drys, expressing their distrust of the "corrupt" cities and alcohol-imbibing aliens. When the bans went into effect on July 16, 1920 (many gathered to

mourn as well as to cheer) Billy Sunday summed up the hopes of
the prohibitionists:

> The slums soon will be only a memory. We will turn our prisons into
> factories and our jails into storehouses and corncribs. Men will walk upright
> now, women will smile, and the children will laugh. Hell will be forever for
> rent."

Yet many other citizens viewed prohibition as an intolerable
violation of individual rights and an unworkable attempt to
legislate morality. Resentment ran strongly among many minority
groups, such as the German- and Italian-Americans, accustomed to
the consumption of beer and light wines with meals.

In any case, Prohibition ran counter to the hedonistic
characteristics of the 1920s. It was widely flouted, especially in the
cities and among the upper classes. Illegal bars called speakeasies
sold alcoholic beverages, often with bribed police protection.
Organized crime quickly took over much of the lucrative whisky
traffic, manufacturing liquors (usually redistilling industrial
denatured alcohol) or smuggling them in from abroad
(rumrunning). "Scarface Al" Capone and his gang grew rich and
powerful in Chicago, and criminal elements often combined other
forms of crime, such as prostitution and narcotics, with
bootlegging.

Many stores openly sold equipment and supplies for the illegal
home brewing of wines, beer, or even whisky. Enforcement on the
whole was a farce, with neither Congress nor the executive
particularly vigorous in its duty. Violations in any case were so
extensive as to defy rigid enforcement, yet even so the courts were
clogged with a vast backlog of cases. Although surveys indicated
that by 1926 large numbers of citizens favored repeal or
modifications of the Volstead Act, politicians feared the largely
rural dry vote and continued to pay lip service to the noble
experiment in legislating morals. Not until the Twenty-first
Amendment repealing prohibition was adopted in 1933 did
government and the people at last admit failure and even then only
over the strenuous opposition of the dry forces.

RELIGIOUS CURRENTS IN THE TWENTIES

The flowering of new religious cults and a popular "mind-cure" seemed symptomatic of the growing dismay at the loss of traditional values and beliefs. Jehovah's Witnesses, established in 1884, preached the imminent end of this world and the beginning of the reign of Christ. The Witnesses aroused much hostility when they refused to permit their school children to salute the flag. The Four Square Gospel of Aimee Semple McPherson was less orthodox and more bizarre. A former schoolteacher and carnival barker, and a divorcee, Sister Aimee invaded Los Angeles and within a few years built an enormous Angelus Temple and won 30,000 members. Her theology was crude and simple, but its stress on love and hope, and her highly unorthodox services marked by filmy gowns, bright lights and color, musical bands, and dramatized sermons proved enormously appealing. The temple owned its own radio station, KFSG, and sent missionaries into the Pacific slope and midwestern states. A mystic cult, the "Great I Am," flowered in California, while a number of New York blacks and whites ascended to Father Divine's earthy Heavens. Frank Buchanan launched the Oxford Movement, or Moral Rearmament its later name. He gave theology little attention and advocated individual "spiritual silence" and group confessions to obtain "God guidance" in life. Many other Americans in this secular decade seemed to find Coué-ism more appealing than any religious approach. Combining ideas drawn from mental healing and psychoanalysis, Emile Coué of France advocated auto-suggestion to assert the primacy of the will over the emotions and the body. Spreading to America, Coué-ism soon had large numbers of Americans chanting to themselves at all hours:

> Day by day, in every way,
> I am getting better and better.

The principal reaction to the growth of religious liberalism and scepticism in urban America, however, came from an upsurge of Protestant fundamentalism and religious conservatism, particularly strong in rural areas and small towns but also affecting the cities. The "warfare between science and theology" that had characterized the late nineteenth century had seemed to be over, as an increasing number of Christian ministers and laymen—"Christian modernists"—had come to terms with the implications of science and evolutionary theories and had adopted the social gospel to improve the social and civic aspects of American life. Yet after World War I an upsurge of religious conservatism, determined to cleanse the church, seminaries, and public schools of modernism, seemed to threaten the preservation of intellectual freedoms.

Fundamentalism apparently owed its name to the efforts of two oil millionaires in Los Angeles, California, who in 1910 had subsidized the publication of ten small pamphlets entitled "The Fundamentals: A Testimony to the Truth." These rejected the findings of modern science and the Biblical Higher Criticism and presented as essential Christian doctrines belief in the absolute accuracy of the Bible and its account of creation, the virgin birth of Christ, the incarnation and historical resurrection of Jesus, and other dogmas. Fundamentalists distributed over three million copies of these pamphlets through churches, schools, and other organizations.

Apparently stimulated by the postwar reaction, many of the religious traditionalists attributed all of America's strains and stresses, from radicalism to crime, to a departure from strict Scriptural faith and standards. Appealing largely to the rural and less educated, fundamentalism reflected a fear of change and a quest for certainty and was intensely emotional and even violent in denunciation of such leading exponents of liberal or modernist Christianity as the Rev. Harry Emerson Fosdick. Some fundamentalists described Fosdick as a seducer of the minds and souls of youth. Evangelists such as Billy Sunday continued to exhort audiences with the simplistic old time religion at revival meetings across America. Such organizations as the World's Christian Fundamentals Association, the Bible League of North America, and the Bible Crusaders of America assumed the offensive against the tides of liberalism, scepticism, and atheism. The Bible Crusaders even sought a constitutional amendment to proclaim "America a Christian nation."

In 1922 the World's Christian Fundamentals Association launched a drive for state laws prohibiting the teaching in public schools and colleges of Darwinism and other scientific theories contradicting the Biblical account of the creation of the world. William Jennings Bryan with magnetic oratory threw himself into the leadership of this crusade to refute scientific heresies. As he put it, "It is better to trust in the Rock of Ages than to know the age of rocks." Local school boards, especially in the southern and midwestern states, banned books on evolution and pressured teachers into compliance. An obscure Georgia legislator expressed the anti-intellectualism of the fundamentalist current:

> Read the Bible. It teaches you how to act. Read the hymn book. It contains the finest poetry ever written. Read the almanac. It teaches you to figure out what the weather will be. There isn't another book that is necessary for anyone to read, and therefore I am opposed to all libraries.

The anti-evolutionists made some progress in the South in their drive for prohibitory legislation. Although checked in North Carolina, where educational leaders courageously spoke up, crusading fundamentalists scored partial victories in Oklahoma and Florida. The Tennessee legislature passed a bill that prohibited all state supported schools from teaching "any theory that denies the story of the divine creation of man as taught in the Bible and to teach instead that man has descended from a lower order of animals." Educators remained silent, and the governor reluctantly signed the measure in 1925. Bryan wired him his congratulations: "The Christian parents of the State owe you a debt of gratitude for saving their children from the poisonous influence of an unproven hypothesis...The South is now leading the nation in the defense of Bible Christianity." Fear of other states following Tennessee's example caused the American Civil Liberties Union to resolve to challenge the law in the courts and to offer aid to anyone involved in such a case.

The opportunity came in the small community of Dayton, Tennessee. John T. Scopes, a twenty-four year old teacher of science in the local high school, allowed himself to be arrested and tried on a charge of violating the new law. The trial commanded national and world wide attention as a supposed battle to the death between Christianity and evolution. Scores of reporters, observers, and the curious flocked to Dayton and the little town took on all the color and excitement of a circus. The World's Christian Fundamentals Association persuaded Bryan to aid the prosecution, while the noted criminal defense lawyer and agnostic, Clarence Darrow, joined the defense. Darrow came to Dayton fresh from his triumph in a celebrated trial in which he had helped Nathan Leopold, Jr. and Rich Loeb, two brilliant youths from wealthy families in Chicago, escape the gallows by receiving life sentences for their senseless murder of thirteen year old Bobby Franks.

At Dayton the key issue of academic freedom versus the right of local authority to control education seemed almost lost sight of in the feverish atmosphere. Although Bryan declared that the real question was the right of the taxpayers to regulate their schools, he too acted as if the trial were one between Christianity and evolution. Many felt disappointed when the judge ruled against the plan of the defense to call noted scientists and liberal clergymen to testify that no real conflict existed between science and the Bible. Unfortunately for his cause, Bryan then unwisely allowed himself to be called to the stand as an expert on the Scriptures. Darrow's merciless examination revealed that Bryan was abysmally ignorant of science, history, and comparative religion and philosophy. Moreover, Bryan's replies seemed to indicate that even he did not interpret literally everything in the Bible.

Although the court found Scopes guilty and fined him, it seemed to many that fundamentalism had been convicted by an enlightened public opinion. Bryan, humiliated and partially discredited even before his own followers, died a few days after the conclusion of the trial. Deprived of his leadership, fundamentalism went into eclipse, although it did not disappear. The spread of education, the battle over the repeal of prohibition, and the coming of the Great Depression soon shunted aside the anti-evolution crusade.

ALIENATION OF THE INTELLECTUALS

Whereas the prewar literary generation had rebelled against the genteel tradition in art, literature, and morals and had exuded optimism about the promise of American democratic life, the postwar generation tended to be pessimistic about social issues. The attitude of this so-called "Lost Generation," whose youth presumably had been sacrificed in the recent war, often was corrosive and fatalistic. For many, World War I had ended the age of American innocence—moral idealism now seemed to many ridiculous, and faith in human progress through reason and science had been shaken or destroyed. Yet the alienation of the intellectuals had begun before the war. The influence of William James's pragmatism and psychology, Dewey's instrumentalist thought, and Freudianism, among other currents, inspired avantgardists prior to 1917 to challenge the optimism and faith in progress of the Progressives. The disillusioning experiences of the Great Crusade merely deepened the currents of pessimism and the rejection of traditional ideals and beliefs.

While businessmen and many others, including historians and economists, contentedly regarded the decade as a "new era," marked by the use of scientific technology and efficiency to produce prosperity for all, much of the intelligentsia could only see decline and retrogression. Literary critic Frederick J. Hoffman wrote of these "disinherited sons and daughters" of the middle class: "The vigor of anti-bourgeois criticism in the 1920s came, not from the proletarian critics, but from middle-class men and women who were disgusted with their cultural heritage." Reacting against middle-class culture, standards, and morals, these rebels often loosely used the term "Puritanism" to describe society as repressive of the natural desires and potentialities of human beings. Americans seemed to them hopelessly materialistic, afflicted by "moral and cultural philistinism." In 1922, Harold E. Stearns published a symposium of thirty essays on *Civilization in the United States*, a savage criticism of virtually every aspect of American life. America, in the view of the critics, was a cultural wasteland. A number of disillusioned intellectuals denounced democracy and praised European fascism; many demonstrated their disgust with American life either by flocking to the bohemian retreat of Greenwich Village, in New York or leaving for self-exile in Europe.

H. L. Mencken, editor of *The American Mercury*, reigned as the chief iconoclast of the Twenties. A mordant critic of middle-class democratic society, he mercilessly attacked almost everything admired by the average citizen whom he described as the "booboisie." He described democracy as an unworkable but amusing form of government and jabbed at crass politicians, smug businessmen, and "Bible Belt" rural Protestants. But though a generation of rebellious youth saw only revolt in Mencken's writing, in fact he surgically exposed the ills of the times. His most enduring contribution was far removed from satire: *The American Language* (1919), a scholarly study of American speech.

Theodore Dreiser was the major representative of literary naturalism in America. Born in Indiana in 1871, the son of a poverty-stricken German immigrant, his career as a novelist spanned much of modern American history—he died in 1945. From his own bitter experiences and influenced by Darwinist currents of thought, Dreiser derived the major themes of his writings, the conflict between human instincts, desires, and ambitions versus social convention and restraints. Dreiser therefore has been classified as a naturalist or realist novelist, guided by a philosophy of scientific determinism. His first important novel, *Sister Carrie* (1900), focused upon a sensitive young girl trying to escape her lowly environment through use of her sex. *An American Tragedy* (1925) presented the central figure of Clyde Griffiths caught in the trap of biological forces and society, culminating in the drowning of his sweetheart and his own subsequent execution in the electric chair. This work was not a tragedy in the Greek sense, but rather was a tragedy of biology and society.

Sinclair Lewis, a native of Sauk City, Minnesota, wrote in a type of regional vein, concentrating on the area of rural countryside and small towns and cities that he knew intimately. He became the best known novelist of the decade by 1930, when he won the Nobel Prize for literature. Literary critics view Lewis as less of a rebel against the older ideals, though he was often so interpreted, than as against their corruption and distortion in the Twenties. *Babbitt* (1922) portrayed the crassness and materialism of life in the city of Zenith, while *Main Street* (1925) did the same for the small town of Gopher Prairie where nearly everything was measured in terms of money. *Arrowsmith* (1925), one of the first novels of medicine, depicted the conflict between ideals and a commercial society, while *Elmer Gantry* (1927) described evangelical Protestantism as corrupted also by crass materialism. Yet, as *Dodsworth* (1929) revealed, Lewis did not lack sympathy for businessmen; he sought reform, not the supplanting of old values.

F. Scott Fitzgerald, another Minnesotan, attended Princeton and after the Armistice plunged into the gay, frenetic, party life of the postwar period. He expressed the generation's shaken faith in noble ideals and crusades for reform and democracy and a restless cynical hedonism in *This Side of Paradise* (1920), *Tales of the Jazz Age* (1922), and *The Beautiful and Damned* (1922). In *The Great Gatsby* (1925), his most tightly written novel, the idealist is a bootlegger. Rich and famous after his first book, Fitzgerald married Zelda Sayre of Alabama, an accomplished dancer and writer, and plunged into dizzy revelry here and in Paris. He returned to the United States in 1931, with funds exhausted and Zelda diagnosed insane; drinking heavily, Fitzgerald went to Hollywood to write, where he died of a heart attack in 1940. Zelda died in tragic circumstances in a hospital fire in 1948.

Encouraged by Gertrude Stein, the high priestess of the American postwar exiles living in Paris, Ernest Hemingway developed a clear and simple writing style glorifying the more basic physical and emotional experiences of men. Born in Illinois in 1898, the son of a physician, Hemingway had been a reporter— he remained one off and on throughout most of his life—and he served in the First World War as an ambulance driver in Italy where he was seriously wounded. He reflected the disillusionment and pleasure-loving mood of the Twenties in *The Sun Also Rises* (1926), in which postwar expatriates in France and Spain aimlessly spent their days in lovemaking, drinking, and watching bull fights. *A Farewell to Arms* (1929) is generally considered his best novel and one of the best of all the novels arising from World War I. Obviously based on Hemingway's wartime experiences, the novel at one point has the hero remark:

> I was always embarrassed by the words sacred, glorious, and sacrifice and the expression in vain...I had seen nothing sacred, and the things that were glorious had no glory and the sacrifices were like the stockyards at Chicago if nothing was done with the meat except to bury it.

In many of his subsequent novels and stories prior to his apparent suicide in 1961, Hemingway concentrated on a nihilistic world of action and adventure for its own sake.

William Faulkner, a contemporary of Fitzgerald and Hemingway, came from a distinguished Southern aristocratic family and spent most of his life in Oxford, Mississippi. Using a stream of consciousness technique in *The Sound and the Fury* (1929), followed by *As I Lay Dying* (1930), *Sanctuary* (1931), and later novels, Faulkner wrote of the decay of the older Southern way of life. Critics at first viewed him as a naturalistic novelist of a world of decay, terror and cruelty, but now they see him as utilizing romantic and naturalistic techniques to arrive at ethical ends. When he accepted the Nobel Prize in 1950, he briefly stated his creed: "Man will not merely endure: he will prevail...because he has a soul, a spirit capable of compassion and sacrifice and endurance." Therefore, "the writer's duty is to write about these things."

John Dos Passos, a realistic novelist who had not given up hope for social reform, joined a number of radical causes during these years. *Three Soldiers* (1921) expressed disillusionment with the Great Crusade, and in his trilogy *USA*, published in the 1930s, he penned a trenchant indictment of the materialistic and corrupt aspects of American life.

A literary-artistic "Black Renaissance" was centered in New York City. Developing growing confidence as well as race consciousness, black writers bitterly attacked racial oppression in America and demanded equality and opportunity for their race. Among the more significant black writers must be listed W.E.B. DuBois, *The Gift of Black Folk* (1924); James Weldon Johnson, *The Book of American Negro Poetry* (1922); and Langston Hughes, *Not Without Laughter* (1930) and *The Ways of White Folks* (1934). Black artists and performers, such as Paul Robeson and Marian Anderson, received increasing recognition from white Americans. Growing out of black life while borrowing from many other sources, jazz in its various moods, joyful funeral marches, original contributions to western culture swept across the United States in the 1920s and was taken up by white musicians. George Gershwin utilized it in his "Rhapsody in Blue" and other compositions.

The great Armory Show in New York City in 1913 displayed not only the realistic paintings of the "Ash Can School" but also called attention to new trends in European art. One of the most talked of pictures at the display was Marcel Duchamp's *Nude Descending the Staircase*. Cubism, derived from Henri Matisse and Pablo Picasso in France, sought to probe beneath the outward appearances of objects to their underlying geometric forms. This movement in America received great encouragement with the founding of New York's Museum of Modern Art in 1929 and the Whitney Museum in 1931, the latter devoted to American art. Throughout the 1920s and 1930s, the artistic world divided into realistic painters and the abstractionists. Although the pendulum swung back toward such realistic painters as Grant Wood, Thomas Hart Benton, and Edward Hopper in the Thirties, new modes of abstractionism such as expressionism and surrealism invaded America from Europe. Whatever its artistic merits, abstractionism in its several expressions has been interpreted as a graphic mirror to the ambiguity, confusions, and chaos of modern life and thought.

Irving Babbitt, a literary critic, wrote in 1924 that while American achievements might be impressive quantitatively, they were not qualitatively. What else could one expect, he asked, of a country that lavished admiration, even hero worship, on such individuals as Bryan, Billy Sunday, and Henry Ford. Yet behind all the glitter and crassness of the materialism of the Twenties there lay a genuine idealism that a life free from poverty and drudgery was possible for all in America. To be sure, the rich got richer but the middle and lower classes also made advances. Unquestionably life for the majority of Americans became far more pleasant during this decade than it had ever been before. Living and health standards improved, leisure time increased, and both recreational and educational opportunities were available on a hitherto unimaginable scale. Material advance cannot be equated with cultural development, but it does make it possible; and despite the attacks by the self-disinherited critics of the 1920s, the decade also witnessed much of lasting value in the arts and literature. Finally, the progressive impulse had not altogether vanished during the decade. Conservation of natural resources broadened to include the preservation of natural beauty. Social service groups remained active and, though their goals often had to be deferred, they contributed much to the coming New Deal in the fields of women and children labor legislation, unemployment and old age insurance, public works and housing, and collective bargaining. The New Deal drew heavily upon these ideas and called many former social workers to high positions in government.

SUGGESTED READINGS

Allen, Frederick Lewis. *Only Yesterday* (1931).

Buckingham, Peter H. *America Sees Red* (1988).

Chalmers, David M. *Hooded Americanism* (1965).

Fass, Paula. *The Damned and Beautiful* (1977).

Fink, James J. *The Car Culture* (1975).

Fitzgerald, F. Scott. *The Great Gatsby* (1925).

Hemingway, Ernest. *The Sun Also Rises* (1926).

Hoffman, Frederick. *The Twenties* (1955).

Huggins, Nathan. *Harlem Renaissance* (1971).

Kennedy, David M. *Over Here: The First World War and American Society* (1980).

May, Lary. *Screening Out the Past* (1980).

Murray, Robert K. *Red Scare* (1955).

Nelli, Humbert S. *The Business of Crime* (1976).

Sinclair, Andrew. *Prohibition* (1962).

Sklar, Robert T. *Movie-Made America* (1976).

Chapter Four

THE POLITICS BUSINESS

The election of Warren G. Harding in 1920 inaugurated a decade of Republican predominance in the national government. These were lean years for the Democrats, the lowest dip in their political fortunes since the Civil War. Progressivism seemed dead and political conservatism supreme. Yet the progressive impulse in fact was still alive, and the period cannot be dismissed merely as one of conservatism and reaction in politics. The trend toward governmental involvement in the economy continued as Republican administrations sought to cooperate with business rather than attempting to regulate it.

WARREN G. HARDING

In so far as the Harding administration had a policy it was the politics of business leadership. The business community asked and received from the new administration more economy and efficiency in government, tax reductions, the elimination of government competition with private enterprise, and freedom for business self-regulation.

Warren Gamaliel Harding provided an apt symbol of the new age of business politics. He often compared himself with William McKinley, whose administration had represented the quintessence of the middle-class ideal in the late nineteenth century. Born in Ohio in 1865 and raised in a rural community, young Harding moved to the town of Marion, Ohio and tried first salesmanship and then journalism. He married a divorcee, the daughter of the wealthiest man in the town, and became the owner-editor of the Marion *Star*. Attracted to politics, Harding was aided by his handsome looks, florid oratory, and genial manner. A "joiner," he belonged to the Elks, Odd Fellows, and the Moose, among other organizations. In the course of politicking, he met a lawyer, Harry M. Daugherty, who became his lifetime friend. Yet while many writers have assumed that the allegedly lethargic Harding was managed by his wife, whom he called the Duchess, and by Daugherty, in fact he was an ambitious and skilful politician who made his own key decisions. Daugherty merely exploited his relationship with Harding to rise from obscurity to power and eventual eclipse.

After holding several state offices in Ohio, Harding won a seat in the US Senate in 1914, one of the first to be chosen by popular vote under the Seventeenth Amendment to the Constitution. There he compiled a conservative record in a progressive era and cooperated with Lodge in the Treaty fight. His nomination in 1920 was not an accident nor was it the result of a boss-ruled convention. A dark horse candidate from Ohio, Harding moved cautiously at the convention while the front-runners monopolized public attention. Hiram Johnson, a contender for the nomination, charged his competitors, Leonard Wood and Frank Lowden, with spending millions of dollars in attempts to control the convention and to buy the nomination. The three candidates cancelled themselves out and threatened a deadlocked convention. Not one but many smoke-filled rooms occurred at the convention as delegates sought a compromise between the bitterly divided contending forces. Harding emerged with the great prize because he was highly available, a man with few enemies, from a key state, and with a politically attractive personality. Senator Lodge in formally notifying the candidate of his selection lectured him on the new balance to be sought between the executive and legislative departments of the federal government and Harding humbly promised to accept Senate tutelage. Lodge was to be disappointed in his hopes for a subservient president.

Harding offered a sharp contrast to his predecessor in office. He could not be accused of advocating social reform at home or idealistic crusades abroad. Something of an isolationist in foreign policy, he disliked the League of Nations and advocated an independent nationalistic course for the United States. He shared the political outlook of rural small-town America, which no doubt helped account for his victory in 1920 and his unquestioned popularity. Harding viewed America as a classless society, with economic equality of opportunity for all, functioning in a free market climate of private property and initiative. He greatly admired the very rich and shared the speculative and booster spirit of the age. Harding's private morals were not beyond reproach— according to recent biographers, it seems that he had at least two mistresses, one of whom, Nan Britton, unfortunately for his reputation was later to write *The President's Daughter*. Easy-going Harding often could be found in the White House playing cards and drinking whisky with his cronies. As Alice Roosevelt Longworth, Theodore Roosevelt's daughter and a caustic observer of the Washington scene, later remarked, "Harding was not a bad man. He was just a slob."

The cabinet appointed by Harding contained a mixture of competent and incompetent men. Virtually ignoring the Senate, whose leaders had expected to dominate him, Harding named the very able Charles Evans Hughes Secretary of State; Herbert Hoover Secretary of Commerce; and Henry C. Wallace Secretary of Agriculture. Andrew Mellon, reputedly the second richest man in the country, headed the Treasury Department. Other appointees tended to be mediocre. Harding's good friend, Daugherty, became Attorney General, and Senator Albert B. Fall, a known foe of conservation (later sent to prison for bribe-taking) served as Secretary of the Interior. Lesser appointments, to Harding's subsequent regret, went to a group of old supporters and hangers-on known as the "Ohio Gang." This group maintained a sort of headquarters at "the little green house" at 1625 K Street. There Harding cronies received bootleg whisky and engaged in the selling of government influence and favors.

THE RETURN TO NORMALCY

In his inaugural remarks, Harding called for "an end of government's experiment in business and...more efficient business in government administration." One of the first acts signed by Harding was the Budget and Accounting Act. Heretofore each executive department had approached Congress separately for its appropriation, thus precluding overall budget study and planning. The act provided for a Director of the Budget to help the President plan an annual executive budget and a Comptroller General to audit accounts and to oversee expenditures in a more efficient way. Faced with a postwar economic slump, Harding frankly stated that business cycles were inevitable and that all government could do was to curtail its own expenditures and to maintain the national credit.

World War I veterans had formed the American Legion in 1919. Arguing that "stay-at-home" civilians had prospered while doughboys risked health and life in the army camps and trenches, the Legion asked for veterans a bonus of one dollar a day for each day of service at home and a dollar and a quarter for overseas service. Harding appeared before the Senate to block passage of such a bill in 1921, but as the congressional elections approached Congress capitulated to pressure and passed a bonus in 1922 in the form of paid up insurance. Harding vetoed it as unwise special interest legislation and costly to the Treasury (it was finally passed over Coolidge's veto in 1924). Secretary Mellon urged Congress to repeal the wartime excess profits tax and to reduce income tax rates on higher incomes, claiming that they penalized initiative and investments. He obtained a large part of his request in the 1921 revenue act, which eliminated the excess profits tax and cut the maximum income rate in half. Subsequently he obtained further reductions, and he also gradually cut back the war swollen national debt.

Agricultural distress and the postwar economic slump caused a return to protectionism, long a cardinal plank of the Republican Party. Conservatives as well as many progressives supported protectionism. Farm prices had declined sharply as European agriculture recovered and American production increased. Although a higher tariff was of doubtful benefit to most farmers, since the United States was primarily an exporting nation, the emergency Tariff of 1921 threw the "Farm Bloc" in Congress a sop by imposing nearly prohibitive duties on twenty-eight agricultural items. The 1922 Fordney-McCumber Tariff, with an average rate of 33 percent, continued farm protection but also raised sharply the rates on industrial goods. Protectionists obtained extremely high duties, intended virtually to embargo imports of dyes, chemicals, silk and rayon, textiles, cutlery, and other products of Japan and Germany. Yet the act retained the low Underwood Tariff rates on most other items.

The Tariff Commission, first established in 1916, was authorized to study the costs of production at home and abroad and to recommend to the administration further rate increases, or decreases, based upon its findings. Originally conceived as one of the progressive reforms using impartial experts in government, the Commission in the Twenties became highly protectionist. In fact, of the 37 changes it recommended that were adopted by Harding and Coolidge, 32 involved increases in rates. The high tariff by its restrictions on imports probably increased industrial profits and the tendency toward monopoly by large businesses. It also had an adverse effect on trade with Europe, eased only by the fact that vast amounts of private American capital was being invested in Europe. Consequently the European debtor countries found it difficult to repay the war debts, while their total private indebtedness to the U.S. financiers also increased.

The federal government withdrew from competition with business as rapidly as possible. Harding's appointees to the Shipping Board sold government-owned vessels for a fraction of their value. He named men to federal regulatory agencies such as the Federal Trade Commission who were interested less in regulation than in cooperation with business interests. The Justice Department also revealed a marked disinterest in enforcement of the anti-trust laws. In this favorable climate, trade associations and cartel arrangements with foreign firms were able to monopolize markets and fix prices. For example, two American sulphur firms formed an agreement with an Italian company, a large supplier, and through the Sulphur Export Corporation controlled the supply of sulphur; and in 1928 General Electric and Krupp of Germany regulated the price of tungsten carbide in Germany and America. Trade associations had been organized earlier to limit competition and stabilize markets, and the movement increased during the war mobilization period. Each trade association had its own code of fair practices and changed competitive industries into semi-noncompetitive ones. Standardization of products and greater efficiency resulted but at the cost of free competition. The federal government in the 1920s looked kindly on these developments and the courts upheld them as long as there was no overt price fixing.

The progressive current lingered on in the 1920s, though more divided and weakened than before. Theodore Roosevelt's party bolt in 1912 had damaged progressive influence within the Republican party, and his return to the fold in 1916 further disorganized progressive ranks. What can be viewed as the Wilsonian mainstream of progressivism had largely accomplished its reform ends by 1917; in any case war and disillusionments with the peace had wrecked Wilson's coalition by 1920. The postwar decade, therefore, found progressivism lacking both unity and dynamic leaders of the prewar type and unable to capture control of either major party. It still manifested some influence in the Congress but not much in the White House.

Progressivism's political role in the postwar Republican era was to be largely negative, as the fight over the disposal of Muscle Shoals revealed. During the war the government had built two plants at Muscle Shoals, Tennessee, using power from federal dams to manufacture nitrogen for the munitions industry and as fertilizer for agriculture. The Harding administration wanted to turn the entire complex over to private enterprise. Henry Ford bid for its lease at a small part of the original cost and, in addition, wanted exemption from federal regulation and a one hundred year renewable lease. Progressive-minded senators, led by George W. Norris of Nebraska, Chairman of the Committee on Agriculture, successfully prevented congressional approval of this lease. Norris advocated cheap public power and wanted the government to use Muscle Shoals as the key to the development of the Tennessee Valley. Congress twice passed such a measure only to encounter vetoes by Coolidge and Hoover. Progressive sentiment was strong enough to frustrate the executive but too weak to compel action.

On the positive side of the ledger, enactment of the Sheppard-Towner Act in 1921 illustrates the link provided by the Twenties between the Progressive Era and the New Deal. Supported by women's groups and endorsed by President Harding, the bill provided for modest federal support of state-established maternity and infant health programs designed to reduce high mortality rates.

Congress passed the measure despite opposition from conservatives and from the American Medical Association, whose House of Delegates denounced the proposal as an "imported socialistic scheme." The government finally permitted federal funding to lapse in 1929, not to be revived until 1935 by the New Deal's Social Security Act. Other progressive contributions involved an enlarged concept of conservation to include preservation of areas of natural beauty and recreation as well as of natural resources. Social service groups continued to advocate reforms, and although their goals usually had to be postponed during the Twenties, they formulated programs in the fields of women and child labor legislation, unemployment compensation and old age insurance, public works and housing, and bargaining rights for labor that contributed greatly to the coming New Deal.

THE HARDING SCANDALS

The Harding administration shares with the earlier Grant regime the dubious distinction of being the most scandal-ridden in American history. Both chief executives governed in postwar eras characterized by disillusionment, moral slump and material prosperity. Private and public chicanery flourished. Even as individuals Harding and Grant had certain similarities, for both men were personally uninvolved in the scandals, victimized by their poor choice of friends and subordinates.

Harding had appointed Charles R. Forbes as director of the Veterans Bureau. On hearing that Forbes was misusing federal funds and accepting payments from contractors, Harding forced his resignation. Forbes's second-in-command, Charles F. Cramer, committed suicide during a congressional investigation and Forbes subsequently received a prison sentence for his conduct. Jess Smith, a crony of Attorney General Daugherty, also committed suicide when he feared his activities in influence peddling in government were about to be exposed. A later investigation revealed that Smith had worked closely with the Alien Property Custodian, Thomas Miller, in fraudulent settlements. Miller, after dismissal from office, was tried and convicted in 1927 of accepting bribes. Many suspected Daugherty also of being involved, but after Harding's death and Daugherty's resignation at the request of

President Coolidge, he managed to escape conviction when brought to trial. Daugherty refused to testify personally and intimated, probably falsely, that he was shielding the dead President's reputation.

The top scandal, breaking after Harding's death, involved his Secretary of the Interior and the lease of naval oil reserves. A rancher in New Mexico, and a former prospector, the picturesque and arrogant Albert Fall had formed a friendship with Harding while both men served in the Senate. Fall's appointment to the Interior Department—he was regarded as a friend of those interested in despoiling the public domain—had greatly disturbed conservationists such as Gifford Pinchot and Harry A. Slattery who kept close watch on him. As Pinchot had remarked of Fall's appointment, "On the record, it would have been possible to pick a worse man for Secretary of the Interior, but not altogether easy." Conservationists also regarded Edwin Denby, Harding's choice for the Navy Department, as questionable. Earlier in the Taft presidency, the government set aside two great oil reserves, at Teapot Dome, Wyoming, and Elk Hills, California, for the Navy's future needs.

Shortly after he took office, Fall with Denby's concurrence had these reserves transferred from the Navy to the Interior Department by an executive order approved by President Harding. Slattery and the conservationists were disturbed by the transfer and also at Fall's attempt to have the Forest Service moved from the Agriculture to the Interior Department. Fall resigned in early 1923 on the grounds of private financial sacrifices; apparently his departure also reflected his resentment of Harding's refusal to approve all his plans. Reports leaked out that Fall was prospering on his ranch at Three Rivers, New Mexico. A Senate inquiry, after Harding's death, eventually uncovered evidence that Fall had secretly leased, without competitive bidding, offset drilling rights at Teapot Dome and Elk Hills to two oil men, Harry F. Sinclair and Edward L. Doheny. In return for these favors, Fall had received so-called loans and gifts of $100,000 from Doheny, delivered in cash in a little black bag, and $25,000 from Sinclair. Although Doheny and Sinclair escaped punishment, Fall was convicted of accepting bribes in 1929, fined $100,000, and sentenced to a year in prison.

Most of these scandals became public only after Harding's death, but he knew enough of them to be deeply disturbed as he embarked on a political fence-mending western tour in mid-1923. According to the Kansas Republican newspaper editor, William Allen White, Harding complained, "My God, this is a hell of a job. I have no trouble with my enemies...But my damned friends, my God-damn friends, White, they're the ones that keep me walking the floor nights!" Harding had long suffered from heart trouble—his wife had not wanted him to run for the presidency in 1920 for that reason—yet he could not relax on the tour, making 85 speeches in five weeks, playing bridge almost constantly in the intervals and sleeping little. He collapsed in Seattle, where physicians at first diagnosed his condition as a digestive illness; rushed to San Francisco, he died of a cerebral attack on August 12, 1923.

Although several recent studies have attempted to rehabilitate Harding, revealing that he had more intelligence and decisiveness than is usually credited, it seems unlikely that his administration will ever be regarded as other than mediocre. Perhaps the fairest evaluation is that he had tried to cope with a job too large for his modest talents. At the time of his death, however, that seemed less clear. A great outpouring of popular grief and mourning attested to his genuine popularity. Only later, when the scandals became fully known, did his reputation plunge. Liberal journalists and muckrakers, alienated by the passing of the Progressive Era and the craser aspects of the 1920s, also aided greatly in fastening the image of failure to Harding.

COOLIDGE PROSPERITY

Vice President Calvin Coolidge fell heir to Harding's office and policies. The new President's personality, his politically skillful but undemanding and unchallenging leadership, coinciding with a period of booming prosperity, seemed to fit the mood of the times. Sometimes called a latter-day Puritan presiding in a most non-Puritan age, Coolidge continued the pro-business policies of his predecessor.

Born in Vermont on the Fourth of July, 1872, Calvin Coolidge grew up in a small town in a small state that clung to the rural

Yankee folkways of the past. Young Coolidge absorbed the values of hard work, thrift, and frugality from his unimaginative and conservative family and community. His mother died when he was twelve; his father, prosperous by local standards, seems to have been an extraordinarily withdrawn, laconic man. Young Coolidge, frail of health and with a thin, quacking voice resulting from nasal congestion, also grew up extremely shy and withdrawn, uncommunicative and outwardly unemotional. His dour visage once caused Alice Roosevelt Longworth to quip that he looked as if he had been weaned on a pickle. Graduating from Amherst and entering law practice, Calvin Coolidge settled in Northampton, Massachusetts. In 1905 he married Grace Goodhue, a gracious and outgoing lady who compensated for many of her husband's social deficiencies.

An astute student of politics, if prosaic and of limited horizons, Coolidge served in both houses of the state legislature, then as Lieutenant Governor, and was elected Governor in 1918. As Governor, he lived in two rented rooms in the capital and saved much of his salary, as he did also when he dwelt in the White house. Coolidge's political principles perhaps are best summarized as economy, honesty, and efficiency in government and order and stability in society. Coolidge respected wealth and confidently believed that the wealth and prosperity created by businessmen would trickle down to benefit the masses of the people. Riding the crest of his unearned fame for ending the Boston police strike, Coolidge won an overwhelming gubernatorial re-election in 1919 and was mentioned as a dark horse candidate for the Republican presidential nomination in 1920. After Harding had won the first prize, the convention ignored the leaders' wishes and nominated Coolidge for the vice presidency in a burst of rebellious enthusiasm.

After the inauguration, Harding invited Coolidge to attend cabinet meetings, but the President only rarely consulted him— Mrs. Harding apparently disliked both of the Coolidges. Coolidge became known as "Silent Cal," a somewhat exaggerated taciturnity that nevertheless had a certain political usefulness. With few close friends and overshadowed in politics and at social functions, Coolidge within his family and staff occasionally sought emotional release in fits of rage and tantrums, sulking and shouting his frustration at those around him. Apart from politics and the reading of history, he had few interests or pastimes except walking and riding a mechanical hobby-horse. Like many of his predecessors and successors, Coolidge regarded the vice presidency as a mockery, an empty and powerless pretension.

Suddenly Harding's death catapulted this discontented man into the White House. At the news, Senator Lodge exclaimed to a reporter, "My God! That means Coolidge is President!" Taking the presidential oath administered by his father, a notary, by the light of an oil lamp in his Vermont home, Coolidge assumed his new responsibilities determined to continue the cabinet and the basic course of the Harding administration.

Coolidge envisioned his presidential duties as essentially to execute the laws while Congress, an independent branch of government, legislated. He wanted to promote stability, unity, and harmony; he thought that big business would promote general prosperity, good for the nation and good for the individual. Accumulated wealth provided the fountain of prosperity and of art and learning as well. Coolidge rejected anything resembling federal paternalism; in his view, the government should keep its own affairs and finances in order and not try to run the economy but let it run itself. Legislation should never be hurried, and government should act or spend only when absolutely necessary. As columnist Walter Lippmann wrote, "Mr Coolidge's genius for inactivity is developed to a very high point. It is far from being an indolent inactivity. It is a grim, determined, alert inactivity which keeps Mr. Coolidge occupied constantly." Coolidge himself once said that Theodore Roosevelt had kept himself constantly in trouble by prematurely taking a public stand on issues:

> It seems to me public administrators would get along better if they would restrain the impulse to butt in or be dragged into trouble. They should remain silent until an issue is reduced to its lowest terms, until it boils down into something like a moral issue.

These concepts of the economy and a highly limited government was in accord with a majority of Americans during the 1920s. Coolidge's administration, therefore, would be a popular and even a successful one within the context of the times.

If the policies remained the same, the atmosphere of the new administration changed sharply. Alice Roosevelt Longworth commented that the White House under Coolidge, in contrast to Harding, was "as different as a New England front parlor is from a back room in a speakeasy." Coolidge enjoyed his role as master of the White House and minutely supervised its operations. He rose early and went to bed early and social affairs were few and stilted. He met reporters, usually twice a week, and often lowered his guard as he selected written questions for comment, although he would not permit direct quotation. The record of his press conferences reveal dry wit and political astuteness but also lack of interest in ideas or abstract speculation. Coolidge's speeches, boringly delivered, were platitudinous and pedestrian. He depended heavily on his cabinet and largely followed departmental recommendations. Secretary of State Hughes towered over the others and had great freedom in running his department. Coolidge greatly admired Mellon, his Secretary of the Treasury, who not only was rich but shared the President's belief in the virtues of budget balancing, tax reductions, and debt retirement. Hoover, the ambitious Commerce Secretary, commanded Coolidge's respect but apparently not his liking.

Coolidge at first held a rather precarious position within his party. He had neither the confidence of the conservative Old Guard Republicans nor that of the progressive wing of the party. Moreover, the Harding scandals just coming fully to light caused him much embarrassment. It was by no means certain, therefore, that Coolidge would receive his party's nomination in 1924. Carefully maneuvering his way out of these dilemmas, Cooldige's first message to Congress concentrated on domestic affairs. It sounded neither a progressive nor a reactionary note. The message emphasized tax reductions and economy in government and called for a constitutional amendment to restrict child labor and to permit the fixing of a minimum wage for women employees. He submitted the lowest budget since before the war with surplus revenue to be applied to the national debt. As Coolidge stated, "I have in mind that the taxpayers are the stockholders in the business corporation of the United States, and if this business is showing a surplus of receipts the taxpayer should share therein..."

Coolidge moved cautiously to investigate the Harding scandals, allowing outraged Senators to take the lead. Fortunately, the Teapot Dome affair seemed to implicate prominent Democrats as well as Republicans—some critics charged former Navy Secretary Daniels with being involved in the removal of the naval oil reserves from the national domain and it became known that McAdoo, a leading potential Democratic nominee for the presidency, had accepted (innocently) a legal retainer from oilman Doheny. Denby resigned from the Navy Department and Coolidge dismissed Daugherty and cancelled the fraudulent oil leases. Coolidge thus emerged untarnished and in a greatly strengthened political position. By his use of patronage Coolidge weakened the Old Guard and dominated the 1924 Republican convention. A dull affair, the convention had the distinction of being the first to be broadcast by radio.

By then prosperity had returned to the country, and accompanied by his vice presidential running mate, Charles G. Dawes, Coolidge campaigned on the slogan "Keep Cool with Coolidge." Dawes, a Chicago banker who had favored a number of progressive reforms, had made a notable reputation as an efficient manager and economizer during World War I and as first Director of the Budget. A colorful character, press and public delighted in his underslung pipe and his favorite oath, "Hell and Maria."

Democrats gathered in Madison Square Garden for fourteen days of public brawling, a donnybrook of a national convention. New York City had to delegate additional police to keep order among delegates and spectators. The faction-ridden party was split between the eastern urban machines that backed New York's Governor Alfred E. Smith and the rural-oriented West and South, Protestant and dry, that supported William Gibbs McAdoo. The Ku Klux Klan became a divisive issue and a specific platform condemnation of it, backed by the eastern wing but opposed by many rural delegates from the South and West, went down to a narrow defeat. After 96 ballots neither Smith nor McAdoo could obtain the two-thirds majority necessary for nomination. The prize went on the 103rd ballot to a compromise candidate, the conservative and colorless John W. Davis of West Virginia. The addition to the ticket of Charles W. Byran of Nebraska, brother of

William Jennings Bryan, as the vice-presidential nominee, failed to mollify more liberally inclined Democrats. Davis, a former Solicitor General of the United States and Ambassador to Great Britain, had close Wall Street connections and failed to appeal to farmers, labor, or progressive elements.

Meanwhile, a revival of progressivism developed to voice the discontent of farmers and laborers with their minimal share in the prosperity of the Twenties. Wisconsin's maverick Republican Senator Robert M. LaFollette became its chief spokesman. A nominating convention was called in 1924, with delegates representing labor, farmers, and independents and socialists. At LaFollette's request, the convention rigidly excluded the Communists. The convention nominated LaFollette for the presidency, with Democratic Senator Burton K. Wheeler of Montana in the second place. The delegates agreed not to establish a formal third party in order not to damage progressives running for congressional and state offices on major party tickets. The platform, advanced in contrast to those of the two major parties but hardly daring or new, condemned monopoly and advocated public ownership of railroads and water power sites, abolition of anti-labor court injunctions, the election of federal judges, and protection of the right to collective bargaining. The Socialist Party endorsed LaFollette's candidacy, as did the AFL.

The election aroused comparatively little popular interest, half of the eligible voters not bothering to go to the polls despite the recent enfranchisement of women. No significant differences separated the positions of the Republican and Democratic parties, and both tended to focus their attack on the LaFollette Progressives. Dawes, bearing most of the Republican campaign burden, repeatedly denounced LaFollette and made an especial effort to identify his followers with the Communists and other radicals, despite LaFollette's repudiation of Communist support. Elderly and in poor health, LaFollette suffered severe handicaps from lack of funds and the absence of local party organization. The Republicans, claiming credit for the return of prosperity, freely spent an estimated $4 million; the Democrats expended about $900,000, and the Progressives only a little over $200,000. Coolidge and Dawes scored a smashing victory, polling 15.5

million votes to Davis' 8.33 million and LaFollette's nearly 5 million votes. The Republicans also won solid control of Congress.

Policies favorable to business seemed even more marked after 1924 than before, reflecting the effective control conservative Republicans had in Congress and the White House. Coolidge exalted fiscal economy in government, declaring in his inaugural that "Economy is idealism in its most practical form." By the revenue act of 1926 the Republicans sharply reduced the maximum income surtax and estate taxes and eliminated gift taxes, although they made a few concessions to the small taxpayer. Despite tax reductions, the Treasury ran a surplus which it used to reduce the national debt from $24 billion in 1920 to $16 billion by 1930. Coolidge continued Harding's practice of appointing business-oriented men to the regulatory agencies. The Federal Trade Commission, for example, did try to prevent fraudulent advertising and misbranding, but it did little to curb holding companies and other monopolistic devices. The President basked in business admiration and often invited prominent industrialists and financiers to the White House. His administration adhered to an easy credit policy to encourage the already booming prosperity. By 1928, however, even Coolidge felt disturbed by the fevered speculation on the stock market, but he would not voice a public warning nor take other action to curb the excesses. Only an actual emergency, he felt, would justify presidential action.

Agriculture conspicuously failed to share in the apparent affluence of the decade. In many ways agriculture had made great progress, marked by new farming methods, machinery, improved seed, and fertilizer that greatly increased acreage production. Wartime prices had been good, land values boomed, and investments and acreage in cultivation grew. But as production continued to increase after the armistice, prices fell precipitously. Foreign markets contracted after World War I, and at home the supplanting of the grain-consuming horse with the gas-burning internal combustion engines in automobiles, trucks, and tractors and a national dietary change toward less starchy or fattening foods reduced the demand for staples. Tradition-bound farmers responded to falling prices by raising more of the same commodity, thus furthering the decline. Most farmers found themselves caught in a cruel squeeze between the rising costs of manufactured goods and sagging farm prices. The total value of farm goods declined from $21.5 billion in 1919 to $11.8 billion in 1929. That decline resulted in increasing poverty, bankruptcies and mortgage foreclosures, more farm tenancy, and agitation for federal relief.

The Congressional farm bloc, representing largely rural constituencies, had been able in the early 1920s to obtain some favorable legislation for agriculture. The 1921 and 1922 tariff acts, at least in theory, had conferred benefits on farmers, the 1921 Packers and Stockyards Act prohibited monopolistic practices by the meat packers, the Capper-Volstead Act in 1922 freed marketing cooperatives from the anti-trust laws, and grain exchanges came under federal regulation in 1921 and 1922. But plans for more direct federal aid, although commanding large support in Congress, could not get by the roadblock of conservative presidents.

Pro-farmer spokesmen advanced a scheme known as McNary-Haugenism as a panacea for farm problems. Nurtured by George N. Peek and Hugh S. Johnson of the Moline Plow Company, the plan called for a two-price system. The government would purchase the surpluses of a certain staple crops at a price based upon the world market price plus the tariff rate charged against such imports and sell them abroad for the going rate; meanwhile the portion consumed domestically supposedly would rise to the higher level paid by the government, compensating itself for the difference by levying a special tax on the producer or the distributor. The Coolidge administration adamantly refused to approve the McNary-Haugen bill in any of its several forms, denouncing it as inherently unworkable and as improper paternalistic legislation. Coolidge vetoed such bills in 1927 and 1928. Instead, in addition to endorsing tariff protection, he encouraged farmers to curtail production and to form cooperatives as authorized by the 1922 Capper-Volstead Act—excellent advice, but manifestly beyond the capacities of most farmers.

THE ELECTION OF 1928

In 1927 Coolidge, at his vacation retreat in South Dakota's Black Hills, suddenly and enigmatically announced that he would not seek a second elected term. The announcement aroused much debate about his motives and true purposes, some suspecting at first that he was merely feigning reluctance and wanted to be drafted to run again. But apparently Coolidge meant just what he said. He felt physically and emotionally weary of the labors and irritations of the presidency. He also, it seems, feared that prosperity might not continue much longer and thought if that happened more vigorous executive leadership would be required. In any case, his statement left the path open for the candidacy of Herbert Hoover. It was fitting that the decade of the Twenties, inordinately admiring the ideal of engineering efficiency, should end with the Great Engineer in the White House.

Hoover's life is the story of the self-made man. Born in West Branch, Iowa in 1874, Hoover suffered the loss of both his devout Quaker parents during his childhood. He entered Stanford University in its first class, studying geology, and after graduation worked for a wealthy Western miner. At age 23 he went to Australia as a mine scout for a London firm, already well-advanced on a mining career that would take him across much of the world and make him a fortune of perhaps $4 million by 1913. During World War I he achieved worldwide fame, first as director of Belgian relief, then as Food Administrator in the Wilson administration, and subsequently in postwar relief activities in Europe. A movement developed to give him the Democratic nomination for the presidency in 1920 until he announced he was a Republican. He accepted an appointment from Harding as Secretary of Commerce, after securing a promise that he would have a role in all important economic policies. To take this new position Hoover declined an offer of a Guggenheim partnership with a guaranteed minimal salary of $500,000 per year. In the Commerce Department he enhanced his reputation both as a great humanitarian in the disaster and relief areas and as the efficient engineer in government encouraging greater productivity by American industry.

Hoover summed up his political philosophy in his *American Individualism*, published in 1922. He had an abiding faith in the individualism and democracy which he believed had made America great—equality of economic opportunity for all and freedom from political or economic domination, protected by a government encouraging cooperation for maximum production. The individual should combine social responsibility with opportunity and freedom, to promote both the individual and the common good. Government, therefore, should umpire the economy and encourage cooperation; government should not compete with private enterprise. Any extension of government beyond that point would undermine the all-essential quality of "rugged individualism" or initiative. He professed to favor collective bargaining though he in fact supported the open shop, a manifest contradiction, and he encouraged private unemployment, disability, and old-age insurance plans. Hoover believed in business-labor cooperation and business self-regulation, and he encouraged formation of trade associations for those purposes. He considered overzealous use of the anti-trust laws as unwise and unnecessary.

With the withdrawal of Coolidge from the race, Hoover easily eclipsed his rivals and secured the Republican presidential nomination in 1928. Although viewed an amateur by professional politicians, Hoover had genuine popularity with the nation at large. His nomination also represented a victory for business and industry, and the business would contributed handsomely to the costs of his campaign. The platform in 1928 praised Coolidge prosperity, lauded the tariff, promised to enforce prohibition, and opposed any program putting the government into agriculture or business.

The Democratic Convention could not deny Al Smith the prize he had vainly sought in 1924. The big-city machines were determined to run Smith, the Happy Warrior as Franklin D. Roosevelt had called him in the 1924 nominating speech, and the rural South and Midwest had to accede reluctantly. The convention chose a Protestant "dry", Senator Joseph T. Robinson of Arkansas, for the vice presidency, in order to balance the Catholic and "wet" Smith. The platform, not particularly daring or inspiring, promised among other things tariff reform, collective bargaining and restriction of court injunctions against labor, enforcement of the anti-trust laws, farm relief, and an "honest effort" at enforcing prohibition.

Smith's nomination symbolized an important urban revolution in American politics. Born in 1873 in a New York City tenement house, Al Smith had dropped out of school and worked in a fish market before entering politics. He made his way up through the Tammany Hall machine and served as sheriff and in the state assembly. Elected Governor of New York in 1918, he held that office, except for a two-year interval, until 1928. An astute but principled politician, Smith never developed a wide political vision, despite his numerous reform achievements relating to such issues as better health and safety laws and his sympathy with the urban lower classes. Yet his nomination in 1928 represented the surge to political consciousness of the urban masses of immigrants and their descendants, the ethnic and religious minorities on the lower end of the economic and social scale.

Smith's defeat by Hoover often has been attributed, understandably if incorrectly, to the religious issue. In the campaign the confident Hoover dealt in generalities while Smith endorsed farm relief and the repeal of prohibition. Despite the Democratic candidate's spirited defense of religious freedom, large numbers of Protestants apparently feared that a victory for Smith would destroy the barrier between church and state, impair the public school system and, some warned, would enable the Pope to dominate the White House. Probably even more importantly, the campaign revealed rural "drys" hostility to city "wets" and their dislike of Smith's East Side New York accent that came so gratingly over the radio. Methodist Bishop A.W. Leonard called for "Anglo-Saxon unity, against foreigners...who trample on our flag," and proclaimed himself "100 percent, Anglo Saxon....We are the keepers of the Constitution, of the flag and of American citizenship." A fundamentalist spokesman railed at urban immorality with its "card playing, cocktail drinking...divorce... dancing, evolution...and modernism," all of which Smith seemed to symbolize. Some progressive Democrats also reacted adversely to Smith's choice of General Motor's John J. Raskob as campaign manager, in a largely futile bid for business support. The election results gave Hoover a smashing victory of nearly 21.5 million votes. Yet Smith ran better than Cox and Davis had earlier, polling 15 million votes or 40 percent of the popular total. Undoubtedly his religion and his urban background cost him support in the rural South and West, but these same factors gained votes for him in the large cities and industrial states. In 1920 and 1924, the Republicans had carried the twelve largest cities in the United States, but in 1928 Smith narrowly won these cities—a trend the Democrats continued and expanded in the Thirties. Moreover, the Democrats during this decade also gained steadily in congressional elections. The Democratic party thus had begun a transformation away from ruralism and Bryanism toward an urban base and urban-oriented interests and policies.

Smith probably had run better than any other Democratic candidate could have in 1928. He was defeated primarily by a combination of Hoover's great popularity and the still booming prosperity of the decade. The Republicans had carried 40 states, several in the upper and border South, and won control of Congress. Yet an urban trend toward the Democrats was emerging.

MIDDLE ROAD TO INTERNATIONALISM

The American government in the Twenties tried to develop middle-road policies somewhere between the isolationism of the past and Wilsonian internationalism. Policy-makers had little other choice, granted the realities of America's great economic power, its interests in foreign markets and stability, and its decisive role in the World War I. The Harding adminstration and its successors marked out a middle path of limited cooperation with the League, participation in the movement for arms limitations and peace, and a vigorous expansion of private American finance and trade abroad, all without binding political commitments or treaty obligations. In short, Republican leaders sought a world safe for America and its economic-political interests, without the potentially troubling obligations symbolized by Wilson's League of Nations. Foreign policy thus complemented the domestic policy of cooperation with business. The Senate reinforced this cautious approach by attaching to treaties reservations or "understandings" that the U.S. would not assume any enforcement obligations.

A majority of Americans had reverted to at least a mild isolationism by the mid-1920s, if indeed they had ever felt otherwise. Most had come to regard intervention in the World War I as a mistake. Isolationist currents ran particularly strong in rural areas and, because of rural over-representation, in Congress as well; most of the great newspaper chains, such as the Hearst and Munsey papers, were also isolationist. Senator William E. Borah of Idaho, after 1924 chairman of the Senate Committee on Foreign Relations, became the self-appointed Congressional watchdog for the isolationists. The "Idaho Lion," tall, massive of frame, and white maned, has been described as a noble man of ideals and principle but lamentably naive and ignorant, particularly about foreign affairs. He believed that the nation's duty consisted of avoiding foreign entanglements while setting a moral example to the world. He viewed the League as an immoral trap, a plot of the bankers and the European allies to entrap the United States and ensure their power and investments. Yet Borah did espouse disarmament conferences, the outlawry of war, and recognition of the Soviet Union.

Wilsonian internationalists continued to try to educate their fellow citizens in the nation's duties to the cause of world peace and stability. Internationalist groups, some pro-League, concentrated on membership in the World Court or the movement for arms reduction, including among others the World Peace Foundation, the Carnegie Endowment for International Peace, the National Council for Prevention of War, and the Women's International League for Peace and Freedom. Millionaire Edward W. Bok gave a Bok Peace Award of $50,000 in 1924 to the best plan for joining the World Court and cooperating in a limited way with the League. The Foreign Policy Association carried on broad-scale educational work in international affairs. The Council on Foreign Relations, established in New York in 1921 and later broadened to include committees in major cities across the country, published *Foreign Affairs* quarterly and concentrated on promoting an interest in international affairs among the more influential members of the community. Internationalism scored particular success among secondary and college teachers and students. Many liberal internationalists focused their attentions upon membership in the World Court and responsible participation in the disarmament movement. Unfortunately for their cause, however, internationalists did not agree on a program, could not capture control of either major political party during the 1920s and had to contend with a hostile Congress.

When World War I ended, the Untied States, Great Britain and Japan stood on the threshold of a naval arms race. The 1916 Naval Act provided for a vast increase of 156 American vessels, including 39 battleships and 12 battle cruisers. Obviously these plans would compel both the British and Japanese governments to make heavy expenditures in an effort to keep up. But in fact, after the Armistice the public and Congress made it clear they were against a costly arms race. Members of peace groups especially expressed dismay and advocated the calling of conference to resolve the problem. Congress, having defeated the League, now pressured the President to adopt a program to promote peace without binding obligations. In 1921 Senator Borah introduced a resolution in Congress for a 50 percent reduction in naval building and the calling of a conference of the three major naval powers. Although he resented the Senate's intrusion into foreign policy and apparently preferred to continue naval construction until achieving parity with Britain, Harding gave way before the growing public clamor and issued invitations to a conference in Washington, to include also Far Eastern problems at the insistence of the British. To ensure the conference's success the administration appointed senators from both major political parties to the delegation. Harding left out the unpredictable Borah, however, in the group he named to assist Hughes: Lodge, Root and Democrat Oscar Underwood.

Invitations went to Great Britain, Japan, France, Italy, China and other powers particularly interested in Far Eastern problems. Japan, fearful of losing recent gains in China, agreed to come because nearly half its annual budget involved military expenditures. Britain, while its leaders spoke bravely of maintaining naval supremacy at all costs, faced harsh economic facts that made it willing to accept naval equality with the United States. Soviet Russia wanted to attend the conference, but the

American government refused to invite a government it did not recognize.

The Washington Conference marked the first time that a major international conference had met in the United States, a fitting tribute to American status as the greatest economic and potentially military power in the world. Secretary of State Hughes, dignified and grey-bearded, boldly seized the initiative in his opening statement to the body on November 12, 1921: "The time has come...not for general resolutions or mutual advice, but for action." He then stunned the assembled diplomats and naval experts, who had expected the usual generalities, with his proposal for a sweeping program halting capital ship construction for ten years and scrapping vast amounts of existing tonnage. According to Hughes, the United States should scrap 15 capital ships then under construction (some were over 80 percent completed), and 15 older battleships or a total of 845,740 tons of vessels; Britain similarly should junk 19 older capital warships of 583, 375 tons and abandon plans for four new battleships, while Japan, the third ranking naval power, should give up 15 ships planned or under construction and ten older vessels for a total displacement of 448,928 tons.

The British and Japanese (and American) naval experts were staggered by Hughes' proposal that sank more battleships "than all the admirals of the world had destroyed in a cycle of centuries." That ardent proponent of peace, William Jennings Bryan, present as an observer, listened to Hughes with tears coursing down his face. The American public and Congress reacted with enthusiastic and overwhelming approval. One church minister summed up the mood of the hour when he called Hughes' speech "one of the greatest events in history."

Because his proposals aroused overwhelming popular support throughout the world and neither Britain nor Japan cared for a costly naval race, Hughes obtained most of his objectives. The Five Power Pact provided for a ten-year construction halt of capital vessels except for replacement of obsolete units, limited battleships to no more than 35,000 tons and 16 inch guns each, and established a 5:5:3 ratio in battleships and aircraft carriers for the United States, Great Britain, and Japan, with 1.75 ratios for France and

Italy. Because France insisted upon a larger submarine tonnage, lesser craft remained unregulated. Japan received compensation for its smaller ratio by pledges that the U.S. would not increase fortifications west of Hawaii nor would Great Britain east of Singapore and north of Australia.

The Anglo-Japanese Alliance was ended, replaced by the Four Power Pact between Great Britain, France, Japan, and the United States that declared mutual respect for each others' possessions in the Pacific and promised consultation if problems arose endangering the peace and stability of the area. In the Nine Power Pact, the delegates—plus China—solemnly pledged to uphold the independence and integrity of China and to observe the principles of the Open Door. In related arrangements Japan agreed to return Shantung to China and to evacuate Siberia, and the United States obtained cable rights on the Japanese mandated island of Yap.

The Senate approved these treaties—strongly endorsed by the press, internationalists, and peace groups—but attached a reservation to the Four Power Pact that made it clear that the American government assumed no obligation to uphold these commitments by force or by alliance. That action of course made this and other treaties signed in the Twenties worthless when subsequently challenged by aggressors. Although Republicans hailed the Washington pacts as the "greatest peace document[s] ever drawn," the Washington settlement obviously fell far short of membership in the League of Nations. However, it ended the capital ship arms race and promoted stability in the Pacific for a decade.

Critics then and after argued that because of the factors of distance and two-ocean or more responsibilities for the United States and Britain, the settlement in effect conceded Japan's naval predominance in the far Pacific. Yet the United States gave up little that it actually had. Even if the government had tried to achieve the planned expansion of the navy, Congress might well have refused to appropriate the funds—during the 1920s it was to fail to build the navy even to the treaty limits—and of course America's rivals would have had to counter-build. At most, therefore, the United States at the conference only traded a potential superiority for a naval and political settlement that saved it money, stabilized the Pacific, improved relations with Japan, and apparently protected China. On the other hand, perhaps the most unfortunate consequence of the conference was that it encouraged Americans in the easy belief that vital national interests and peace could be ensured without the assumption of binding commitments and obligations.

It proved almost impossible to extend meaningful limitations to lesser naval vessels. A conference at Geneva in 1927 failed to reach agreement on cruisers, primarily because Britain wanted more smaller vessels (6" gun cruisers) to guard its overseas empire while America wanted fewer but larger ships with longer cruising range (10,000 ton craft with 8" guns) to compensate for inadequate bases overseas. The threat from Congress of a construction race in cruisers—it authorized 15 heavy cruisers and an aircraft carrier in 1929—and Hoover's diplomacy cleared the way for the London Naval Conference in 1930. The United States obtained full parity with Britain, but Japan was compelled to abide by the 5:5:3 ratio for capital ships while being compensated by a 10:10:7 formula for light cruisers and parity in submarines. The addition of an escape clause in case either of the three major powers felt threatened by a nonsignatory raised serious questions about the value of the agreement.

The movement to outlaw war illustrated the bright optimism about world peace that prevailed in the United States and Europe during the Twenties. Internationalists viewed it as a way of linking the United States indirectly to the League and its concept of collective security, but moralists, pacifists and isolationists rallied to it because of its simplicity and lack of obligation. A Chicago lawyer, Salmon O. Levinson, and Professor James T. Shotwell and President Nicholas Murray Butler of Columbia University, aroused popular interest in the scheme. They won Borah's invaluable support; he called the resulting pact "the only kind of treaty the United States could sign" with the rest of the world. Borah and most Americans viewed outlawry as a simple and universal solution, resting solely upon world moral opinion for enforcement.

Aristide Briand, the French Foreign Minister, fired the opening diplomatic volley in 1927 when he appealed publicly for a Franco-American treaty outlawing war between the two countries.

Apparently Briand hoped to tie a security hungry France more closely to the United States. President Coolidge and Secretary of State Frank B. Kellogg—the latter dubbed "Nervous Nellie" by reporters because of his fear of the isolationists in Congress— resented Briand's unorthodox public diplomacy, and at first they ignored his suggestion. Because of growing public pressures, however, they decided to turn the tables on Briand by proposing a multi-national treaty to ban war. Although many diplomats were skeptical, world opinion rallied behind Kellogg's proposal. Fifteen nations signed the Kellogg-Briand Pact, or Pact of Paris, in August 1928 and eventually 64 nations ratified the pact. Signatories solemnly promised to renounce aggression and to rely upon peaceful processes to settle international problems; no provisions were made for enforcement. The Senate granted its approval by a vote of 85 to 1, along with an interpretation reserving the right to self-defense and the preservation of the Monroe Doctrine and disavowing any obligation to uphold the treaty against violators. Not all Senators voted enthusiastically for the pact. Carter Glass of Virginia called it not "worth a postage stamp in the direction of accomplishing permanent international peace." Although millions here and abroad hailed it as a notable achievement for peace, the Pact of Paris seems at best an innocuous international gesture. In another sense it proved disastrous because it encouraged the misleading assumption that peace and security could be obtained without costs and obligations.

Any lingering doubts that President Harding and Secretary Hughes—the latter had favored membership in a league emphasizing judicial rather than political measures for peace—had of joining some type of world association quickly foundered before isolationist opposition in the Senate. Harding assured a cheering Congress on April 12, 1921, that in the "existing League of Nations, world-governing with its super powers, this Republic will have no part." The State Department concluded a separate peace treaty with Germany in 1921 reserving privileges under the Treaty of Versailles but none of its obligations. Despite the opposition of ex-President Wilson and many Democratic Senators, who viewed such a separate peace as cowardly, the Senate approved the Treaty of Berlin.

The Harding administration at first declined even to answer League correspondence; when criticism finally drove it to reply it was only informally and indirectly. Nor would the United States permit international agencies to which it belonged to come under League sponsorship. By mid-1922, however, the administration began to view the League with more tolerance. Coolidge told Congress in 1923 that while membership in the League was a closed question, the United States would cooperate with other nations in humanitarian efforts. The State Department began to send observers and later official representatives to attend technical and specialized conferences dealing with matters such as copyrights, pornography, prostitution, health, and suppression of the opium traffic. In other words, while America would not join the League in enforcing peace, it would cooperate in non-political international affairs. Thus the State Department rejected several attempts to tie the United States indirectly to collective security, such as the League's 1923 Draft Treaty of Mutual Assistance and the 1924 Geneva Protocol for the Pacific Settlement of International Disputes (which called for economic sanctions against aggressors). Under President Hoover the United States greatly increased its involvement in League activities, even to the extent of some cooperation with the League Council during the Manchurian crisis in 1931-32.

Peace groups and internationalists wanted the United States to join the World Court. They argued that Americans had been in the forefront of the movement for arbitration and international adjudication and that the World Court in a very real sense represented an American creation. Many supporters of the World Court also saw it as a first step toward closer relations with the League. Harding and Hughes endorsed membership in the Court and by the mid-twenties both major political parties favored it. Although most Americans apparently agreed, the isolationist bloc in the Senate managed to defeat the project. One irreconcilable opponent referred derisively to the Court's judges and asked rhetorically, "Who are these who would place above the American flag the bastard banner of internationalism?" After lengthy hearings and compromises, in 1926 the Senate finally approved joining, but it attached reservations that were unacceptable to members of the Court. Another try in 1935 failed by seven votes to obtain the necessary two-thirds majority in the Senate. The internationalists had won over the majority of Americans, but they could not overcome the die-hard isolationists in the Senate.

Unfortunately all the cooperation with the League, the movement to join the World Court, and participation in arms limitation conferences fell short of the full participation and assumption of League responsibilities that might possibly have prevented the outbreak of World War II. Events in the thirties soon demonstrated the futility of this middle-of-the-road foreign policy to serve America's best interests.

ECONOMIC FOREIGN POLICY

European governments in 1920 owed the American government about $10.33 billion for wartime and post-armistice loans, most of it spent in the United States for war purchases. Despite the pleas of the war-weakened Allies, the American government, from the Wilson administration on, insisted that the loans were straight-forward financial arrangements to be repaid in full with interest. As Coolidge reportedly remarked, "they hired the money, didn't they?" Washington therefore rejected proposals for cancellation or sharp reduction as America's contribution to the general war effort. Moreover the United States officially denied European debtor claims that their ability to repay depended upon Germany meeting her reparations obligations. Despite European resistance and ill will—one French cartoon portrayed the United States as Uncle Shylock—the American government forced funding agreements upon the debtor countries providing for full repayment of the principle over a period of 62 years. Britain agreed to repay her debt of nearly $4.3 billion at an average rate of 3.3 percent interest, while the interest rate on Italy's $1.6 billion was reduced to 0.4 percent in view of her financially straitened condition. France proved most reluctant to sign an agreement for her debt of $3.4 billion, coming to terms at an interest rate of 1.6 percent in 1926 only after economic pressure in the form of an embargo against private loans to France. Yet America's war debt policy should be viewed as more short-sighted than grasping.

America had emerged from the war as the leading industrial and financial power in the world. Its industrial production by the late 1920s amounted to 46 per cent of the world's total. The United States largely replaced Europe as the supplier of outside capital to Latin America and the Far East, while its imports from Europe declined sharply. By 1928 the combined governmental and private debts owed America reached a total of $21 billion. New York City had become the financial capital of the world, while American firms penetrated foreign tariff walls through branch factories and subsidiaries overseas. American exports also captured markets previously dominated by Europe, as for example Latin America.

The State Department tried with limited success to guide overseas investments and loans, but investors attracted to risky foreign ventures by high interest rates frequently ignored its advice. In Germany large sums flowed in from America for purchases of what turned out to be unsound provincial and municipal governmental bond issues. By the mid-twenties, American economic and diplomatic leadership had helped establish an apparently stable open-door world. Unfortunately, that world order had serious defects; too many unsound American investments abroad, not enough investments in the development of economically backward countries, and insufficient trade between the industrialized nations.

Despite the fact that the United States had become a creditor nation on both the government and private levels, Republicans with a "debtor complex" insisted upon returning to a high protective tariff. As Harding put it in one of his characteristically muddled comments, "We should adopt a protective tariff of such a character as will help the struggling industries of Europe to get on their feet." The 1922 Fordney-McCumber Tariff, as noted earlier, sharply increased rates on numerous imports. The Great Depression led to a further hike in tariff rates under the Hawley-Smoot Tariff of 1930 from the previous average of 25.9 percent to 50.02 percent on dutiable imports. President Hoover ignored the warnings of over a thousand economists and signed the highest tariff measure in American history. European countries, already running an adverse balance of trade with America and also feeling the effects of the depression, retaliated by erecting tariff walls against American goods. By 1932 the combined effects of the depression and tariff wars had reduced American foreign trade to the level of 1905.

American protectionism made it harder for Europe to recover from the war, thus the State Department recognized some responsibility to promote European readjustment. Despite a formal refusal to acknowledge any connection between war debts and reparations, the State Department encouraged private American bankers to join Europeans in formulating the Dawes Plan in 1924 to lend Germany money to enable it to resume reparations payments—Charles G. Dawes headed the group and American bankers supplied over half of this loan. As a result of the Dawes Plan, France withdrew from occupation of the Ruhr and Germany seemed on the road to economic and political stability. In 1930, the American Owen D. Young headed another unofficial commission to reduce Germany's reparations debt from the original $33 billion to $9 billion. In 1931, as the economic depression spread around the globe, President Hoover initiated a one-year moratorium on all inter-governmental debts. He hoped the breathing spell would promote world economic recovery (and shore up questionable American loans in Germany), but the only long term result was to end virtually all payments on the war debts. The Allies and Germany then met at Lausanne and agreed to cancel virtually all reparations if the Untied States would sharply pare the war debts— Hoover declined, as American public opinion demanded. After the moratorium expired, all debtors but Finland defaulted on debt payments and soon even stopped payments of interest. The American public, caught in the toils of the depression, reacted with a bitterness that remained as late as 1967-68 when France's President Charles DeGaulle seemed to be attacking the stability of the American dollar and its gold reserve.

Ironically, the war debts paid to the United States almost equalled private American loans to Germany and Germany's payments to the Allies. About $2.25 billion had been invested in Germany, while reparation payments amounted to about $2 billion. This unsound chain broke down with the depression and the cessation of the flow of private American funds abroad. In retrospect, the United States would have been wiser to have cancelled or sharply reduced the war debts which would have aided Europe's recovery and the reabsorption of a democratic Germany into a peaceful world.

Republican foreign policies appeared to be successful as the Twenties drew to an end. They had curbed the naval arms race and stabilized the Pacific, and Europe apparently had recovered from the First World War. The United States enjoyed prosperity and its interests abroad seemed adequately safeguarded in a stable world order, all without paying a price of entanglement and obligations. This illusion of prosperity and a cost-free security collapsed with the economic debacle that reached America in 1929. The great stockmarket crash dispelled optimism about prosperity and international stability. In the next decade foreign perils gradually compelled the United States painfully to swing back toward Wilsonian internationalism, while at home the puncturing of the prosperity balloon forced government to move from cooperation with business to direct intervention in the economy.

SUGGESTED READINGS

Adler, Selig. *The Uncertain Giant* (1965).

Buckley, Thomas. *The United States and the Washington Conference, 1921-1922* (1970).

Burner, David. *The Politics of Provincialism* (1967).

Carter, Paul A. *Another Part of the Twenties* (1977).

___. *The Twenties in America* (1975).

Dingnan, Roger. *Power in the Pacific* (1976).

Ellis, L. Ethan. *Republican Foreign Policy, 1921-1933* (19680.

Feis, Herbert. *The Diplomacy of the Dollar* (1950).

Farrell, Robert H. *Peace in Their Time.* 1952.

Hicks, John D. *Republican Ascendancy: 1921-1933* (1960).

McCoy, David R. *Calvin Coolidge* (1967).

Murray, Robert K. *The Harding Era* (1969).

___. *The Politics of Normalcy* (1973).

Noggle, Burt. *Teapot Dome* (1960).

O'Connor, Richard. *The First Hurrah: A Biography of Alfred E. Smith* (1970).

Pusey, M.J. *Charks Evans Hughes* (1951).

Silverman, Dan P. *Reconstructing Europe After the Great War* (1987).

White, William A. *A Puritan in Babylon* (1938).

Chapter Five

THE GREAT DEPRESSION

Prosperity seemed a fact of life to many Americans by 1929. The stock market soared to astronomical highs as Herbert Hoover, the Great Engineer of the new business era of the twenties, prepared to enter the White House. *Time* magazine honored Walter P. Chrysler, the manufacturer of the Plymouth and DeSoto automobiles and builder of the then world's largest skyscraper in New York City, as "Man of the Year." A new magazine, *Fortune*, emerged on the promise of the "generally accepted commonplace that America's great achievement has been Business." Calvin Coolidge, despite some private qualms, in his last State of the Union message succinctly expressed the national mood of self-congratulation:

> No Congress of the United States ever assembled, on surveying the State of the Union, has met with a more pleasing prospect than that which appears at the present time. In the domestic field there is tranquillity and contentment...and the highest record of years of prosperity...[We can] regard the present with satisfaction and anticipate the future with optimism.

Rarely have hopes been higher or so speedily and cruelly disappointed. By the end of 1929 the disastrous stock market crash raised questions about the soundness of the business system—and years of bleak, grinding depression faced the American people. Revered prophets of the Twenties, businessmen, economic soothsayers, and politicians, almost overnight became figures of scorn and ridicule. Cherished values and traditions of free enterprise and economic opportunity suddenly acquired a hollow cynical ring, as people frantically sought panaceas for the stunning economic blight. More than ever before in American history, the multitudes trapped in an apparently inexplicable economic debacle looked to Washington for rescue. Government, reluctantly under Herbert Hoover and more readily during the era of the New Deal, felt compelled to prod, regulate and tinker with the economy in desperate attempts to halt the downward spiral and to stimulate recovery. The interventionist welfare state emerged, as so-called *laissez-faire* policies of the past were abandoned for those of at least a partly planned and managed society.

BOOM AND BUST

The urge to get rich quick was a logical, if distorted, reflection of the mood of the Twenties. Hopes of obtaining wealth without effort and without serious risks seemed almost universal, as the frenzied booms in real estate and the stock market revealed. Prior to 1924 the stock market had been comparatively restrained and the dividends paid on most stocks corresponded reasonably to their market prices. The real bull market got under way in the later part of that year. The average of the *New York Times* index of selected industrial stocks rose from 106 at the beginning of 1924 to 245 by the end of 1927. This did not indicate speculation, defenders of the market claimed, but only a delayed catching up of stock prices to increased corporate earnings. In 1928 the rise in stock prices became even steeper, prices advancing as much as twenty points a day. The *New York Times* index reached 331 or a gain of 86 points during the year. Some stocks that had never paid a dividend rose even more spectacularly. In this sense, the majority of the stock market transactions reflected gambling rather than long-term investments.

Buying on margin, where a purchaser pays only part of the cost of the stock and a broker lends the remainder, increased rapidly. Banks and insurance companies, attracted by the high interest rates for "call money" used in margin transactions, diverted funds from capital investments and construction to the stock market. Such funds jumped from about $1 billion in 1924 to nearly $8.5 billion prior to the crash in 1929. Money also poured in from all over the world, attracted by the high returns of the American market. Prices advanced to new highs in 1929, with little if any relationship to the actual earning power or worth of the stocks. Investment trusts multiplied, offering portfolios of stocks to those too inexperienced or cautious to invest directly. Local stock exchanges flourished across the country, and many banks set up special facilities for investors. By the summer of the first year of the Hoover administration, the *New York Times* index recorded a high of 449, up 110 points in three months.

The crash came with stunning force. A few voices had warned of the dangers of such wild gambling, but most spokesmen continued optimistically to predict even greater gains. The Federal Reserve Board, acting cautiously to avoid precipitating a crash, cautioned member banks in 1929 not to lend money for speculation and raised the discount rate to six percent, but without a noticeable effect. In September and early October, the market began to fluctuate uneasily. On October 23, thousands of speculators suddenly lost confidence and tried to dispose of their holdings. Panic struck on the next day, "Black Thursday," when brokers sold nearly thirteen million shares of stocks and prices fell disastrously. Rumours attracted crowds outside the stock exchange, drawn by reports that eleven speculators had jumped to their deaths in despair. Inside the exchange, many frantic sellers found it impossible to find buyers for their holdings. Brokers, facing ruin, sold out margin buyers with heavy losses.

At noon on October 24, a group of bankers representing J.P. Morgan and Company and several major New York banks met to try to stem the tide. They pledged a pool, estimated to have been as much as $240 million, to halt the decline. Thomas W. Lamont of the Morgan firm spoke for the group: "There has been a little distress selling on the Stock Exchange," but "It is the consensus of the group that many of the quotations on the Stock Exchange do not fairly represent the situation...." Widely hailed as saviors, the financiers acted in part to save their own skins by stabilizing the market and gaining time to get out without heavy losses. Richard Whitney, the agent of these "Lords of Creation," then entered the stock exchange and dramatically placed large purchase orders for major stocks at above the current bidding price. The gesture had only a temporary effect, for all across the nation thousands of stockholders frantically dumped their holdings.

The bottom fell out on Tuesday, October 29, the worst single day in the history of the market. Brokers sold nearly sixteen and a half million shares and the tickertape ran hopelessly behind as more sellers than buyers appeared. Prices continued to decline, within a few weeks wiping out paper values of nearly $30 billion. Despite optimistic statements by President Hoover, Treasury Secretary Mellon and industrialists such as John D. Rockefeller, the collapse continued. By the end of the year, the *New York Times* average had fallen to 224 from the previous high of 452. Investment trust stocks became nearly worthless, and even such giants as American Telephone and Telegraph fell from 310.25 to 193.25. The downward spiral continued throughout the next two years, until the *New York Times* index stood at an all time low in mid-1932 of 58 points. An estimated $74 billion in stock values had been lost.

Signs of an economic recession existed even before the stock market crash. Residential construction had fallen a billion dollars below the 1928 rate, consumer spending slowed, unsold business inventories rose sharply, and industrial production fell off with an increase in unemployment. Businessmen and consumers found credit tight and costly, and the rate of industrial plant growth declined. In addition, agriculture and certain other industries had never experienced prosperity throughout the decade.

After the crash, the economic cycle dipped even lower. Production dropped as factories responded to reduced consumption by laying off employees and curtailing operations, leading to still lower consumer demand and more layoffs in an ever worsening spiral. By 1932 industrial production had fallen to less than half the pre-crash level, and the annual national income had dropped from $82 billion in 1928 to $40 billion. Bankers found themselves hard hit as debtors defaulted, real estate loans lost value, and speculative ventures collapsed. Loss of public trust and unsound practices resulted in numerous bank failures, especially among the smaller state banks unaffiliated with the Federal Reserve System.

Unemployment steadily grew. From an average of about two million in the Coolidge era, unemployment rose to three million in the spring of 1930, nearly four million by the end of that year, and almost seven million in late 1931. By 1932 between twelve and fifteen million Americans lacked jobs. Even those still employed often experienced sharp reductions in wages or were on part-time work. Farm prices, already depressingly low, fell 64 percent below the 1929 level. Some farmers burned corn for fuel, since they had unsold supplies and coal was relatively expensive. Farm income dropped proportionately, with the inevitable results of more indebtedness, mortgage foreclosures (a fourth of all farmers lost their farms), farm tenancy, and grinding poverty. Professional groups also felt the squeeze in lowered income and mounting debts.

The social effects of the depression were deep and destructive. As economist John Kenneth Galbraith notes, it raised serious questions for many, and especially for the young, about the old verities that thrift, hard work and diligence would inevitably be rewarded by prosperity. The diligent and the improvident alike experienced the same fate. Relief and charity weakened habits of self-reliance and prolonged joblessness caused despair and fear. Security rather than advancement or daring enterprise seemed to have become the new universal goal.

Local relief and philanthropy proved hopelessly incapable of meeting the staggering burden of unemployment. Philadelphia had 300,000 people out of work by 1932, in contrast to the normal figure of 40,000; 55,000 families were on relief, receiving $4.23 a week which it was estimated provided only two-thirds of a minimum healthy diet. New York City found it necessary because of lack of revenue to reduce the weekly relief allowance to $2.39 a family and even then could provide for only half of the needy, while the Toledo, Ohio, commissary could spend only slightly above two cents per meal for those in want. In the larger cities, groups of ragged men, women, and children scavenged garbage dumps for scraps of food or clothing. In Chicago, according to one reporter,

Around the truck which was unloading garbage and other refuse, were about thirty-five men, women, and children. As soon as the truck pulled away from the pile, all of them started digging with sticks, some with their hands, grabbing bits of food and vegetables.

So-called "Hoover-villes" or makeshift settlements festered around the larger cities, where homeless families dwelt in worn-out cars, tin shacks or caves. Hundreds of single men and women slept in the parks even during inclement weather, while others sought warmth and food in the jails. New "industries" sprang up, such as apple selling on the streets or shoeshine "boys" of all ages and backgrounds. Illustrating the desperate mood of the unemployed, Soviet Russia advertised in 1931 for 6000 skilled workers to go to Russia and was flooded with over 100,000 applications.

As always, youth was especially hard-hit. A survey in New York City in 1932 revealed that 20 percent of the children suffered from malnutrition—starvation in a land of plenty. Teachers in Chicago fed 11,000 hungry school children from their own meager resources. Hundreds of thousands of jobless youth took to the road and drifted aimlessly across the country in search of opportunity, hitch-hiking or riding the rails on freight trains. Whole families packed their belongings and set off in ramshackle cars, attracted by rumors of jobs in California or elsewhere. Teachers received sharp salary cuts, and their salary was often in arrears. Chicago, whose teachers went unpaid for six months, issued promissory notes or scrip as tax revenues fell off. A number of schools closed their doors, particularly in rural areas and in the South. Georgia, for example, closed 1318 schools with a total enrollment of over 170,000 pupils.

Writers of the depression again became absorbed by social issues rather than with problems of individual fulfillment. There was a reawakening of national self-consciousness, as authors in volumes or articles bearing such titles as "My America," "Tragic America," or "The American Earthquake," analyzed the nation and the emergency it confronted. Erskine Caldwell's *Tobacco Road*, a ribald novel about the plight of the rural poor, became a popular Broadway play. John Steinbeck, in *The Grapes of Wrath*, described the forlorn migration of "Okies" and "Arkies," refugees from farm poverty and the dust bowl, many of whom sought a new life in the golden state of California only to encounter new disappointments. In *Native Son*, the gifted black writer Richard Wright related the obstacles facing a young Negro boy emigrating to the North. James T. Farrell wrote a trilogy of young Studs Lonigan growing to manhood in depression-ridden Chicago. A brilliant writer, Thomas Wolfe, wrote in an autobiographical vein about boyhood in North Carolina and life in the North in *Look Homeward, Angel, Of Time and the River,* and *You Can't Go Home Again.* As the decade wore on and problems of the depression became compounded with dangers of fascism and war, Ernest Hemingway wrote of the Spanish Civil War in *For Whom the Bell Tolls*, and Sinclair Lewis in *It Can't Happen Here* warned of the menace of totalitarianism.

It seemed to many observers in the early 1930s that the United States faced an imminent revolution. Hunger riots occurred in several cities, mobs smashing and pilfering stores and warehouses in search of food and clothing. On May 1, 1930, as President Hoover was assuring the US Chamber of Commerce of imminent recovery, a group of the jobless, organized by the Communists, demonstrated before the White House until dispersed by police with tear gas. In New York City, 35,000 people tried to march on the city hall. Detroit, the automotive capital, had such vast unemployment that William Z. Foster and the Communist Party picked it as the target for a major effort at unionization and increased party influence. Three thousand unemployed advanced from the city in an orderly procession on Henry Ford's River Rouge plant at Dearborn to deliver a petition, only to be turned back by police fire that killed four and wounded several. A funeral procession for the martyrs carried banners proclaiming that "Ford Gives Bullets for Bread."

Desperate farmers frequently prevented or interfered, to the point of violence, with mortgage foreclosure sales. In the midwest, there emerged a movement known as the Farmers' Holiday Association (FHA), which, in the words of its historian, proved "the most aggressive agrarian upheaval of the twentieth century...a final great attempt of the family farmer to save himself from absorption and annihilation." The FHA, like previous expressions of agrarian radicalism, arose in a period of depression and low prices; but, unlike earlier protests when wheat farmers assumed leadership, the depression farmers' protest of the late Twenties and early Thirties was led by corn, hog and dairy farmers. Its leader was Milo Reno of Iowa, its program was the so-called cost of production panacea. Reno argued, with some persuasion, that if the national leadership would guarantee the cost of production, the farmers' purchasing power would soon be restored, a prospect by which the economy as a whole would soon profit. How does one arrive at the cost of production? According to one estimate:

...tabulate all essential operating costs of farm business units and determine an average. Add an annual wage of $1,250 for the operator, a 5 percent return on investments in land and a depreciation allowance. Then determine the percentage of the total farm product of the state derived from each farm community.

By the time of Reno's death in 1936, and despite the threat of a national farm strike in mid-1932, the FHA was a dead letter.

A group of about 20,000 war veterans, known as the Bonus Expeditionary Force because they sought full and advanced payment of the bonus for war services, camped with their families on the outskirts of Washington. Chanting:

> Mellon pulled the whistle,
>
> Hoover rang the bell,
>
> Wall Street gave the signal
>
> and the country went to hell!

Veterans forced Congress to debate the bonus bill. Passed by the House, administration pressure defeated the bonus in the Senate. Although the veterans were orderly and only a handful were Communists, President Hoover refused to talk with them and regarded them as revolutionary. Finally, after the police panicked during a melée, he ordered the army under General Douglas MacArthur to evict the BEF from its encampments. The dashing, bemedaled general carried out the task with tanks and with troops armed with bayonets and tear gas, chasing away the forlorn refugees and burning their tents and shacks. Hoover was to pay in lost popularity for his needless fright.

The Communist Party gleefully hailed the depression as proof of the bankruptcy of the capitalist system and eagerly anticipated revolution. It sent organizers to various cities to win over the jobless, organized protest meetings and marches and in 1931 called for a National Hunger March on Washington. Yet, despite the despair of the times, the Communist Party garnered only a small number of converts. Intellectuals, disillusioned by the crassness of the 1920s and the economic debacle of the 1930s, seemed more attracted to the cause than workers. Michael Gold edited the *New Masses*, a Communist revival in 1927 of the old radical *Masses* of the Progressive era, and printed much crude "proletarian" literature. A number of able writers either joined the Communist Party or contributed to the *New Masses*: John Dos Passos, Granville Hicks, Theodore Dreiser, Erskine Caldwell, and others. The aging muckraker and radical, Lincoln Steffens, in his *Autobiography* (1931) reiterated his earlier conviction that progressive reforms had not been enough; the capitalist system must be replaced and business nationalized as the Communists had done in Russia. As he commented, "All roads in our day lead to Moscow." John Chamberlain's *Farewell to Reform* (1932) agreed that time had revealed the futility of progressivism and liberalism. Yet, despite an apparently unparalleled opportunity, by 1932 the Communist Party only had about 12,000 members. Obviously most Americans felt alienated by the revolutionary jargon of the communists and still clung to faith in law and order and the private property system. Even the small number of intellectuals won over tended to become speedily disillusioned by the dogmatism of the party and the brutal fanaticism of Joseph Stalin's dictatorship in Soviet Russia.

The causes and cure of the Great Depression were endlessly debated. Economist William T. Foster attributed the collapse to oversavings, reducing ability to consume goods. He contended that recovery would come only from heavier private and especially governmental spending. John Maynard Keynes, the brilliant British economist, agreed in his *Treatise on Money* (1930) that the depression was "a crisis of abundance" resulting from underconsumption. In this and subsequent writings, especially *The General Theory of Employment, Interest, and Money* (1936), Keynes advocated massive government spending via public works and other projects to create purchasing power and to revive the economy. In reality Keynesianism always meant more than mere deficit spending; it called for nothing less than for government to plan for full employment and consumption. A Utah banker, Marriner Eccles, reached similar conclusions about the need for federal spending. Gardiner C. Means and Adolf A. Berle, Jr, authors of *The Modern Corporation* (1932), and Rexford Guy Tugwell concluded that the vast growth of corporate power and *de facto* price fixing made meaningless older assumptions about a free market and required a large measure of public planning of the economy and government spending to balance production with consumption.

In the words of the *New Republic*, many critics saw the depression as a great opportunity for the "democratization of industry." The experiences of World War I seemed particularly appropriate, for then, as philosopher John Dewey pointed out, all the belligerent countries had emphasized production for need and use rather than merely for profit. Gerard Swope of General Electric proposed a World War I type of Liberty Bond drive to raise money for large-scale governmental spending; subsequently he advocated the "Swope Plan" for a national economic council to supervise a network of private trade associations that would stabilize production, employment, and prices. McAdoo, formerly Secretary of the Treasury in the Wilson administration, called for a Peace Industries Board, resembling the old War Industries Board, to mobilize the economy in the new crisis. Whether advocating more business self-government, federal planning, or heavy pump-priming spending by Washington, all these voices agreed upon the necessity for greater governmental effort. Startling though their proposals seemed to many, they actually were only logical extensions of the tendency toward greater rationalization and organization of the economy that had been underway since the turn of the century.

It is now generally agreed that the stock market crash, itself largely the result of gambling and speculative mania, contributed to the Great Depression. If the basic economy had been healthier, economist Galbraith points out, the collapse of the boom in stocks probably would have been less acutely felt. Since the reverse was true, the Wall Street debacle triggered a spiral of other collapses in the economy. Examining these underlying factors, it must be borne in mind that much of the prosperity of the 1920s had been founded on consumer industries rather than on heavy industry. Production of basic necessities such as food tended to be surpassed in importance by the production of durable or semi-durable goods, formerly considered luxuries, and by the growth of distributive and service industries. By their very nature, consumption of such goods and services could be sharply curtailed in times of economic distress, whether individual or national. Consequently the maldistribution of income in the decade, when industry retained too much of the gains of increased productivity as profits and passed on a disproportionately small share in the form of higher wages and lower prices, meant a sharp limitation in the ability of the average American to consume an ever-growing flood of goods and services. It has been estimated that 60 percent of American families received less than the $2000 annual income necessary to buy the minimum essentials. Industry simply produced far more than consumers easily could buy under prevailing wages and prices, even when aided by the new system of installment or credit purchasing. Production outstripped consumption, with the inevitable results of gluts of unsold goods, factory cut-backs, unemployment, and a further reduction of consumer purchasing power that touched off more rounds of retrenchment.

Other contributing factors involved a precarious corporate structure of holding companies piled on top of holding companies; a weak banking system marked by unsound credit practices and speculative loans and inadequate state or federal regulation; technological unemployment and the absence of unemployment compensation; and the diversion of profits and dividends from plant expansion or construction to stock market speculation. A series of business-oriented administrations had failed to deal with a depressed agriculture or to enforce existing regulatory laws and had encouraged inflation and cheap money during most of the decade. World conditions undoubtedly contributed, though the depression came first to America and was felt more severely here. Foreign trade was unhealthy and a vast burden of inter-governmental and private international debts existed, made worse by the high tariff and war debt policies of the American government.

HOOVER AND THE GREAT DEPRESSION

Few men have entered the presidency with brighter prospects than Herbert Hoover in March of 1929. Famed for his past services to the nation and mankind, the Great Engineer in politics confidently anticipated consolidation of the business "New Era." Four years later he left office, deeply embittered and near exhaustion from his ceaseless labors to cope with the depression, reviled as few other presidents in American history. Why, in view of his great talents, did he fail in this crisis?

Hoover's personal philosophy seems the primary explanation. Because of his own experiences, Hoover firmly believed in an "American system" based on individualism, economic opportunity, and private enterprise, with the government's role restricted to that of an umpire to regulate and encourage the economy. As he said during the 1928 campaign:

> It is as if we set a race. We, through free and universal education, provide the training of the runners; we give to them an equal start; we provide in the government the umpire of fairness in the race. The winner is he who shows the most conscientious training, the greatest ability, and the greatest character.

A skilled administrator, Hoover was not an effective political leader. Shy and ultra-sensitive to criticism, he detested politics and could not project a dynamic public image during the depression. Contrary to a widely-held opinion, however, Hoover early recognized that a severe depression had hit America, even if like some others he failed to perceive just how grave and prolonged it would be. In past economic crises, recovery had set in by the operation of so-called natural laws. Decreased production had permitted surpluses to be absorbed, and declining costs in labor and raw materials had allowed the prices of goods to fall also with a consequent revival of economic activity, aided by foreign markets and a growing population. These processes, owing to a fairly stable population in the 1930s and to a world-wide depression, operated poorly if at all in the current crisis.

Hoover fully recognized that government must be more active in trying to quicken the economy. Unlike the hands-off attitude of his predecessors during past slumps, he involved the federal government as never before in anti-depression measures. Especially in the last two years of his administration, he clearly foreshadowed some of the approaches of Franklin D. Roosevelt's New Deal. Yet he changed too slowly, when the times demanded rapid and even desperate measures. Above all, he clung stubbornly to his belief that while the national government must help the people to recover, the public would have to bear the major burden and should not expect miracles. A prisoner of his earlier experiences and of Republican policies, he relied too much upon voluntary effort, cooperation, and persuasion. He viewed direct federal aid as dangerous, for it might weaken private initiative and responsibility and lead to federal control of the economy. America had been built on the principle of individual self-help and local responsibility, he firmly believed, and to weaken that by federal actions would endanger the very qualities that had made the nation great.

Hoover called a special session of Congress, prior to the 1929 crash, to cope with the farm problem and the tariff. Congress authorized the creation of a Federal Farm Board with a revolving fund of one-half billion dollars to encourage farmers to plan production and marketing, especially through the formation of nationally organized cooperatives. According to this self-help theory, farmers could be educated voluntarily to restrain production in order to raise market prices. With the encouragement of the Farm Board, farmers formed national cooperative associations or corporations for those producing grain, wool, cotton, livestock, fruits and vegetables, and other commodities. Using pool selling, loans on products stored for later sale, and other devices, the Farm Board hoped to provide for more orderly marketing and improving prices. As a temporary device to remove surpluses and generate a price rise, the cotton and grain stabilization corporations lent funds and then purchased those crops on the open market.

At Hoover's insistence, the Farm Board could not impose production controls and farmers continued overproduction of cotton and wheat, despite Farm board recommendations for restraint and the plowing under of cotton. The stabilization corporations accumulated huge unsalable stocks before admitting failure and abandoning their efforts in 1931 to prop up prices. As the depression deepened, wheat prices skidded to fifty-seven cents a bushel in 1931 and cotton sold for five cents a pound by 1932.

After the Wall Street debacle, President Hoover appreciated that the country faced more than a mere financial panic. Publicly, he exuded confidence. In October, he stated that "the fundamental business of the country...is on a sound and prosperous basis," and in November he declared that "any lack of confidence in the economy future or the basic strength of business...is foolish." Privately, however, the President decided not to follow Treasury Secretary Mellon's classic formula of letting the depression run what he described as its natural course until a bottom was reached and recovery began. Instead the President hoped to use governmental persuasion to cushion the shock and generate a more rapid revival of the economy. He called a series of conferences in Washington of businessmen, industrialists, agricultural spokesmen, and labor leaders and obtained promises to maintain wage rates and to continue capital investments.

The conferences and optimistic statements illustrated Hoover's faith in encouraging cooperation between various groups in the private economy. Unfortunately as the depression deepened, the promises he obtained from business leaders could not be or were not kept. The Federal Reserve Board relaxed credit and the Farm Board tried to raise agricultural prices. Hoover proposed to expand federal public works and urged the states to adopt similar programs. The Hawley-Smoot Tariff of 1930 increased duties on agricultural and industrial imports, but proved to be a false hope as a weapon against the depression. Congress also enacted a tax cut in 1929 to stimulate the economy. But since taxes already had been very low, the reduction had negligible results.

At Hoover's suggestion, Julius H. Barnes of the United States Chamber of Commerce invited important businessmen in a National Business Survey Conference to discover and remove the key barriers in the economy in order to restore prosperity. The organization faded away by 1931, obviously a failure. The simple fact, to be repeatedly demonstrated during the depression, was that businessmen and farmers were too individualistic to voluntarily take collective measures to raise wages and to regulate production. When the pinch became tighter most businessmen forgot about cooperation and adopted measures to protect themselves—wage slashes, layoffs, and production reductions—ensuring further declines in the economy. For example, a National Credit Corporation formed by bankers in response to administration suggestions to enable stronger banks to strengthen essentially sound but temporarily endangered banks failed, because the larger banks were unwilling to take the risk. At no time did President

Hoover recommend any fundamental reform of the nation's economic machinery, though reform seemed necessary to most critics in the areas of stockmarket operations, banking, and the corporate structure.

To generate confidence and to minimize the hoarding of money, Hoover and his administration issued an unending stream of optimistic statements. Unfortunately, the President fell victim to his own optimism. Repeatedly he misinterpreted slight upward fluctuations in a generally downward economic spiral to reassure the country. Thus on May 1, 1930, Hoover proclaimed to the US Chamber of Commerce, "we have now passed the worse and with continued unity of effort we shall rapidly recover." The spring upsurge, however, quickly passed and the depression continued. Had the economy been sounder, his methods might have succeeded as similar ones had in the 1921 slump. Unfortunately he let pass a crucial period when a relatively small increase in federal spending might have restored a balance.

Hoover refused to admit the failure of his indirect methods, despite further declines in the economy and growing popular criticism. The 1930 mid-term elections, though not a Democratic sweep, registered large gains for the opposition party. The Democratic National Committee was largely successful in fixing the responsibility for the depression on Hoover. The results of the election gave the Democrats a narrow control in the House of Representatives and a forty-seven to forty-eight balance in the Senate. Because of growing insurgency among western Republicans, Hoover faced an increasingly hostile Congress during the last two years of his term. Yet he resisted pressures for massive federal spending and stubbornly maintained that his recovery measures met the needs of the country.

A new danger disturbed the President. Declining federal revenues threatened to result in a huge public debt and possible abandonment of the gold standard. Falling revenues and the amount of deficit spending that Hoover reluctantly accepted increased the national debt from slightly over $16 billion in 1930 to $19.5 billion in 1932. The deficit for 1931 alone neared $1 billion. To counter the deficit, Hoover slashed outlays for public works in order to avoid throwing the budget further out of balance.

As the depression grew worse, Hoover blamed everything but the American economic system. Earlier he had condemned domestic overspeculation as the cause of the crash, but now he pointed to world conditions as the culprit. When the Creditanstalt Bank in Vienna collapsed, triggering similar financial debacles across much of the continent, Europeans dumped American securities resulting in a heavy flow of gold from America to Europe. To stem the tide, the Federal Reserve Board raised the rediscount rate from 1.5 percent to 3.5 percent saving the gold reserve but making credit tighter for businessmen. In still another attempt to cope with the world depression, Hoover in 1931 proclaimed a moratorium on inter-governmental debt payments in the vain hope of stemming the collapse abroad.

Although state and local and private relief agencies proved obviously inadequate, Hoover stubbornly clung to the conviction that they could meet the problem of unemployment. Even years later he was reluctant to admit the magnitude of unemployment. In his memoirs he explained the large-scale phenomenon of apple-selling on the streets as a shrewd scheme by the apple growers: "Many persons left their jobs for the more profitable one of selling apples." He did appoint an Emergency Committee for Employment, subsequently reconstituted as the President's Organization on Unemployment Relief, to stimulate voluntary and local charity. The first director, Colonel Arthur Woods, concluded that more was required on the part of the federal government and soon resigned. His replacement, Walter S. Gifford of American Telephone and Telegraph, fully concurred with the President's views. With much ballyhoo Gifford launched "a great spiritual experience" to remedy joblessness by persuading more people to employ one another. Testifying before Congress, Gifford insisted upon the soundness of the administration's policy and he condemned all proposals for federal relief. Business leaders claimed there would be recovery if government did not interfere by direct relief. They proposed (courtesy of J.P. Morgan) a "block system" whereby residents in an area would pledge weekly contributions for relief and another plan for the collection of restaurant leftover food to be distributed to the poor.

In Hoover's mind, direct federal relief would destroy individual initiative and self-respect, weaken local government and voluntary charity, and result in a dangerous federal paternalism. Brushing aside unpleasant facts, Hoover repeatedly declared that all the needy were being taken care of. Far from there being any starvation, he assured the nation, the national health standards in fact had improved. Yet agonized appeals continued to flood into Washington for measures to prevent misery and suffering. When one group called on him at the White House in mid-1931 to urge direct federal action, Hoover confidently declared that the depression was over: "Gentlemen, you have come six weeks too late."

Hoover did consent to federal loans to buy seeds and tools for farmers stricken by the great drought in the Southwest's Dust Bowl in 1931, but he balked at a proposal to feed the farmers and their families or to extend direct relief to the unemployed. In the Senate, Robert F. Wagner of New York, who sympathized with the lowly and the unfortunate perhaps because he had been poor, led the fight for more accurate statistics on joblessness, proposed the expansion of public works, and backed other relief measures. The President, however, adamantly opposed such proposals. "Never before," he said on vetoing a relief bill, "has so dangerous a suggestion been seriously made in this country." The President reluctantly signed into law in 1932 the Norris-La Guardia Anti-Injunction Act, sought by organized labor to curb anti-strike court injunctions, but he vetoed a bill to strengthen the Federal Employment Service established in 1907. Hoover's defeat in 1932 can be attributed in large degree to his refusal to use federal resources in direct relief of the unemployed and needy.

The administration did act more boldly in two areas, if only in accordance with Hoover's philosophy. A federal Home Loan Act was passed in 1932 to strengthen building and loan associations. Unfortunately thousands of home owners had already lost their homes—273,000 in 1932 alone. The Reconstruction Finance Corporation, established in early 1932 and based on the War Finance Corporation of World War I, represented a more imaginative measure. Congress authorized the RFC to lend money to banks, insurance companies, railroads, and agricultural credit associations. Although one critic derisively dismissed the RFC as a "millionaire's dole," Hoover intended it to restore confidence in the nation's financial structure. He hoped in fact that its mere creation would be enough so that actual lending could be kept to a minimum. Unfortunately, RFC's first director, Charles G. Dawes, stirred up a triade of denunciations when it became known that shortly after he had resigned from the RFC that agency had loaned Dawes' own bank, the Central Republic Bank and Trust Company in Chicago, $90 million in a vain effort to shore it up. Hoover correctly defended the loan as proper but it seemed to many to demonstrate the willingness of the administration to help only big business. Yet despite such criticisms, the RFC strengthened otherwise sound institutions and was a direct precursor to the New Deal's lending policy. Hoover reluctantly accepted subsequent legislation for the RFC to lend up to $300 million to the states for relief purposes. The nearly bankrupt states, however, responded unenthusiastically because they preferred gifts. The RFC and the states used loans so sparingly that only a few million dollars were actually advanced. The New Deal was to expand vastly the scope of the RFC.

By 1932, Hoover's philosophy of voluntaryism and self-help, with government confining its role largely to encouragement, had failed to overcome the crisis. Yet as Albert U. Romasco has pointed out, President Hoover had made a valiant effort within the limits of that approach and if he had not thus pioneered little would have been learned about how government should cope with a severe depression.

DEPRESSION POLITICS

Hoover was tired of coping with the depression but he sought to vindicate his policies by running for re-election in 1932, and he won renomination, though without any great enthusiasm by his party. Many progressive-minded Republicans either responded apathetically or deserted to the Democrats. Increasingly the rigid and self-righteous President became the target of widespread criticism and abuse. Cruel jokes circulated that he was indeed the world's greatest engineer, having "drained, ditched and damned" the entire country within the span of a few years. One popular joke had Hoover asking Andrew Mellon for a nickel to telephone a friend, and the latter replied, "Here's a dime; call all your friends." Hoover's very name became an epithet, a symbol for despair and misery: "Hoover wagons" were old broken-down cars, "Hoover blankets" referred to newspapers that covered forlorn men sleeping in the parks, and lean jackrabbits were re-christened "Hoover hogs."

Opening his campaign in Iowa, Hoover encountered protest picketers carrying placards. One sign read, "In Hoover We Trusted; Now We Are Busted." People booed him in Philadelphia and Salt Lake City, and he was jeered at in Detroit by several thousand veterans, unemployed, and some communists who surrounded his train. The hapless President reassured the nation that no "deserving American fireside" would experience cold or hunger that winter, small comfort to the millions of presumably "undeserving" who did.

Franklin D. Roosevelt, one of the most charismatic figures in American political history, held the front-runner position among Democrats in 1932. Born in 1882 into the aristocratic Roosevelt family at Hyde Park, New York, young Franklin grew up imbued with a sense of duty and service to family and the community. After education at Groton and Harvard, where his grades were gentlemanly but not outstanding, Franklin briefly went into law before he decided to emulate his famous cousin, Theodore Roosevelt, by entering politics. He married Eleanor Roosevelt, Theodore's niece, in 1905. A sensitive woman with an unhappy childhood, and deeply sympathetic with the less fortunate of this world, Eleanor had an incalculable influence in the development of her husband's social conscience and his interest in reform. Roosevelt received an excellent political education while serving in the New York State Senate. For the first time aware of the plight of the lower classes, he began to reveal attitudes and convictions regarding labor and agriculture that subsequently shaped the New Deal. He also learned invaluable political lessons about party regularity, and he perceived firsthand that machine politicians, such as Al Smith, could also be men of honesty dedicated to public service. During the Wilson administration, he served ably as Assistant Secretary of the Navy under Josephus Daniels. In 1920

Roosevelt received the vice-presidential nomination on the ticket with Governor Cox of Ohio and campaigned energetically in a lost cause for the Democrats.

Stricken with infantile paralysis in 1921, Roosevelt courageously fought back to a partial recovery; he often visited Warm Springs, Georgia, and founded a center there for the treatment of polio victims. Roosevelt remained actively interested in politics despite his illness. He formed a political friendship with New York's Al Smith and supported him in his bids for the presidency in 1924 and 1928. At the 1924 convention, Roosevelt on crutches hailed Al Smith as the "Happy Warrior" of politics and made a moving impression on the delegates. After Smith obtained the nomination in 1928, Roosevelt won the governorship of New York. Despite the defeat of the national ticket, Roosevelt battled for regional planning to help both the farmer and the state in general. He got a constitutional authorization in 1931 for state acquisition of abandoned farms for reforestation, and backed other conservation measures. Roosevelt continued Smith's program for public power development on the St. Lawrence River.

When the depression came, Roosevelt operated "a little left of center" in his efforts to cope with state problems of unemployment and relief. He established a Commission on the Stabilization of Employment within the state and approved the concept of unemployment insurance. He created a state emergency relief administration, under the direction of Harry Hopkins. But even Roosevelt, probably the most progressive state governor then on the national scene, at first showed a marked unenthusiasm about expanding public works, and he tried to finance relief by raising taxes until compelled to accept larger deficits. He had not yet fully envisioned the positive role government intervention could play in the economy, still sharing the conservative belief in an unhampered free enterprise system. At any rate, he managed to create an image of himself as a dynamic political leader fighting the depression, in contrast to Hoover's do-nothing approach. Aided by able political advisers such as James Farley, Louis M. Howe (his private secretary), and speech-writer Samuel J. Rosenman, Roosevelt won reelection as Governor in 1930 by a heavy margin. Thereafter, his national political star was on the rise and he began to challenge the Republicans. In several addresses early in 1932 Roosevelt sharpened his attack on the Hoover policies. The emergency was worse than 1917, he declared, and it required similar planned effort to "build from the bottom up" and not to neglect the "forgotten man."

Roosevelt thus was in a good position to win the Democratic presidential nomination in 1932, though he first had to brush aside Smith who had sacrificed himself in the Republican year of 1928 and thought he deserved another chance. Despite primary election setbacks in Massachusetts and California (Smith won by a three to one margin in the Bay State and Roosevelt came in a poor second in California), the Roosevelt forces beat back Smith and such rivals as Governor "Alfalfa Bill" Murray of Oklahoma. Roosevelt won the nomination on the fourth ballot at the Democratic convention in Chicago. John N. Garner of Texas got the second place on the ticket.

Roosevelt set the tone of the campaign in his precedent-shattering appearance before the convention to accept the nomination. Dramatically flying to Chicago, he proclaimed to the assembled delegates and the nation, "Ours must be a party of liberal thought, of planned actions, of enlightened international outlook, and of the greatest good to the greatest number of our citizens." He then spoke in general terms of the necessity for government aid and encouragement for agriculture, business, and the unemployed. "I pledge you [the delegates at the convention], I pledge myself, to a new deal for the American people...this is more than a political campaign; it is a call to arms. Give me your help, not to win votes alone, but to win in this crusade to restore America to its own people." His stirring promise of a New Deal captured the public's imagination and furnished a label for his subsequent administration.

Roosevelt was criticized then and later for giving vague speeches that failed to spell out the details of his plans for defeating the depression. The *New Republic*, for example, evaluated Roosevelt as a man of good intentions but without great intellectual or moral force. Commentator Walter Lippmann dismissed him as "a pleasant man who, without any important qualifications for the office, would like to be President." True, he did not present a clear-cut program to the electorate, but that usually has been the pattern in American presidential elections. Roosevelt sought to win an election and naturally wanted to alienate as few voters as possible. He found it far safer to condemn Hoover's policies than to specify his own. Moreover, Roosevelt as a practical politician did not indulge much in theorizing or dogmatic philosophy. Yet he should not be viewed as an opportunist in the crass sense, for he believed in certain principles of responsible democratic government and its obligations to promote the welfare of all its citizens. Roosevelt in office revealed a pragmatic and experimental approach, willing to borrow ideas and programs from diverse sources in the desperate battle to relieve suffering and restore national prosperity.

Roosevelt did indicate in a general way the course his administration subsequently followed. Aided by his "brains trust"—Felix Frankfurter of Harvard, and Raymond Moley, Adolf Berle, and Rexford Tugwell of Columbia—he outlined some of the essentials of the subsequent New Deal program in a series of major speeches. At Topeka, Kansas, Roosevelt indicated the need for a federal crop-control program to rescue the farmers. He talked of regulation and aid for the bankrupt railroads in Salt Lake City, the dangers of a high tariff at Seattle, and in Portland, Oregon, he called for federal dam and power projects.

He made his most radical proposals before the Commonwealth Club in San Francisco. There the candidate spoke of the need for an economic bill of rights including a decent minimum living standard, economic order, and government planning. When Hoover attacked him for advocating collectivism, charging that the New Deal would enslave America, Roosevelt toned down his speeches and began to criticize the Republicans for an unbalanced budget and a growing national debt. Hoover's $2.75 billion deficit, he declared, represented "the most reckless and extravagant [one]...that I have been able to discover in the statistical record of any peacetime Government anywhere, anytime." While pledging himself to greater economy in government and a balanced budget, in which he sincerely believed, Roosevelt left a loophole that more federal funds would be expended if necessary to relieve dire need and avert starvation. An experimental approach, more governmental regulation and intervention in the economy, some economic and social planning—the welfare, interventionist state— came to epitomize the New Deal.

The elections resulted in a Democratic landslide. Having claimed credit for the prosperity of the 1920s, the Republicans now were caught by the depression in a trap of their own making. Most voters remained impervious to Hoover's warning, a few days before the balloting, that if Roosevelt won "the grass will grow in the streets of a hundred cities, a thousand towns; the weeds will overrun the fields of millions of farmers....Their churches and school houses will decay." Roosevelt won the votes of nearly 23 million Americans, or 57.5 percent, to Hoover's 15.75 million votes and 39.6 percent of the popular total. Despite the obvious breakdown of the capitalist system, Socialist Norman Thomas only polled 881,951 votes, less proportionately than in 1912, and the Communist Party candidate, William Z. Foster, managed to attract slightly over 100,000 votes. Hoover carried only six states and was as badly defeated as Smith had been in 1928. As Hoover later wryly commented, "Democracy is not a polite employer. The only way out of elective office is to get sick or die or get kicked out." The Congress became overwhelmingly Democratic, as the party not only capitalized on the urban minorities of the great cities but even broke into traditional Republican strongholds in the agricultural midwest. The political revolution symbolized by Al Smith in 1928, when the Democratic party first significantly benefited from the growing political consciousness of urban ethnic and religious minorities and organized labor, approached fulfillment.

INTERREGNUM

Between November, 1932, and inaugural day in March, 1933, President Hoover found himself a lame duck chief executive as all eyes focused on the president-elect. The two met in the White House in late November, 1932, and their representatives held several conferences. Pleading the need to bolster business confidence, Hoover tried to persuade Roosevelt to continue Republican policies and not to embark on the experimental tack indicated in the recent campaign. Specifically he urged pledges not to tamper with the dollar nor to unbalance the budget (which Hoover already had unbalanced). When Roosevelt warily declined to assume responsibility or to commit himself prior to taking office, the embittered Hoover blamed him for the further deterioration of the economy and the banking panic that became acute in the early months of 1933.

Hoover left office persuaded that his methods had turned the corner on the depression until Roosevelt's election had shattered business confidence by the threat of federal tinkering with an otherwise sound economic system. Later he repeated that conviction in his *Memoirs*: "If the New Dealers had carried out our policies instead of deliberately wrecking them and then trying to make America over into a collectivist system, we should have made complete recovery in eighteen months after 1932...." Few historians and economists have concurred with Hoover's analysis. None the less, Hoover deserved credit for struggling with the depression, and some of his measures were to be continued in greatly expanded form by the New Deal. But the crisis was too severe for his palliatives to succeed. The times doubtless required a less conventional and more responsive leadership, and that his successor supplied in abundance.

SUGGESTED READINGS

Allen, Frederick Lewis. *Since Yesterday* (1940).

Burner, David. *Herbert Hoover: A Public Life* (1979).

Chandler, Lester V. *America's Greatest Depression* (1970).

Daniels, Roger. *The Bonus March* (1971).

Friedman, Milton and Schultz, Anna L. *A Monetary History of the United States* (1963).

Galbraith, John Kenneth. *The Great Crash* (1955).

Hawley, Ellis W., et al. *Herbert Hoover and the Historians* (1989).

McElvaine, Robert S., ed. *Down and Out in the Great Depression* (1983).

__. *The Great Depression* (1984).

Romasco, Albert U. *The Poverty of Abundance: Hoover, the Nation, the Depression* (1965).

Schlesinger, Arthur M., Jr. *The Crisis of the Old Order: 1919-1933* (1957).

Schwarz, Jordan A. *The Interregnum of Despair: Hoover, Congress and the Depression* (1979).

Smith, Gene. *The Shattered Dream: Herbert Hoover and the Great Depression* (1970).

Sternsher, Bernard, ed. *Hitting Home: The Great Depression in Town and Country* (1970).

Wecter, Dixton. *The Age of the Great Depression* (1948).

Wilson, Joan Hoff. *Herbert Hoover: Forgotten Progressive* (1975).

Worster, Donald. *Dust Bowl* (1979).

Chapter Six

FDR AND THE NEW DEAL

Inaugural Day, 1933, dawned cold and overcast in Washington. The prevailing mood across the nation, however, was one of hope. As the *New York Times* summed up: "No President...ever came to greater opportunities amid so great an outpouring of popular trust and hope." The economy was continuing its sickening and bewildering downward lurch amidst misery and ruin. The very existence of the republic seemed imperiled and the people looked to the new chief executive for leadership.

ROOSEVELT TAKES COMMAND

Franklin D. Roosevelt radiated confidence and determination. His inaugural address, vague on specific proposals but exuding hope and the promise of energetic action, galvanized the American people and renewed their spirit:

> This great Nation will endure as it has endured, will revive and prosper. So, first of all, let me assert my firm belief that the only thing we have to fear is fear itself—nameless, unreasoning, unjustified terror which paralyzes needed efforts to convert retreat into advance.

Although the outgoing Hoover visibly shuddered at what he regarded as the demagoguery of Roosevelt's inaugural remarks, the people were impressed.

In his first two weeks in office, President Roosevelt quickly dispelled the national mood of despair. Rising early on his first full day in the White House, Roosevelt was wheeled by his aides into his still bare study, and the new Deal began. It was not so much what he did—at this stage his acts were rather conservative and orthodox—but that, in contrast to Hoover, Roosevelt seemed to be grappling decisively with the depression.

The new chief executive faced an immediate crisis in banking. The annual number of bank failures had increased from 167 in 1920 to 2,294 in 1931, and to an incredible 4,004 in 1933. Loss of confidence among depositors led to runs on many otherwise sound banks and to the hoarding of gold. By Inaugural Day, 38 states had been forced either to close all banks or permitted only limited operations. Responding to desperate pleas from the financial world and anxious to protect hundreds of thousands of large and small depositors, Roosevelt on March 5 proclaimed a national bank holiday. All banks would be closed, to gain time to reopen sound institutions and to liquidate others with minimum losses. Called into special session, Congress quickly passed the Emergency Banking Act, the House of Representatives voting by acclamation and without seeing a copy of the bill that authorized issuance of new federal currency and gave the President full authority over gold transactions.

In this first week Roosevelt met the governors of the states in conference and assured them of federal help. Two days later he held his first press conference, where he abolished Hoover's requirement that all questions from reporters be submitted in written form. Then in his first "fireside chat," an informal radio report to the nation that he was to use repeatedly and effectively, Roosevelt announced the reopening of the sound banks and urged the return of withdrawn funds. In an impressive demonstration of confidence in the President, on the following day long lines formed across the country as recently frightened depositors returned their money to the banks.

Roosevelt's handling of the banking crisis revealed the essentially conservative nature of the early New Deal. In view of the public's loss of faith in the banking system and hatred of bankers, Roosevelt probably could have obtained congressional approval for truly drastic measures, even nationalization of the system. Instead he remained content with legislation to restore confidence and improve the banks by closer federal regulation, while still leaving them under private ownership and management. The Glass-Steagall Act of 1933 separated commercial from investment banking, increased the powers of the Federal Reserve Board to curb speculation by banks, and established the Federal Depositors Insurance Corporation to insure all deposits in Federal Reserve banks up to $2,500. Another measure two years later reorganized the Board of Governors of the Federal Reserve System and further increased its regulatory authority over bank credits and reserves. These measures helped reduce the annual rate of bank failures to forty or less, and most of these were small banks outside the federal system.

At the President's request, Congress passed the Beer Act, legalizing the sale of light wines and beer. Repeal of Prohibition by the Twenty-first Amendment to the Constitution followed soon thereafter. Keeping his campaign promises to reduce federal expenditures and to balance the budget, Roosevelt persuaded a rather reluctant Congress to approve the Economy Act. That act slashed about $500 million from veterans' benefits and the salaries of federal employees. These and other planned actions caused thousands of congratulatory telegrams to flood into the capital, while newspaper columnists and editors lavished praise on the new administration. Congress reflected the national mood of urgency by passing legislation hastily and almost without debate. The temper of Congress in fact seemed to favor even more drastic and sweeping action than the executive proposed. In the remainder of his first hundred days in office, Roosevelt obtained congressional approval for measure after measure with minimal debate and controversy. Congress enacted fifteen major bills and numerous lesser acts, a legislative record unsurpassed in American history.

FIRST NEW DEAL

It is traditional to view Roosevelt's administration as falling into two rather clear divisions or periods. The so-called First New Deal, 1933-1935, presumably concentrated on relief and recovery activities; the Second New Deal, from 1935 to 1938, emphasized broad social and economic reform intended to preclude future economic catastrophes and to promote a larger degree of social justice for all citizens. Historian Arthur M. Schlesinger, Jr, prefers a different set of interpretative labels: the "New Nationalism" for the first period, characterized by greater emphasis on government planning, integration, and regulation of the economy; versus the return to "New Freedom" approaches in 1935, when the administration manifested greater suspicion toward big business and placed more reliance upon trust-busting and punitive measures to cope with abuses in business and finance.

Both interpretations have much validity and are useful tools in understanding the thrust and nature of the New Deal. They should not be taken too rigidly, however, for concern with issues of relief, recovery, and reform remained a constant preoccupation of the administration until the outbreak of the World War II. Moreover, President Roosevelt manifested a non-theoretical or dogmatic approach to politics and government. Far from being radically inclined, the President leaned toward economic orthodoxy and conservatism. The depression compelled him to experiment and improvise, to borrow ideas and programs from a variety of sources, but his personal preferences remained to avoid radical changes and to return the government to a balanced budget as soon as possible. In short, Roosevelt hoped to reform capitalism as a bulwark of American democracy.

Columnist Walter Lippmann once commented that the major difference between the Hoover and the Roosevelt administrations seemed to be the willingness of the New Deal to spend larger sums with less regret. That interpretation had validity for early New Deal relief activities, but not later when the administration placed greater emphasis upon conserving human skills and dignity while providing relief. Hoover also had run deficits in fighting the depression, but he had refused to involve the federal government in direct relief to the needy and unemployed. Critics had condemned his approach as too timid and many argued that conditions required direct pump-priming expenditures to revive mass consumer purchasing power. The existing system of private, local, and state relief by 1933 obviously proved incapable of coping with the problem.

Although Roosevelt preferred a balanced budget (he made a distinction between the ordinary budget that would be balanced and the emergency one that required compensatory expenditures), he plunged into direct federal relief. The President continued to anticipate an early end to such outlays and a return to fiscal solvency and a reduction of the national debt. He never accepted the Keynesian argument for protracted and massive federal spending and did not venture beyond comparatively modest emergency measures. While he managed to relieve acute suffering, he failed to eradicate unemployment and restore full prosperity. These goals remained unachieved until World War II at last mobilized the national wealth and energies and increased the national debt by truly astronomical sums.

The New Deal contributed to the language a new glossary of alphabetical agencies, many of them created to cope with relief. Harry Hopkins, a highly controversial figure and a New York state relief director under Roosevelt, assumed the primary responsibility in this area. One observer once described the outwardly cynical and often profane Hopkins as having "the purity of St Francis...combined with the sharp shrewdness of a race track tout." Hopkins viewed the essential challenge as how to administer relief not only to feed people but to preserve their skills and self-respect. While he accepted the immediate necessity for direct handouts, he sought with the President's approval to supplant the dole with work-relief as soon as possible. Congress in May 1933 appropriated $500 million for relief through the states and local agencies, largely handled through Hopkins' Federal Emergency Relief Administration. Hopkins insisted that relief hand-outs be given to the needy in cash rather than scrip redeemable in food and that relief include not only food but housing, clothing, and medical needs.

The administration established the Civil Works Administration, a subsidiary of the FERA, in late 1933 as a makeshift effort to give emergency jobs to the unemployed during the winter of 1933-34 at a minimum wage eventually fixed at thirty cents an hour. By early 1934, Hopkins had expended close to $1 billion through the CWA and provided temporary employment to over four million people. Convinced that such heavy expenditures had achieved little beyond emergency relief, Roosevelt terminated the CWA in the spring of 1934. Other forms of aid continued, however, and over $2 billion had been spent for relief by the end of the year.

The administration launched a second major attack on relief in 1935. FDR asked for nearly $5 billion for a massive program of federal emergency employment, the largest single appropriation to that date in world history. Conservative critics preferred the less expensive dole and opposed the bill as an unwise extension of executive powers. Republican Senator Arthur H. Vandenburg of Michigan reflected the view of the minority in Congress: "This measure requires Congress to abdicate; it requires the country to lean on a dubious dream; it requires posterity to pay the bills...." Many supporters, however, feared that not enough funds had been requested. Congress passed the measure after much debate. Roosevelt divided the funds between Hopkins' newly created Works Progress Administration and Harld Ickes' Public Works Administration. Hopkins and Ickes were in a sharp rivalry for funds; because Ickes' PWA expended money more slowly on carefully planned public projects, his funds tended to be diverted to the freer spending WPA.

Charges of worthless, "boondoggling", make-work projects to the contrary, the WPA represented a notable attempt not only to conserve skills and to relieve unemployment but also to perform socially useful work. It paid "security wages" that were higher than the dole but sufficiently below private wages to provide incentive to seek regular employment. Normally, as Professor Kenneth Galbraith comments, in a private profit economy such as that in the United States genius and money are lavished on the private sector of the economy while the public sector is sadly neglected. Now during a national emergency, the WPA and other New Deal agencies could perform invaluable work. By 1941, the WPA had expended nearly $11 billion, employed a grand total of about eight million people, and completed 250,000 projects. Some waste inevitably occurred, but the gigantic effort remained remarkably free from overt politicking, while performing much useful labor that normally would not have been undertaken. Relief agencies built around 600 air fields; constructed 500,000 miles of roads; completed over 100,000 bridges or viaducts; built or repaired 110,000 public libraries, schools, post offices, auditoriums, and hospitals; and served 600 million school lunches. These deeds represented remarkable achievements in view of the fact that the WPA had to choose projects that could be completed quickly and that would not compete with private industry or regular and more substantial public works.

To utilize and improve existing skills, Hopkins established under his agency a Federal Theater Project that employed 13,000 people and staged plays for thirty million people, while the Music Project in its first fifteen months presented live concerts before audiences totalling fifty million. The Federal Writers Project produced numerous publications from historical projects to state and local guides. The Federal Art Project employed needy artists to beautify public buildings and stage educational art displays. Another agency, the National Youth Administration, provided part-time jobs for 600,000 college students and 1.5 million high school students and aided an even larger number of non-school youths in acquiring vocational training. A veritable cultural revolution occurred under New Deal auspices, encouraging creativity and making its achievements accessible to the people. An impressed English critic, no doubt exaggerating, exclaimed that "Art in America is being given its chance and there has been nothing like it since before the Reformation." Although denounced by conservatives as frivolous and havens for radicals, Hopkins' agencies undoubtedly reduced the appeal of the Communists.

The New Deal created other agencies that combined goals of relief, recovery, and reform. President Roosevelt's personal brainchild, the Civilian Conservation Corps, organized under civilian direction with Army reserve officers in charge, removed thousands of jobless youths from the city streets and gave them useful employment in more healthful rural environments. Thought of as a sort of moral equivalent to war, uniformed CCC youth fought fires, reseeded forests, and engaged in flood prevention work.

In 1932 when some 273,000 home owners lost their homes through mortgage foreclosures, Hoover had approved a system of Federal Homer Loan Banks to bolster building and loan associations. Since that offered little direct help, Congress approved a Home Owners' Loan Corporation in 1933 to lend money to refinance home mortgages and repairs. By 1935 HOLC had lent over $3 billion and held one-sixth of the national home mortgage indebtedness. The administration obtained a Federal

Housing Agency in 1934 to encourage new home building, followed by a US Housing Authority in 1937 that advanced money for slum clearance and low cost housing projects. A modest success, about one-third of the housing projects benefitted low-income Negro families.

The Farm Credit Administration extended similar relief to threatened farmers. The Resettlement Administration under Rexford Tugwell established three "greenbelt towns" of 500 to 800 families each near Washington, Cincinnati, and Milwaukee and tried to help rural people move from worn out farms to better land. Faced with conservative southern opposition, the Resettlement Administration never could obtain sufficient funds to reduce sharply farm tenancy. After two years, it had only purchased five million acres of land and resettled 4,441 families. A southern Tenant Farmers' Union tried to organize sharecroppers and complained that most of the federal rural aid went to the larger landowners. The Farm Security Administration replaced the Resettlement Administration in 1937, to lend money to tenants to buy farms and to improve the lot of migrant farm laborers.

The Rural Electrification Administration advanced funds to cooperatives to build electric power transmission facilities, so that where only 580,000 farms had been electrified in 1929, the number increased to about 2 million by 1941. Among other effects, rural electrification created a whole new market for electrical equipment and appliances, a good example of how government programs often benefit the private economy. Additionally, Ickes' PWA from 1933 to 1939 built nearly two-thirds of the nation's new school buildings, county courthouses, and city facilities, one-third of the hospitals and public health service buildings, and a number of warships for the Navy including the aircraft carriers *Yorktown* and *Enterprise*.

The Tennessee Valley witnessed one of the boldest and most controversial experiments in planned recovery and reform. In 1933 Congress authorized creation of the Tennessee Valley Authority to operate the existing Wilson Dam at Muscle Shoals and to construct new dams to prevent floods, to manufacture fertilizer and explosives, and to generate and distribute electrical power in the area. The activities of the TVA helped transform the lives of the people in seven southern states, freeing them from floods, supplying cheap power, and encouraging development of diversified agriculture and industry. By 1940 per capita income in the Valley had risen 73 per cent over 1933. Despite criticism of this type of governmental regional planning as socialistic, the vast experiment aroused world-wide interest and created industrial facilities that proved of enormous national value during World War II. Opponents, however, prevented other power projects, such as Bonneville Dam on the Columbia River and Grand Coulee in Washington, from undertaking a similar experimental approach.

The New Deal turned Hoover's Reconstruction Finance Corporation into one of the most successful ventures in the struggle for recovery from the depression. Under the direction of Jesse Jones of Texas, the RFC lent funds not only to the larger financial institutions, as under Hoover, but to needy railroads, medium and small businesses, farmer cooperatives, and rural electrification projects. By 1938 the RFC had lent $10 billion and had become the largest single source of credit and investment funds in the nation. Nearly all of the loans eventually were repaid in full.

FDR pinned his main hopes for quick knockout victory over the depression on the National Industrial Recovery Act, passed by Congress in June 1933. The idea, another example of the influence of the Progressive era on the New Deal, derived from the War Industries Board of World of World War I that had been remarkably successful in obtaining business and governmental cooperation during that great emergency. Now an equally great emergency seemed to require a similar mobilization. The National Recovery Administration, directed by the flamboyant General Hugh Johnson, undoubtedly constituted a departure from the *laissez-faire* attitudes of the past. Yet it was not a radical one, for apart from World War I experiences, the NRA had a precedent in the trade associations that had flourished during the Twenties. It went a step beyond, however, placing federal authority behind attempts to regulate production and prices. The NRA encouraged various industries to frame codes of fair competition, exempt from the anti-trust laws but subject to governmental approval. Business in effect agreed to these codes on minimum wages and maximum hours in exchange for federal help in stabilizing production and prices. Section 7(a) of the NIRA recognized the right of workers to organize and to bargain collectively with employers and prohibited compulsory company unions (employer unions established to offset independent national unions). Consumers theoretically had representation in the NRA but never effectively.

The NRA initially had the support of most businessmen. The administration hoped it would promote friendly cooperation between business and labor by eliminating wasteful competition and stabilizing prices and wages. Despite the objections of a few industrialists such as Henry Ford, who charged a plot by his competitors and what he called the "bankers' international," Johnson obtained codes for the major industries. He also launched a nationwide campaign with parades and flashy appeals to sign up over two and a quarter million employers under the NRA Blue Eagles (the Blue Eagle symbol was patterned after the Navajo thunderbird emblem). The NRA in fact drew up far too many codes, many for unimportant "industries"; the 800 codes included the dog food industry, mopstick manufacturers, and the burlesque theater.

Johnson relied upon persuasion and appeals to patriotism, rather than legal action, to enforce the codes against violators and chiselers. After the first flush of enthusiasm, it proved to be a losing struggle. Complaints swiftly multiplied. Businessmen objected to organized labor's aggressive use of Section 7(a) to unionize workers. Small businessmen and liberals complained that the codes were fascistic and facilitated the growth of big business and monopoly, while consumers reacted unhappily to production curbs and increases in prices. An investigation by a review board under Clarence Darrow confirmed many of the charges and caused President Roosevelt to restrict price fixing and the proliferation of codes for small industries. The administration soon eased out the quick-tempered and often rash Johnson, noted for heavy drinking and "shooting from the hip."

Although many observers viewed the NRA as a failure, President Roosevelt though otherwise and was displeased when it was invalidated by the Supreme Court in 1935. The NRA had tended to reduce production and raise costs and prices, but it could take credit for increasing employment by an estimated two million, reducing child labor, and improving working conditions across the nation. Above all, the NRA helped restore the nation's confidence during the darkest days of the depression.

The first Agricultural Adjustment Act, adopted in May 1933, constituted another long step toward the interventionist state and a planned economy. The desperate plight of farmers, resulting from over production and declining prices, worsened by the depression, seemed to require a new remedy. Henry A. Wallace, the Secretary of Agriculture, can perhaps be called a mystic and faddist—he once tried to live on a diet of corn meal and milk after the example of Caesar's troops in Gaul—but he had a profound knowledge of agriculture. Wallace saw his task as leveling off farm production to avoid over production and to achieve "parity" in farm income comparable to other groups in the economy. The AAA went beyond the Hoover farm program to include not only price supports but curtailment of production. It levied a special tax on food processors to finance government purchases of surpluses and set acreage and production limitations on cotton, wheat, corn, and hogs. The first year the AAA slaughtered six million young pigs and 200,000 sows (salvageable meat was used to feed the needy) and plowed under ten million acres of cotton. Aided by a drought in 1934, the program sharply reduced production and farm income had risen by 50 percent at the end of Roosevelt's first term. Like the NRA, however, the AAA and its successors benefitted the large producers, who could control the local agencies, more than small farmers, tenants or sharecroppers.

Searching for still other ways to speed recovery, and under great pressure from inflationists, Roosevelt with Congress' authorization turned to money manipulation. The theories of Cornell University's George F. Warren and others that the price of gold controlled the general commodity price level persuaded FDR to experiment with the gold content of the dollar. Roosevelt incurred the wrath of the orthodox by taking the country off the gold standard and then by buying gold at rates above the current world market price, hoping to encourage foreign trade and raise domestic price levels. Al Smith echoed the sentiments of the traditionalists when he sneered at the new "baloney dollar." The

President finally abandoned the experiment and under the Gold reserve Act of 1934 fixed the reserve gold content of the dollar at 60 percent of the 1933 rate of $35 per ounce. In 1936 an agreement with Britain and France achieved stabilization of currency exchanges. To satisfy the silver interests and inflationists, the Treasury purchased silver at well above the world market price. The only appreciable effect, besides bringing prosperity to silver miners, was to endanger the silver based currencies of China, Mexico and Peru. Conservatives were horrified—one feaedr that the monetary experiments signalled the end of civilization.

ATTACKS FROM THE RIGHT AND THE LEFT

Up to 1934 Roosevelt had followed the "politics of consensus," asking and getting support from all groups including business. As the midterm elections loomed, his coalition began to break down under assaults from the right and the left of the political spectrum. However, he retained the support of the farmers, labor, the unemployed, and the underprivileged, and the Democratic party in the 1934 elections substantially increased its control of Congress.

By 1934 a number of conservatives and businessmen had become highly disenchanted with the New Deal. The NRA had proved a disappointment, the national debt had mushroomed, and new agencies such as the Securities and Exchange Commission and the Federal Communications Commission, supervising the radio, telephone, and telegraphic systems, seemed to presage even greater federal control. In August a group of alarmed conservatives founded the American Liberty League to battle the New Deal and to expose its allegedly drift toward socialism. Led by such bitter anti-New Dealers such as Al Smith, Raskob, John W. Davis, and top industrialists from DuPont and General Motors, the Liberty League crusaded to preserve the free enterprise system. Its adherents believed firmly in the Social Darwinist *laissez-faire* world expounded in the late nineteenth century by William Graham Sumner. Natural economic law governed the world and, left unmolested, would bring recovery as surely as it had brought the depression. They viewed the New Deal as trying to replace these economic laws with a planned socialist society.

Many conservatives were outraged at the large number of academicians and experts used by the New Deal, the so-called "Brains Trust." The Chicago *Tribune* repeatedly printed a cartoon caricaturing a college teacher in academic gown offering ridiculous advice to people wiser than he. The Hearst and Scripps-Howard newspapers, among others, joined the outcry. The *Saturday Evening Post* shrilly declared, "it is our country and not a laboratory for a small group of professors to try out experiments." One New Deal intellectual, Tugwell, wryly retorted that such criticisms of brains caused him to wonder by what other part of the human anatomy government should be guided. In fact the Brains Trusters differed greatly among themselves, from the orthodox Raymond Moley to the liberal Harry Hopkins. In any case, they did not dominate Roosevelt for he used them as he saw fit.

The reason for conservative discontent of course went deeper than this. The depression had toppled the high priests of finance and industry from their exalted status and influence and, stunned by their loss of prestige, embittered businessmen vented their spleen against the essentially conservative Roosevelt. The President viewed his administration as remarkably moderate in its efforts to avert national collapse, and he reacted with hurt and anger to conservative attacks. He thought of himself as the savior, not the destroyer, of the capitalistic system. Roosevelt's "swing to the left" in 1935 in large part reflected a reaction to what he regarded as uncomprehending and unfair criticism.

Attacks came from the left as well. Soothsayers peddled easy panaceas to exploit social ills and grievances. In Louisiana, Senator Huey P. Long, called the "Kingfish" after a character in the popular Amos 'n Andy radio comedy act, seriously worried Roosevelt with his "share our wealth" program. FDR once referred to Long as "one of the two most dangerous men in the country," comparing him to Germany's Adolf Hitler; the other man, in his view, was General Douglas MacArthur, whom he thought an ideal leader for those citizens willing to discard democracy for strong-man rule.

The seventh of nine children, Long had been born in a log cabin in the uplands of Louisiana. After education at Tulane he practiced law and entered politics as the defender of the popular interests against the entrenched railroad, oil, and utility interests that dominated Louisiana and gave it the reputation as one of the worst governed states in the union. An intelligent man despite his hillbilly attitude and his intentionally crude and offensive manners and flashy clothes, Long won the governorship in 1928, appealing to the poor "red-necked" farmers. He pushed through reforms in Louisiana and by ruthless methods built a powerful state machine. Long obtained from the legislature measures to build roads, schools and hospitals, taxed the privileged industries, and smashed the former ruling oligarchy. Not a die-hard racist, Long conferred benefits on both poor whites and blacks through free schools and other programs. On the other hand, Long did little to raise wages or aid the unemployed or needy through welfare legislation.

After Long was elected to the U.S. Senate in 1930 he first supported Roosevelt, but he soon broke with the New Deal and tried to attract a national following of his own. He confidently predicted that he would win the White House in 1936. Aided by a fundamentalist revivalist minister, Gerald L.K. Smith, Long called for confiscating all large fortunes and redistributing the wealth. Each family should be guaranteed a minimum living wage, pensions for the elderly, and free college education for all who wanted it. By early 1935 Long claimed 27,000 Share-our-Wealth Clubs with a mailing list of 7.5 million people. Meanwhile he made himself virtual dictator in Louisiana and ruled by force and intimidation, until assassinated in the corridor of the state capital building in September 1935, by the son of one of his opponents whom the Long machine was trying to ruin.

In California, already a mecca for the retired and the elderly, sixty-seven year old Dr. Francis Townsend promoted a scheme to cure the depression by aiding the millions of needy oldsters. Known as the "Ham and Eggs" movement, Townsend's plan called for payment of $200 a month to each person over age sixty. Since the money would have to be spent in the month it was paid and would be financed by a two percent sales tax, the rapid turnover would generate vast purchasing power and restore prosperity. Although financial experts pronounced the scheme absolutely unworkable, Townsend had established 12,000 clubs by 1934 and enlisted millions of members. Meanwhile, the old socialist warrior, Upton Sinclair, had another cure for the depression. EPIC, or End

Poverty in California, advocated state operation of uncultivated farms and idle industry for the benefit of the jobless. Land colonies and workers' villages would produce for their own use rather than for profitable sale, and this socialist-syndicalist system would eventually spread across the nation to transform society and the economy.

A strange movement known as Technocracy also had emerged. Inspired by the writings of an unorthodox economist, Thorstein Veblen, its advocates called for discarding democracy and the capitalist system and allowing the engineers to run the economy on the basis of full production where everybody "produces what he uses and uses what he produces." Father Charles Coughlin, the Roman Catholic radio priest of Detroit, proposed still another cure-all. He had turned against the New Deal in 1934 and founded his National Union for Social Justice. He preached a type of Christian fascism to his radio audience of between thirty and forty-five million listeners, flailing at evil bankers and advocating nationalization of the banks and inflation of the currency. These groups cooperated ineffectively in an effort to defeat FDR, forming the Union Party in 1936 and running William Lemke for the presidency.

A rash of strikes began in 1934, triggered in part by long standing grievances and in part by the more favorable climate for unionization created by the attitude and policies of the Roosevelt administration. Radical leaders directed severe industrial action against such cities as San Francisco, Minneapolis, Toledo and Milwaukee; the majority of these actions, including the general strike in San Francisco, failed. In the Twenties the American Federation of Labor, with its craft philosophy had proven unequal to the challenge of unionizing the mass industries. In fact, AFL membership dropped from nearly four million in 1921 to slightly over two million in 1933. Clinging to the traditional emphasis on voluntary, self-reliant unionism—the hallmark of the movement's foremost spokesman, Samuel Gompers who died in 1924—some of the leaders of the AFL either opposed or were lukewarm at first to proposals for government support of collective bargaining, as well as federal unemployment insurance and old age pensions. Section 7(a) of the NIRA, however, offered unprecedented opportunities for combatting company unions and organizing semi-skilled and relatively unskilled labors in the major industries such as steel, automobiles and coal. For its part, the majority of the AFL leadership preferred to recruit these workers not into one industrial union but into separate craft unions.

Among others, John L. Lewis, president of the powerful United Mine Workers, Sidney Hillman of the Amalgamated Clothing Workers, and David Dubinsky of the International Ladies Garment Workers established a Committee for Industrial Organization for recruitment on an industry-wide basis in 1935. After sharp fights with older craft unions—Lewis, the Iowan-born son of a Welsh miner, actually exchanged blows with one craft leader at the AFL convention in 1935—the rebel faction split off from the AFL in 1936 and set up what became known as the Congress of Industrial Organization (CIO). The AFL, under the direction of the mild-mannered William Green, fought back, mobilizing local opposition to the CIO, as well as collaborating with employers in resisting the unionizing efforts of the new organization.

Within a short period the CIO set out to organize the steel and automobile industries, the latter of which provided the CIO with its first great test of strength. On New Year's eve, 1936, several hundred workers seeking to gain recognition of the newly-organized United Auto Workers, seized a number of General Motors plants at Flint, Michigan, staging what was to be the beginning of a spectacular "sit-down strike" in which strikers barricaded themselves inside factories. The strike, which saw violent clashes between the strikers on one side and strikebreakers and police on the other, lasted forty-four days and involved 150,000 workers—directly and indirectly. Fortunately for the strikers, the Roosevelt administration and the governor of Michigan, Frank Murphy, assumed a tolerant position toward labor and thus ruled out governmental intervention. At the time, the President noted: "It [the strike] is illegal, but shooting it out...[is not] the answer." In February 1937, General Motors, which feared the destruction of its plants, and the United Auto Workers came to terms, giving the CIO its first significant victory. The other automotive manufacturers followed suit.

Sit-down strikes, which were ultimately declared illegal by the Supreme Court in *Hague v CIO* in 1939, quickly spread to other industries, including rubber, textiles, oil refining, shipbuilding, and steel. Within a brief space of time the CIO achieved a second stunning success, this time in the steel industry. In March 1937, after a bitter strike, US Steel yielded to the demands of the Steel Workers' Organizing Committee, recognizing that body as the bargaining agency of its employees, and agreeing to a wage increase of 10 percent and a 40-hour week with time and a half for overtime work. Lesser steel companies—known collectively as "Little Steel"—led by Tom M. Girdler of Republic Steel proved adamant in refusing to follow the lead of US Steel. The issue reached a climax when a group of union demonstrators were fired upon by police at the Republic plant in South Chicago on May 30, 1937. In the so-called "Memorial Day Massacre" that ensued 10 people were killed and 84 injured; by the end of the year "Little Steel" had defeated unionization. Other industries, however, fell into line, and by 1939 the CIO had become a major rival to the older AFL. Union membership in general had grown prodigiously under the New Deal, reaching a figure of almost nine million by 1938.

"SWING TO THE LEFT"

Responding to pressures from the left and attacks from the right, Roosevelt's annual message to Congress in January 1935 outlined a bold new approach. "In spite of our efforts and in spite of our talk," Roosevelt declared, "we have not weeded out the overprivileged and we have not effectively lifted up the underprivileged." He called for measures to provide adequate housing, social security and a decent living standard for all. Flaying obstructionism by big business and the wealthy, the President also advocated a new and more equitable tax policy to shift the burden of public expenditures to those better able to bear it. Two days later, Roosevelt asked Congress for billions of dollars for a massive assault on unemployment, to be waged primarily by Hopkins' WPA.

During the summer of 1935 Roosevelt cracked the whip over Congress and launched the Second New Deal. Advisers, such as

Felix Frankfurther and Supreme Court Justice Louis Brandeis, argued that cooperation with big business had failed and that an all-out effort was necessary. A second Hundred Days ensued. The Wagner Labor Relations Act, accepted by Roosevelt as a replacement of Section 7(a) of the NIRA, reaffirmed the right of labor to organize and to bargain collectively with employers. Congress approved creation of a National Labor Relations Board to outlaw unfair labor practices and to conduct elections in industry to certify union bargaining agencies. The NLRB understandably enraged business leaders. This measure was supplemented by 1938 by the Fair Labor Standards Act banning child labor under sixteen and fixing a national minimum wage, at first at forty cents an hour, a maximum forty hour work week, and time and a half for overtime work. Although its terms were to go into effect over a period of years and a minimum wage of $16 per week was obviously inadequate, many businessmen and others, especially in the low-wage South, roundly denounced the measure. Other measures launched slum clearance and public housing projects and strengthened the TVA.

A furious battle was waged over the Utility Holding Company Act. Drafted by New Dealers Thomas C. Corcoran and Benjamin V. Cohen, the bill provided for federal regulation and coordination of utility companies to obtain greater efficiency and contained a highly controversial "death sentence" clause allowing the Securities and Exchange Commission to dissolve holding companies that could not demonstrate that they contributed to the efficiency of the actual operating firms they controlled. The utility companies fought back, led by Wendell Wilkie of Commonwealth and Southern, flooding Congress with lobbyists and letters of protest. Congress finally passed a compromise measure that was still very tough: the government would have to defend dissolution orders for utility holding companies.

Two other measures, the income tax and social security, also aroused business and conservative hostility. Roosevelt told Congress and the nation that past tax laws had "done little to prevent an unjust concentration of wealth and economic power" and a new approach was needed that would promote "a wider distribution of wealth." The resultant Wealth Tax Act of 1935 increased the graduated income tax on the upper brackets to a maximum of 75 percent, and imposed higher inheritance, gift, and corporate income levies. Though denounced as a socialistic measure to redistribute wealth, the tax hike was rather moderate by later standards; in any case, such taxes failed to reduce significantly the share of wealth received by the upper-income groups. Studies in the 1970s revealed that while the overall living standard had advanced greatly since the depression, wealth remained concentrated in a few hands. In 1922 the top two percent of all families held 33 percent of the nation's private wealth, versus 32 percent in 1958; the top tenth of income recipients got around a third of the total income in 1910, versus 30 percent in 1960.

The Social Security Act of 1935 dealt with a problem that was of growing public concern. In 1861 only one of forty Americans was sixty-five years or over, but by 1940 the number had increased to one out of every fifteen and was mounting. This increase reflected a declining birth rate, the drastic slowing of immigration, and improved medical care. Most major industrial countries in Europe had recognized the problem long before and had adopted compulsory old-age insurance programs. The elderly particularly suffered from the depression, as they exhausted savings and private insurance and could not find employment. Yet conservatives denounced any government plan for aiding these unfortunates as socialistic and destructive of self-reliance. Introduced in Congress by Senator Wagner of New York, the Social Security Act provided old age insurance for those aged sixty-five and over, to be financed by taxes on wages and payrolls. Supporters added a system of federal-state unemployment compensation, plus aid to dependent mothers and children and the physically handicapped. Although the act had defects, especially in failing to provide for the elderly indigent already retired, it represented a notable landmark in catching up with the social problems of the twentieth century. As Roosevelt remarked at its formal signing, the Social Security Act did not remove all the dangers and risks of life, but it gave "some measure of protection to the average citizen."

THE NEW DEAL AT HIGH TIDE

Ignoring Al Smith's disgruntled plea to pick "some genuine Democrat," the Democratic convention in 1936 renominated President Roosevelt by acclamation. The platform, which reflected the New Deal's turn against big business, pledged a vigorous enforcement of the anti-trust laws. The Republicans chose Governor Alfred M. Landon of Kansas; Frank Knox, owner and editor of the Chicago *Daily News* and a strong opponent of the New Deal, received second place on the ticket. The Republican platform realistically conceded many of the New Deal reforms, merely promising to administer them more efficiently and economically. The colorless Landon, often called a Kansas Coolidge, had moderately liberal views but he was embarrassed by support of the conservative Liberty League. Al Smith, who deserted the Democratic party to support Landon, called the New Deal a "dismal, dull, dark, and dreary failure." Other dissident Democrats, among them Bainbridge Colby and John W. Davis, declared for Landon.

To his great distress, Landon also found himself upstaged in the closing weeks of the campaign by Hoover's unwonted and increasingly bitter denunciations of the New Deal. Meanwhile, the anti-New Deal Hearst newspapers printed a jingle:

> The Red New Deal with a Soviet Seal
>
> Endorsed by a Moscow Hand.
>
> The strange result of an alien cult
>
> In a liberty-loving land.

Hearst urged voters to choose Landon since the Communists had denounced the Republican nominee. As for Roosevelt, Hearst stated: "Naturally the Communists flock to him. 'Every bird knows its own nest.'"

FDR waged a vigorous campaign. In his acceptance speech, he excoriated what he described as the "economic royalists," those special interests that sought to preserve their privileges and to block reform and regulation. In moving phrases he proclaimed that "This generation of Americans has a rendezvous with destiny." It was good politics, even though critics accused him of stirring up class hatreds. In subsequent speeches he emphasized the anti-big business orientation of the Second New Deal and the need to increase individual opportunity and freedom. With an efficient political organization directed by Postmaster General James Farley, Roosevelt attracted the support of organized labor, farmers, the reliefers, and small businessmen. Most newspaper owners and editors opposed FDR, but working reporters overwhelmingly favored him. Attesting to his successful undercutting of the radicals, the Union Party of Lemke ran poorly, polling only 882,479 votes instead of the 10 million or more predicted by Father Couglin; the Socialist vote declined to less than 200,000, and the Communists fell to a low of 80,159 out of 44 million votes cast.

The black population outside the South had increased rapidly since World War I and comprised an important element in the urban vote. Traditionally Republican since the Civil War, even as late as 1932, northern Negroes voted Democratic in 1936 by heavy margins. The New Deal had won their support not only by non-discriminatory relief measures but also by appointing some blacks to political office. Mrs. Roosevelt was known to sympathize with blacks, and FDR often consulted black leaders. The New Deal gave racial equality only token support, but it seemed a clear improvement over the past. Roosevelt thus carried by huge majorities the larger cities and eastern industrial states.

The final tally in 1936 revealed that Roosevelt had polled 27,751,597 million votes to Landon's 16,679,583 million, or 60.4 percent of the popular vote. FDR carried every state except Maine and Vermont. As Roosevelt quipped about his tidal wave triumph, it had been a baptism by total immersion in which the other fellow nearly drowned. The Democratic party had become the new majority party, exploiting an urban political revolution through its appeal to the city masses. Yet ironically 1936 marked the high water of the domestic New Deal, for Roosevelt subsequently encountered increasing resistance in his efforts to extend reform.

DEFEAT: THE COURT PACKING PLAN

The federal judiciary during Roosevelt's first term remained heavily Republican and conservative in tone. Only an estimated 28 percent of the 266 federal judges were Democrats. The Supreme

Court contained four very conservative justices, George Sutherland, Willis Van Devanter, James C. McReynolds, and Pierce Butler; three more liberal justices, Harlan F. Stone, Louis Brandeis, and Benjamin N. Cardozo; while Justice Owen J. Roberts and Chief Justice Charles Evans Hughes apparently sought to preserve a balance between the two groups. The average age of the Justices was nearly seventy-two.

The federal judiciary at all levels seemed to be mounting an attack upon New Deal legislation, issuing 1600 injunctions against the government in 1935-36 alone. The administration watched anxiously as some of these cases moved up to the Supreme Court. A series of blows fell quickly as the Court ruled adversely on the "hot oil" case (a law banning interstate shipment of oil produced in violation of state quotas) and the Railroad Retirement Act. Then in May 1935 the Court unanimously struck down the NRA in the Schechter Poultry or "sick chicken" case. The Court majority ruled that the selling of poultry did not come under the interstate commerce powers of the federal government and that Congress unconstitutionally had delegated legislative powers to the executive.

The Court invalidated the AAA in 1936 by a vote of six to three, on the grounds that the processing tax constituted an improper delegation of legislative functions and an invasion of the reserved powers of the states. The justices also struck down the Guffey-Snyder Bituminous Coal Act in a five to four decision, and restricted the powers of the Securities and Exchange Commission in another decision. The Court, in a case directly affecting presidential powers, ruled that the chief executive could not remove members of such quasi-judicial bodies as the Federal Trade Commission. Clearly many of these decisions reflected not so much the requirements of the Constitution as the personal preferences and prejudices of the Justices. The deeply disappointed Roosevelt exclaimed to reporters, "We have been relegated to the horse-and-buggy definition" of the Constitution.

Apparently Roosevelt had decided to attack the Supreme Court even prior to his reelection in 1936. Meanwhile he sought to repair much of the damage done by the adverse decisions by obtaining stop-gap legislation from Congress. As noted earlier, the Wagner

Act in 1935 saved the labor provision of the NRA. The Soil Conservation and Domestic Allotment Act of 1936 managed to curtail agricultural production through voluntary and compensated withdrawal of acreage for conservation purposes. In 1938 Congress enacted the second AAA to limit production and achieve parity prices for crops via subsidies on a voluntary basis. Yet the administration feared that the Court might also strike down these and other measures. In his annual message in January 1937, Roosevelt called for legislation to promote opportunity for all citizens as "the deeper purpose of democratic government." Again, in his second inaugural address, the President spoke of "one-third of a Nation ill-housed, ill-clad, ill-nourished," and declared that the goal of his second administration would be to eradicate these ills.

But would the Supreme Court abide by the election returns and accept new sweeping social measures? Or would these too be doomed by hidebound justices? To forestall that possibility, Roosevelt in early 1937 suddenly sprang his "court packing" plan on a stunned Congress and nation. He believed that he had a popular mandate to achieve additional reform and he resolved not to let the "Nine Old Men" on the Court frustrate the national will. To do otherwise, he feared, would entail the risk that society might break down and collapse into anarchy or fascist reaction.

Roosevelt had committed a serious political blunder, probably the greatest of his career. He failed to consult congressional leaders prior to his decision and he underestimated the popular reverence for the Supreme Court as a body above politics. Instead of openly advocating a constitutional amendment to restrict the Court's powers, he presented to Congress a scheme that claimed to be a reform to improve the efficiency of the judiciary. For each Supreme Court Justice reaching the age of seventy and not retiring, a new Justice could be appointed up to a total membership of fifteen; additional judges would also be appointed on the lower levels of the judiciary, and other measures would be adopted to quicken the processes of adjudication.

Chief executives since Jefferson's day had often fumed about the obstructionist role of the Supreme Court and had contemplated attempts to curb its review power. Yet conservatives condemned Roosevelt's plan as destroying the constitutional balance of the national government, bar associations denounced it, and so did a number of liberal supporters of the New Deal such as Senator Burton K. Wheeler of Montana. Voluntary organizations to "save the Constitution" sprang up across the nation, and several state legislatures adopted resolutions against what Hoover labeled a court-packing scheme.

Too late to repair the political damage, Roosevelt in a fireside talk tried to explain his case to the people. His proposal, he declared, sought to "save the Constitution from the Court and the Court from itself." He unwisely refused compromises such as requiring a seven to two majority by the Court to invalidate federal laws or enlarging the Court by the addition of two more justices. Roosevelt was supremely confident after his reelection and determined to curtail the power of the Court. His case received a blow when Chief Justice Hughes publicly denied that the Court lagged in its work.

Finally the Court undercut the president by reversing its recent trend. (Apparently the change was not a response to Roosevelt's attacks and had begun to take place before he announced the court scheme.) By a vote of five to four the high court upheld the Wagner Act in the Jones and Laughlin Steel case and thereby seemed to presage acceptance of other important New Deal laws. Justice Van Devanter also resigned under a new law permitting retirement at age seventy with full salary, and Roosevelt had his first opportunity to fill a vacancy. Subsequently the Court also validated the Social Security Act. Yet Roosevelt persisted in the fight, despite an adverse majority report by the Senate Judiciary Committee. Finally, after his loyal floor leader, Senator Joseph T. Robinson of Arkansas, died of apparent overstrain, FDR had no choice but to retreat. Too many important members of his own party in Congress, many conservative southern Democrats but also a number of moderates and liberals, had opposed his plan. Although he took some comfort in the Court's more liberal turn— he had lost the battle but won the war, many said—Roosevelt had experienced his first serious defeat and a blow to his myth of political invincibility that opened deep rifts within his own party. Yet, the Court fight at least hastened the legitimatizing of the New

Deal's vast expansion of federal powers and the changed role of government.

THE CONSERVATIVE REACTION

A conservative coalition of Republican and southern Democratic congressmen, largely from rural areas, began to take shape. Members of this loose bloc shared a preference for balanced budgets and states' rights and looked with suspicion on welfare programs and the rise of organized labor. Southern white conservatives especially disliked the equalitarian effect of New Deal legislation on the Negro in the South and feared for the southern way of life. Moreover, as Jeffersonian Democrats they disliked the burgeoning bureaucracy of the New Deal and its increasing orientation toward the urban masses after the 1936 elections. Many southern Democratic congressmen had given the New Deal only reluctant support in the past—on occasion not even that—and the Court fight emboldened them to move into more open opposition (Roosevelt's appointment of the liberal Senator Hugo Black of Alabama to Van Devanter's place added to their displeasure). The conservative coalition drew support from the public reaction against sit-down strikes and labor unrest during 1937, widely blamed on New Deal radicalism and "coddling" of the unions. Despite the new bloc's informality and lack of cohesion on all issues, it functioned well enough by 1939 to prevent further significant gains in New Deal legislation.

The Year 1937 proved difficult for FDR. Not only did he experience the Court defeat but Congress refused to endorse his plan for a sweeping reorganization of the executive branch. Roosevelt had proposed combining or subordinating a number of semi-independent executive agencies, the creation of two new cabinet-level departments, for Social Welfare and Public Works, and provisions for six presidential administrative assistants. Many thoughtful observers, including a number of political scientists, had long advocated such reforms. Hoover himself had favored such a reorganization when president. Yet conservatively inclined Republicans and southern Democrats resisted strenuously and charged president with dictatorial ambitions. They blocked the measure in 1937 and 1938, although it finally obtained approval in

1939 in a much weakened version. Even so, the act marked a major advance in managing a modern complex governmental machine.

A sharp economic slump in 1937 added to Roosevelt's difficulties. The president, influenced by his fiscally more conservative advisers led by the Secretary of the Treasury Henry Morgenthau, Jr, and by his own inclinations, had reduced deficit spending and slashed WPA payrolls in 1936 in the mistaken belief that prosperity had returned. A recession promptly set in during the summer of 1937, causing farm prices to decline and unemployment to rise from about five to over nine and half million. Obviously the economy still required heavy federal spending, and Roosevelt by 1938 felt compelled to override conservative opposition to secure approval for increased outlays by the WPA. New Deal measures had not cured the depression but only alleviated it. Probably only really massive federal expenditures, as urged by Keynes and others, would have worked, but Roosevelt was too orthodox to accept that solution.

Despite huge Democratic majorities in Congress, Roosevelt had encountered serious resistance to the program he had presented to Congress in 1937. Resolving to remold his party into a more liberal movement, he attempted in the 1938 primaries to purge certain conservatives. Democratic senators and representatives, mostly southerners such as Senators Walter George of Georgia and "Cotton Ed" Smith of South Carolina. The effort backfired as most of them survived; the new Congress, with a larger Republican minority, thus became even more conservative. The major parties remained as coalitions of divergent interests without clear philosophical and ideological differences. the New Deal virtually came to an end. After 1938 the emphasis shifted to digesting gains already made and to questions of foreign policy that seemed more imperative as the world plunged toward another global conflict.

THE NEW DEAL IN RETROSPECT

Probably no chief executive since the days of Andrew Jackson aroused as much impassioned controversy as Franklin D. Roosevelt and his New Deal. Criticism varied from shrilly intemperate charges of dictatorship, socialism, or communism, to more reasonably expressed disapproval of centralization of federal authority at the expense of the states, impairment of self-reliance and initiative through welfare programs, and wasteful deficit spending and a huge public debt. Roosevelt personally became the butt of many ribald and cruel jokes about his health and family life. Some apoplectic critics could only refer to him as "that man." His wife Eleanor especially drew much abuse because of her clearly expressed sympathy for the lowly and oppressed of all races and her endorsement of liberal causes.

Of course Roosevelt also aroused deep affection and dedicated support, as the million of votes he polled amply attested. Even twenty years after his death the Roosevelt name and political legacy remained powerful assets to the Democratic party. More importantly, he inaugurated profound changes in the role of government in society and the economy that have helped shape the course of subsequent American history.

Was the New Deal revolutionary or evolutionary? Or essentially conservative? Oceans of ink have been used in attempts to answer these questions. Most historians today emphasize the continuity of the New Deal with the past. In their desperate battle against the depression, Roosevelt and his advisers drew freely from the ideas and programs of earlier years. The Populist and Progressive eras supplied a number of specific proposals for regulating workers conditions and assisting less fortunate members of society. The experiences of mobilization in World War I provided another fruitful source of ideas and programs. Even the prosperous years of the Twenties and the Hoover administration offered precedents for New Deal experiments and measures. In fact it is difficult to think of a single New Deal program that in some way had not been suggested or tried in the past. In this sense Roosevelt and his administration were not highly original. Most of his reforms flowed from existing circumstances and reflected public demands to cope with the deep social needs created or emphasized by the Great Depression. Or to express it differently, the New Deal represented the culmination of a half-century of historical change marking the rise of an organizational type of capitalism and the development of the regulatory interventionist state.

Roosevelt's greatest personal contributions probably lay in his dynamic personality and optimism, his sympathy with the underprivileged and distressed, and his willingness to experiment and to use more fully the powers of government in long overdue efforts at relief and reform. Although a good politician, he was not the master politician often assumed, as his defeats in the Court fight and his failure to remold the Democratic party in the 1938 congressional elections revealed. His administrative tactics also left much to be desired, characterized by dependence on conflicting conservative and liberal advisers and his reluctance to grant clear-cut delegations of power and responsibility. New Deal agencies overlapped one another in a crazy-quilt jungle of conflicting authority and personal rivalries.

Moreover, all the New Deal pump-priming spending and relief measures failed to overcome the depression. In 1939, on the even of World War II, millions of people were still unemployed despite the expenditure of billions of dollars through the WPA and similar agencies. Roosevelt could never abandon his hope of returning to a balanced budget and could not bring himself to spend on the really gigantic scale necessary to eradicate the depression—that chance came with the national emergency created by the Second World War. Above all, he sought to preserve a modified capitalist structure, not to destroy it. And clearly, as a practical politician he aimed his programs primarily to benefit the great middle class. Thus although a vast number of citizens were aided the New Deal, millions of blacks, slum dwellers, rural agricultural workers, and unemployed remained in poverty.

Yet even though the New Deal fell short of transforming American society, it still marked a bold new phase in our history. Its reforms when judged against the past remain impressive and enduring. The welfare-interventionist state had come to stay in America. New Deal reforms became a permanent part of the fabric of American life. In subsequent years, political debate raged not about whether gains such as Social Security, unemployment compensation, aid to agriculture, public power and conservation projects, and regulation of the economy should be kept, but about how to improve and better administer them. Thus the Republican candidate in 1952, Dwight D. Eisenhower, declared that "Never again shall we allow a depression in the United States," and he promised to mobilize the "full power" of government if necessary to that end. The New Deal marked an irreversible turning point in American life.

SUGGESTED READINGS

Allswang, John M. *The New Deal and American Politics* (1978).

Bergman, Andrew. *We're in the Money* (1972).

Bernstein, Irving. *Turbulent Years* (1969).

Brinkley, Alan. *Voices of Protest* (1982).

Burns, James MacGregor. *Roosevelt: The Lion and the Fox* (1956).

Conkin, Paul K. *The New Deal*(1967).

Flynn, George Q. *American Catholics and the Roosevelt Presidency* (1968).

Friedel, Frank. *Franklin D. Roosevelt,* 4 vols. (1952-1973).

Hawley, Ellis. *The New Deal and the Problem of Monopoly* (1966).

Leuchtenburg, *William E. Franklin Roosevelt and the New Deal* (1963).

McCraw, Thomas K. *TVA and the Power Fight, 1933-1939* (1971).

Pells, Richard. *Radical Visions and American Dreams* (1973).

Perkins, Van L. *Crisis in Agriculture: The Agricultural Adjustment Administration and the New Deal, 1933* (1969).

Ranch, Basil. *The History of the New Deal, 1933-1938* (1949).

Salmond, John A. *The Civilian Conservation Corps, 1933-1942* (1967).

Schlesinger, Arthur M., Jr. *The Age of Roosevelt,* 3 vols. (1957-1960).

Scharf, Lois. *To Work and to Wed* (1980).

Sitkoff, Harvard. *A New Deal for Blacks* (1978).

___. ed. *Fifty Years Later: The New Deal Evaluated* (1984).

Sussman, Warren, ed. *Culture and Commitment* (1977).

Walters, Raymond. *Negroes and the Great Depression* (1970).

Ware, Susan. *Beyond Suffrage* (1981).

Chapter Seven

THE ROAD TO WAR

The Great Depression not only represented a turning point in the domestic history of the United States, it also marked a watershed in its foreign relations. Threats to the nation's peace and security caused the Hoover administration to begin to move away from the less demanding neo-isolationist policies of the Twenties, and Roosevelt's New Deal completed the return to the collective security approach of the Wilson era.

The year 1931 marked the opening of a decade of economic misery and international crises. While the United States slid deeper into the slough of the Depression, the blight spread abroad, inflicting paralysis and despair on Europe and Asia. Only the rigidly controlled state economy of the Soviet Union remained relatively immune to the deadly disease that cursed the capitalist world. The depression not only inflicted incalculable loss and misery on millions of people across the globe, it wrecked the postwar system established at Versailles and Washington.

The collapse of the economic system seemed to tip the balance almost everywhere toward irrationality, violence, and war. In Germany the frail democracy of the Weimar Republic crumbled as Adolf Hitler grasped dictatorial power; Italy already had succumbed to the posturing and jut-chinned Fascist dictator, Benito Mussolini; totalitarian parties on the left and right proliferated throughout Europe, even in the old democracies of Britain and France; and in the Far East, right wing, super-patriotic, and militaristic groups surged to the fore with their plans for solving Japan's problems through imperialism and conquest.

The Depression intensified isolationist sentiment in the United States. Trying desperately to achieve domestic recovery and fearful of another series of wars in Asia and Europe, most Americans seemed more than ever determined to erect an isolationist wall around their country. The neutrality laws adopted in the mid-Thirties served notice of that determination. A strange paralysis of will seemed to afflict not only the United States but also the great European democracies. Great Britain and France almost supinely observed the rise of totalitarian dictators who openly expressed their contempt for democracy and barely troubled to hide their plans to "rectify" the Versailles settlement. Only belatedly did the western democracies, the United States most tardily of all, recognize the peril and act to meet it.

CRISIS IN THE FAR EAST

The Far East had seemed to promise a new era of progress and stability during the Twenties. The great powers had curbed the arms race and agreed to preserve the territorial status quo in the Pacific at the Washington Conference. In Japan, moderates held power and pursued a policy of conciliation toward China and cooperation with the western powers. Meanwhile, at home they began to curb military expenditures and undertook a number of social reforms. Even China seemed to make progress toward unity and stability. China's failure to obtain the restoration of Shantung at Paris in 1919 had ignited the May Fourth Movement, a sharp surge of nationalist sentiment, particularly among students, aimed at throwing off the unequal treaties (fixed tariff and extraterritoriality) forced upon China by the great powers in the past. Chinese intellectuals and reformers determined to transform Chinese civilization and to modernize China so that she could protect her own interests in the Far East. The American government in general looked favorably upon this nationalist movement, hoping for a unified, strong, and friendly new China able to defend itself. Sun Yat-sen with Soviet aid, revitalized the Kuomintang or nationalist movement in the early 1920s. Chiang Kai-shek, who emerged as his heir, broke with the Communists in 1927 and by 1929 seemed to have succeeded in unifying his country. Time proved, however, that his power depended too heavily upon the warlords, the wealthy merchants, and large land holders, thereby preventing social reforms that might have forestalled the eventually seizure of power by the Chinese Communists.

Chiang Kai-shek's movement disturbed Japan and thereby the Pacific treaty system. The Chinese Nationalists struggled fiercely to cast off the unequal treaties and to "redeem" the lost provinces in Manchuria. Popular boycotts repeatedly broke out against western and Japanese business interests in China. But the principal crisis came in Manchuria, a fertile and strategically important frontier area that long had been a center of rivalry among China, Russia and Japan. Legally belonging to China, Manchuria actually constituted a sort of undeveloped frontier area between the three powers, with Japan entrenched in the south and Russia in the center and north. The Nationalists began a drive to evict the other two competitors. Chiang Kai-shek's movement first attempted to compel Soviet Russia to surrender control of the Chinese Eastern Railway in Manchuria, but his forces met a firm rebuff in 1929. Not much fighting occurred in this brief border war, as Soviet troops invaded the area and Russian aviators frightened the ill-prepared and motley Chinese forces by dropping bags of sand and rotten cabbages on them. The State Department blunderingly tried to invoke the Pact of Paris until rebuffed by a Russian government with which it had no formal diplomatic relations.

Undaunted by the Soviet check, the Chinese Nationalists also tried to undermine Japan's position in Manchuria, built around the Japanese-owned South Manchurian Railway. The Nationalists refused to recognize the validity of past Sino-Japanese treaties relating to Manchuria and carried on anti-Japanese propaganda and boycotts against Japanese goods and merchants in China and Manchuria. Moreover, the Nationalists planned to construct a rival railroad and port to undercut the Japanese in Manchuria. Many Japanese became alarmed and feared that the Foreign Office under Baron Shidehara followed too soft a policy to protect Japan's interests. Most Japanese viewed Manchuria as strategically and economically vital to the island empire, the center of about 90 percent of Japanese foreign investments, while to the north lay the threat of Russian power. Above all, the Japanese feared the emergence of a strong modern nation-state in China, able to challenge Japan's interests in China and her preeminent position in the Far East.

A group of Japanese militarists and nationalist organizations—such as the Black Dragon Society, the Cherry Blossom Society, and the Blood Brotherhood—eagerly awaited an opportunity to seize control and plot a new course for their nation. These militarists and super-patriots, drawn largely from the junior officers of the army, regarded themselves as reformers who would sweep away the alien trappings of western democracy. Japan seethed with change and discontent caused by rapid industrialization and urbanization, and the consequent uprooting of rural people and weakening of older traditions. The reactionary nationalist groups saw the army alone as capable of destroying the strangle-hold of big business and the politicians, and restoring Japan to her ancient ideals and virtues as one great national family under the divine emperor. Japan's true course, they propagandized, dictated reform at home and an aggressive foreign policy to assert leadership over all East Asia.

Unfortunately western blunders helped undermine the moderates in Japan. Sensitive Japanese already resented Japan's small end of the 5:5:3 naval ratio fixed by the Five Power Pact. They were affronted further by other signs of western discrimination and condescension, such as tariff barriers against Japanese goods and the American Immigration Act of 1924 that excluded Japanese and other Asians. The world-wide economic debacle of 1931 that hit Japan along with the rest of the world gave the militarists their chance.

Alarmed at Chinese Nationalist plans in Manchuria, the Japanese army struck suddenly. On the night of September 18, 1931, Japanese agents rigged a small explosion on the rail lines near Mukden. Claiming Chinese provocation, Japanese troops quickly moved out of the leased areas and seized the major cities and evicted Chinese soldiers and officials. By early 1932, most of Manchuria had fallen to Japanese control, and they soon proclaimed the so-called independent state of Manchukuo. Emperor Hirohito and the civilian authorities in Tokyo did not approve of the attack, but they were powerless to halt it. The Foreign Office made apologies and promises to the western powers, only to have them nullified by new aggressions by the military.

The Japanese militarists and super-nationalists combined successful conquest with a campaign of intimidation and assassination of moderate opponents at home. Extremists assassinated the Prime Minister in 1930 in protest against the London Naval Agreement; two years later another Prime Minister and a cabinet member met a similar fate; and in 1936 assassins narrowly missed the Prime Minister but killed his brother-in-law by mistake, along with several other officials. Meanwhile Japanese patriotic pride had been greatly stimulated by the easy victory in Manchuria, where an estimated 60,000 Japanese troops with little difficulty drove back Chinese forces of about 400,000 men. Moderate Japanese thus found their position undermined by the militarists. The militarists gradually took control of the Japanese government and adopted an aggressive course aimed at hegemony in the Far East. After Manchuria, the military began to subvert northern China from the rule of Chiang Kai-shek, pulled Japan out of the League of Nations in 1933, and after failing to obtain naval parity with England and America in 1934 had the government denounce the naval arms limitations treaties.

Chiang Kai-shek at first tried to follow a conciliatory course toward Japan, despite the loss of Manchuria, and conceded her special economic privileges in North China and Inner Mongolia. Growing anti-Japanese sentiment in China, however, particularly among students, compelled the Nationalist chief to adopt a firmer policy against further Japanese encroachments. The Japanese militarists determined to strike again, ignoring the depression-paralyzed western nations and a Soviet power then being weakened by Stalin's bloody purge of Communist leaders. In July, 1937, after a clash in Peiping, the "China Incident" began, an all-out undeclared war intended to reduce China to a protectorate.

THE STIMSON DOCTRINE

Henry L. Stimson, Secretary of State under President Hoover, differed rather sharply with his chief over Far Eastern policy. Hoover had not known Stimson very well and decided on him for the State Department only after three other men had declined the post. Stimson, an old follower of Theodore Roosevelt and a former Governor General of the Philippines, came from a stern mold. Confident, moralistic, and with a Roman sense of duty, he conceived of world relations as governed by strict standards of moral principles and mutual respect. He sympathized with China, but more importantly he viewed Japanese aggression as threatening the entire post-World War system upon which rested world peace. Stimson believed that firmness and a show of force would compel Japan to observe its treaty obligations. In contrast, President Hoover was a "worrier" about domestic and foreign problems. Although not a narrow isolationist by any means, he was determined to limit America's foreign commitments and to keep the nation at peace. Moreover, coping with the Depression monopolized his time and energies. The two men also differed in petty but annoying ways. Hoover, an early riser and hard worker, frequently felt irritated by Stimson's more relaxed pace and shorter working hours. Stimson, over 60 years of age, suffered from a variety of infirmities that kept him away from the State Department for days, and he was fond of golf and other relaxations.

Stimson was at first inclined to trust the Japanese civilian leaders to restrain the military. Like many observers, he overestimated the strength of the moderates and underestimated the determination of the army. By rebuffing a Chinese appeal to invoke the Pact of Paris in September 1931 Stimson unwittingly encouraged continued aggression when a firmer policy might have been more effective. The Council of the League of Nations, though greatly embarrassed, also tended to rely upon the Japanese moderates to restore control and contented itself with a request for a mutual withdrawal of armed forces.

By early October 1931, however, both Stimson and the major League powers realized that the Japanese army was firmly in command. Carefully maneuvering in order to avoid unnecessarily weakening the Japanese moderates or permitting the League to saddle the United States with the responsibility for challenging Japan, Stimson suggested that the League Council invoke the Pact of Paris, with similar American action. When the League powers declined to act and instead suggested unilateral American measures, Stimson refused. Then the League Secretary General proposed that the League Council meet on the problem, with American participation, and Stimson with Hoover's approval agreed. He had won a diplomatic victory of sorts, though valuable time had been lost. A few days after the principal League powers reminded Japan and China that they had been signatories to the Kellogg-Briand international "kiss of peace," the United States dispatched a similar note. The Council fixed a deadline for the withdrawal of Japanese troops to their original positions, but Japan refused to comply. Subsequently the League's Lytton Commission investigated the Manchurian clash and its 1933 report fixed primary responsibility upon Japan, while recognizing some Chinese provocation. Japan thereupon denounced the report and walked out of the League.

Hoover reacted with alarm when possible sanctions against Japan came up for discussion. He would not cooperate with measures that might be adopted by the League. Yet the American attitude was not alone to blame for the failure to follow up condemnation of Japanese aggression. Neither Great Britain nor France felt greatly distressed by Japan's actions, especially as long as they occurred in areas remote from their own interest in the Far East. In fact, important elements in both countries tended to welcome Japanese rebukes to the disorderly Chinese government with its anti-foreign agitation and boycotts, and looked upon Japan as a salutary check to the power and designs of the Soviet Union in Asia. Some conservatives in England even talked of the need to revive the old Anglo-Japanese alliance, in preference to cooperation with the United States.

The President agreed with Stimson that the United States must formally condone the Manchurian conquest. In identical notes to Japan and China on January 7, 1932, the American government refused to recognize any changes in China brought about by force and in violation of the Open Door Policy or the Pact of Paris. The British and French governments at the time failed to adhere to this "Stimson Doctrine," though they did so subsequently under the prodding of the smaller League powers. After the bloody "rape of Shanghai," when Japanese forces brutally bombed and attacked Shanghai early in 1932 in retaliation against anti-Japanese boycotts and riots, Stimson asked for British cooperation in a display of naval force and the invocation of the Nine Power Pact. Some authorities feel that decisive collective action at this point might have forced Japan to halt. Britain, however, distracted by the Depression, left the responsibility primarily to the United States. Stimson interpreted the cautious response of the British Foreign Secretary, Sir John Simon, as a refusal and decided to act alone.

Stimson resorted to a public letter to Senator Borah of the Senate Foreign Relations Committee. In this letter, dated February 23, 1932, he reaffirmed the principles of the Open Door and invited other powers to adopt the non-recognition policy. He also intimated that because the Five Power Pact limiting naval armaments was closely linked to the Nine Power Pact, the United States might regard the violation of one as nullifying the other. His threat of a resumption of the naval arms race had some effect, particularly when the Senate committee on naval affairs recommended passage of a $1 billion construction bill. Tokyo decided on a retreat and arranged a truce in Shanghai. Yet though disturbed, Japan's leaders soon perceived that an isolationist America, preoccupied with the Depression, would not follow words with deeds.

At this point Stimson wanted to threaten Japan with still firmer action, but he could not persuade President Hoover. Stanley K. Hornbeck of the State Department's Far Eastern Division argued that vigorous measures would avert an eventual war with Japan. Japan seemed particularly vulnerable to economic pressures, because of its large export trade with the United States and its heavy dependence on America for oil, scrap iron and steel, and other commodities vital to modern industry. Although Stimson had doubts about actually embargoing trade, he wanted at least to brandish that economic weapon. However, William R. Castle, the Undersecretary of State, agreed with President Hoover that economic coercion or threats would probably lead to war rather than peace. Castle was not necessarily pro-Japanese; he simply saw Japanese predominance in the Far East as inevitable and possibly even beneficial in terms of stability.

The President felt so apprehensive that Stimson had to dissuade him from publicly undercutting his policy of pressure on Japan.

The Secretary hoped that uncertainty in Tokyo about America's next step would have a restraining influence. Yet while he was absent in Europe on an official trip, Castle with Hoover's approval made two speeches revealing that the United States opposed trade boycotts and would not go beyond a moral rebuke of aggression. Upon his return to Washington, the furious Stimson tried to repair the damage and managed to persuade the President to leave the Pacific fleet at Pearl Harbor for the 1933 naval war games. He hoped thereby to continue pressure on the Tokyo authorities, but apparently all that he accomplished was to convince more Japanese that the United States was their chief opponent. Unquestionably, Hoover's position against forceful measures or even threats reflected majority sentiment in America. Most citizens approved non-recognition of Japan's conquests and sympathized with the Chinese victims of aggression, but they also wanted to avoid war.

The United States obviously lacked sufficient naval power and popular will to restrain Japan. Moreover, its moral gestures affronted one of its best customers—American trade with China, despite the old illusion of a vast potential market, was very small while Japan was the third largest purchaser of American exports. American policy toward Japan's aggression in Manchuria reflected a high degree of moralistic outrage and traditional missionary-nourished sympathy with China. There was a realistic element also—Stimson feared that Japan had undermined the postwar settlement and if unchecked would stimulate aggression elsewhere. Yet if the U. S. felt it must condemn Japanese aggression, it should have been prepared to follow words with action. Its moral rebukes merely outraged the militarists and presented them with additional ammunition to persuade their people of American enmity, while leaving them free to pursue their conquests. Many Japanese regarded western condemnation as hypocritical at best. In the words of Yosuke Matsuoka, later Japan's foreign minister, "The Western Powers taught Japan the game of poker but after acquiring most of the chips they pronounced the game immoral and took up contract."

EARLY NEW DEAL FOREIGN POLICY: DRIFT AND INCONSISTENCY

Roosevelt's early foreign policy has aroused much debate. Did he adhere essentially to the neo-isolationist course of his Republican predecessors, avoiding binding political commitments abroad? Or did he recognize American interests in a stable world and seek cooperation with other states to curb aggression and war? Roosevelt took a great interest in international affairs, as his private correspondence amply reveals, reflecting his education and his earlier service in the Wilson administration. But in practice, at least through 1936, he followed a course not greatly different from that of Hoover. Why? In part because domestic issues of recovery and reform absorbed most of his energies. Furthermore, these were years of mounting withdrawal sentiment in America.

A practical politician, Roosevelt well realized the need for caution in foreign affairs in order to obtain the support of powerful liberal isolationists in Congress for his domestic legislation. He once remarked, "It's a terrible thing to look over your shoulder when you are trying to lead—and to find no one there." But equally important, despite his internationalist or Wilsonian orientation, FDR could not be completely impervious to the isolationist current of his day—to some degree he too shared isolationist views and emotions. Consequently, FDR's first administration revealed drift and inconsistency, with isolationist and internationalist policies incongruously intermixed.

Cordell Hull, 61 years old when he took office, would serve longer than any other Secretary of State—11 years and 9 months before he resigned at the end of 1944. A Tennessee politician and dedicated Wilsonian, Hull viewed world affairs from a Wilsonian perspective of idealistic and moral principles. He had a rather simple panacea for world troubles: freer trade, revival of morality, and the application of international law. Hull's absorbing interest was to remove or reduce barriers to international trade. In other areas he lacked specific solutions and was inclined to deliver moral lectures to erring foreign governments. Hull indeed resembled the great leader he so revered—like Wilson, he had a pronounced penchant for expressing moral indignation. He made his most significant contributions to New Deal foreign policy in trade reciprocity and the Good Neighbor Policy. His naive view of power politics and his faith in moral exhortations poorly fitted him to deal with the threat of aggressions in Europe and the Fear East. Hull, although never close to the President and highly suspicious of FDR's very able and sophisticated friend in the State Department, Undersecretary Sumner Welles, nevertheless played an important part in American foreign policy until Pearl Harbor. Thereafter, he found himself increasingly bypassed.

Roosevelt continued his predecessor's short-sighted course toward the League of Nations and the war debts question. During the 1932 election, FDR had conciliated William Randolph Hearst and other isolationist die-hards when he assured an audience that the present League had fallen away from Wilson's ideal and the United States had no place in it. He even failed to name an ambassador to the League, the least that many internationalists expected, and he left it up to Secretary of Labor Francis Perkins to get the United States into the International Labor Organization. After the moratorium, Hoover had shown some interest in scaling down the war debts owed to America. Roosevelt, realizing this would be highly unpopular in the United States, continued to insist upon full payment of the debts. When all the European debtors except Finland defaulted in a whole or in part, he signed the 1934 Johnson Act prohibiting private or governmental loans to foreign governments in default. Subsequently in 1940 and 1941 he regretted thus tying his hands in foreign affairs.

The World Economic Conference that met in London in 1933 has frequently been cited as proof of FDR's isolationism during his first year in office. According to many historians, Roosevelt sacrificed international considerations to the needs of domestic recovery. In fact, most major powers followed narrowly nationalist economic policies.

Roosevelt selected a strangely mixed lot for the American delegation. Hull, without a voice in the appointments, nominally led a group composed of free traders, protectionists, inflationists, planners, and hard-money men. Moreover, as an ardent advocate of lowered tariff barriers, Hull had little sympathy with the domestic planners in the NRA and AAA who sought to raise prices by curtailing production and restricting the entry of competitive foreign products. Senator Key Pittman, chairman of the Foreign Relations Committee of the Senate and a member of the delegation, apparently spent most of his time at the Conference defending higher prices for silver and scandalizing London with his drunken sprees. Another delegate, a Texas banker, revealed ignorance of even the simplest facts of international affairs. An adviser, William C. Bullitt, became preoccupied with trying to discover hidden dictaphones in London and greatly annoyed the British with attempts to pry information from the secretary of the Prime Minister.

Hull had hoped to achieve a reduction of tariffs at the Conference, only to have the President decide against it for the present while the Secretary of State was enroute to London. He arrived, as he noted bitterly, with empty hands and nothing to offer but platitudes. Even the opening of the assemblage was delayed because the President was slow in approving Hull's speech—Europeans were annoyed at this discourtesy. To cap the confusion, New Dealer Raymond Moley arrived as FDR's messenger during the middle of the Conference, capturing the headlines and overshadowing the enraged Hull. Little wonder that an amazed Prime Minister MacDonald asked an American observer how FDR could have chosen such a delegation.

With reduction of war debts and a permanent stabilization agreement ruled out by FDR, hopes at the Conference centered on a temporary exchange arrangement. Just as an agreement had been reached, however, Roosevelt decided that it would be unwise to freeze commodity prices at their existing low level. Therefore on July 2 he sent the famous "bombshell" message vetoing even a temporary stabilization of currencies. Released on July 4 and widely hailed in America as a new Declaration of Independence from the international banking interests, Roosevelt's message expressed satisfaction that the "old fetishes" of the financiers were being supplanted by planned national currencies, and he piously rebuked the European nations for not balancing their budgets and living within their means. The hapless Hull managed to prolong the futile Conference for a few more weeks before it adjourned amid a nearly universal chorus of denunciations of the United States.

Roosevelt no doubt committed a diplomatic blunder in his bombshell message, but he was not alone responsible for the debacle at London. The other major powers also maneuvered for national advantage, seeking currency rates that would favor their own commerce at the expense of others. Moreover, the delegates showed little interest in tariff reductions or any other definite remedies. Roosevelt's mistakes lay in not having decided on a clear policy earlier, and in the unnecessary abruptness of his July message that allowed other governments to blame him for the failure of the Conference. Yet the U. S., the world's foremost economic power, had failed to show any leadership in developing a cooperative approach to international recovery. The fascist nations gleefully hailed the failure in London and drew a parallel between Roosevelt's emphasis on national solutions for recovery and their own methods. International trade after the London fiasco increasingly became a matter for bilateral governmental bartering rather than free private exchanges.

The World Disarmament Conference, convened in 1932, still limped along when FDR entered office. France demanded security before reductions, and Germany wanted equality with France. Hoover previously had attempted to stimulate the conference, first by suggesting the abolition of all offensive weapons and then by proposing one-third reduction in all armaments. Roosevelt tried also, offering a package containing a pledge of non-aggression, overall arms reductions, and an American promise in case of crisis to consult with other powers; if the United States agreed on the designation of an aggressor, it would not interfere with any sanctions the League might impose. Roosevelt apparently dared not go further toward collective security. In any case, the Disarmament Conference ended in failure when Chancellor Adolf Hitler ordered the German delegates to walk out of the meeting and announced that Germany would withdraw from the League.

Hull finally obtained authorization to negotiate tariff reductions in hopes of reviving international trade and promoting a more peaceful world. By the Reciprocal Trade Agreement Act of 1934, regularly renewed in subsequent years, the executive could negotiate agreements with other countries, reducing existing tariff rates by as much as 50 percent. The State Department completed sixteen agreements within the first three years under the act, most of them with Latin America. By 1940, the number had increased to twenty-two. Apart from winning some good will abroad and some quickening of trade, especially in Latin America, the reciprocal trade approach fell lamentably short of Hull's liberal dream. Too many other countries, especially the dictatorships, preferred protectionism or governmental bartering.

RECOGNITION OF THE SOVIET UNION

President Roosevelt realistically decided that the time had arrived to recognize the Soviet Union. His Republican predecessors had continued Wilson's policy of non-recognition, reflecting moral disapproval of communist ideology, methods of government, and the Soviet's repudiation of foreign debts. While most Americans approved non-recognition, a number of liberals always had been inclined toward tolerance, or even endorsement, of the Soviet system as an experiment for the improvement of mankind. Many Americans mistakenly viewed Lenin's New Economic Policy as indicating an abandonment of socialism and a return to the free enterprise system. After Lenin's death in 1924, Americans observed with some pleasure that he was replaced by an obscure Joseph Stalin instead of that well-known and feared advocate of world revolution, Leon Trotsky. Moreover, many American businessmen subscribed to the illusion that recognition would bring increased trade with the Soviets, especially after most European countries had recognized the former outcast and renewed their economic relations. The Depression heightened the lure of trade, which Soviet authorities cleverly exploited to facilitate diplomatic recognition. Moscow initially sought recognition primarily for reasons of prestige. The growth of the fascist threat in Europe and Japanese expansion in the Far East also made recognition attractive for the security it might provide.

By 1933 a number of large American firms, such as General Electric, Ford, and International Harvester, had entered the Russian market. In 1930, the U.S. briefly surpassed all competitors in exports to Soviet Union. Stalin's first Five Year Plan, calling for increased mechanization of industry and agriculture, seemed to promise vast new opportunities for American exporters. They felt acute disappointment, therefore, when the volume subsequently fell off and Germany replaced the United States as the USSR's foremost supplier. Business spokesmen and politicians such as Senators Hiram Johnson and Borah argued that recognition would greatly facilitate the growth of American trade with the Soviets. Of course, many Americans remained opposed to recognition on moral and religious grounds. Patriotic groups such as the American Legion and the Daughters of the American Revolution, members of Protestant and Roman Catholic Churches, the AFL, and the chambers of commerce provided the bulk of the opposition. As long as Hoover occupied the White House, these negative viewpoints prevailed. As the El Paso *Herald* sneered at proponents of recognition on trade grounds, "A dangerous Red is any Russian who appears in America without placing an order for machinery."

FDR favored formal diplomatic relations on the realistic grounds that whatever one thought of it the Soviet regime had existed for sixteen years; moreover, a restoration of official relations hopefully would bolster the status quo in the Pacific against Japan and would strengthen non-aggressive forces in Europe. After preliminary explorations, Soviet Foreign Commissar Maxim Litvinov arrived in Washington. He made it clear that Russia preferred unconditional recognition prior to negotiations on outstanding issues, in accordance with the pattern she had followed in establishing diplomatic relations with other countries. The American authorities, however, insisted on negotiations first. With Roosevelt taking a direct part in the conversations, recognition was completed on November 16, 1933.

The arrangement established diplomatic relations, provided freedom of religious worship for Americans in the USSR, and promised to halt Soviet propaganda and subversion in the United States. Roosevelt and his advisers insisted upon the religious provision, primarily because the American people took such issues seriously and had long objected to the Soviet Union as a godless regime. Public opinion also required the promise that neither government would interfere "in any manner" in the internal affairs of the other, though some of the American negotiators may have taken the Soviet pledge seriously. The USSR dropped its claims for compensation for damages during the American intervention in

North Russia and Siberia and promised further negotiations on the question of debts. American claims totalled over $630 million, including about $187 million owed by the former provisional government in bond issues, private loans, and property confiscations. In their "gentlemen's agreement," Litvinov mentioned a possible settlement for $75 million, while Roosevelt referred to a figure of $150 million.

Most Americans approved the establishment of formal relations. Litvinov was honored at a farewell luncheon at the Waldorf-Astoria Hotel, attended by the representatives of such giant capitalistic firms as J.P. Morgan and the Pennsylvania Railroad. The president of International Business Machines even urged Americans to promote better relations in the future by refraining "from any criticism of the present form of Government adopted by Russia." Unfortunately for such enthusiasts, recognition of the Soviets proved a disappointment. Trade remained small, primarily because Russia lacked the necessary funds and private long-term credits were deemed too risky by businessmen and financiers.

The hoped-for diplomatic benefits also proved illusory, the two powers failing to achieve any notable collaboration either in regard to Japan or Europe. The debt negotiations also ended in deadlock. The USSR in effect refused to agree to any sum unless the U.S. provided double that amount in the form of long-term governmental loans or credits. Since such a settlement would merely increase Russian indebtedness to the United States, the State Department rejected it. The Soviets, needless to say, continued their propaganda and subversion in this country. When Secretary Hull protested the continuation of revolutionary activities, trumpeted at the seventh congress of the Comintern at Moscow in 1935, the Soviet government blandly disavowed the private and separate international Communist apparatus that happened to be meeting on Russian soil. Litvinov reportedly had told an American Communist when he made the agreement in 1933, "The letter [pledge] is a scrap of paper which will soon be forgotten." The State Department did not forget it, however, and lodged repeated protests. A growing number of Americans soon came to view recognition as a serious mistake.

THE GOOD NEIGHBOR

Long before the era of the New Deal, the American government had begun to cultivate better relations with Latin America. The Wilson administration and its Republican successors in the 1920s became aware of Latin American resentment of the Colossus of the North and tried to assuage it. Latin American critics cited a long list of Yankee "crimes" and blunders: the "rape of Panama"; armed interventions and military rule in the Caribbean; economic penetration and exploitation of Latin America; and the refusal of the United States to subject its actions to international restraints by joining the League of Nations. Above all, the Monroe Doctrine and its infamous Roosevelt Corollary— justifying preventive intervention in the Caribbean in the name of security—aroused hatred and fear among neighbors to the south. American businessmen, eager for new markets and investment opportunities, urged a more conciliatory course on the State Department. So did many other Americans, appalled at the often exaggerated accounts of harsh military rule by the marines in Haiti and the Dominican Republic. For these reasons, and because after 1918 the United States no longer felt insecure about the Panama Canal, the government began to abandon its benevolent imperialism.

The new era began during the last year of the Wilson administration. Secretary of State Bainbridge Colby announced America's intention to withdraw soon from Haiti and the Dominican Republic, and he made a brief but successful good will tour of South America in 1920-1921. The wooing became more ardent under his successors. The U.S. marines left the Dominican Republic in 1924, although the State Department retained financial controls until 1941. The Senate approved a treaty with Colombia in 1921 that paid her $25 million for the 1903 Panama affair and cleared the way for eager Yanqui oil concessionaires to operate in that country. American forces decamped from Nicaragua in 1925, only to return the following year when revolutionary disturbances broke out between the Liberal faction supporting Juan B. Sacasa against the pro-American regime of Adolfo Díaz. Henry L. Stimson went to Nicaragua on a special mission in 1927 and arranged a political truce and new marine-supervised elections.

The truce soon collapsed and American troops began to chase the "bandit" forces of Augusto Sandino. The marines remained until 1933 and the financial controls until 1944. The Clark Memorandum, released in 1930, disclaimed any valid connection between the hated Roosevelt Corollary and the Monroe Doctrine, although it did not repudiate interventionism on other grounds.

The Pan American movement, dating back to the first Conference in 1889, drew new strength from Washington's conciliatory policies in the 1920s. Secretary of State Hughes ensured that the United States did not dominate the Fifth Pan American Conference that met at Santiago, Chile in 1923. The Conference endorsed the Gondra Convention for cooling-off treaties on the Bryan model, which eight states including the United States eventually ratified. President Coolidge personally opened the Sixth Pan American Conference, held at Havana in 1928. Hughes, again heading the American delegation at this and a subsequent special conference, helped secure approval of an arbitration agreement along the lines of the Pact of Paris outlawing aggressive war.

Even relations with difficult Mexico improved in the Twenties. Article 27 of the 1917 Mexican Constitution, providing for national ownership of oil and mineral deposits, had caused sharp controversy between Washington and Mexico City. President Carranza threatened to apply these provisions retroactively to Aemrican holdings acquired before 1917. Moreover, the Carranza regime's anti-clerical policies aroused much ill will among Roman Catholics in the United States. After Carranza's fall, Hughes negotiated the Bucareli settlement with his successor, Alvaro Obregón, in 1923. Obregón agreed not to apply Article 27 retroactively and promised compensation to foreign owners for land expropriated for Mexico's agrarian reforms.

Relations quickly soured when the next Mexican regime, under Plutarco Elías Calles, returned to Carranza's position and imposed severe restrictions on foreign oil properties. Foreigners could own land only if they renounced the protection of their governments and oil leases acquired before 1917 were to be limited to 15 years. Moreover, the Calles' regime fought the hierarchy of the Catholic Church by nationalizing Church property, closing convents and religious schools, and requiring priests to register with the state. Catholics in the United States naturally felt outraged and they urged diplomatic intervention. The larger American oil companies resisted the land and oil decrees and appealed to the State Department for protection.

President Coolidge and Secretary of State Frank B. Kellogg (1925-29) at first reacted sharply, implying Soviet influence in Mexico and the supplying of Mexican arms to Nicaraguan rebels. The two quickly adopted a more conciliatory approach, however, when Calles indicted a willingness to arbitrate and a U.S. Senate resolution endorsed a peaceful solution. Coolidge sent his old friend, Dwight Morrow, on a special mission to Mexico City, instructed only to "Keep us out of war with Mexico." Morrow speedily established rapport with Calles and the Mexican people. He arranged a good will visit by humorist Will Rogers and a special flight to Mexico City by his son-in-law, America's new idol, Charles A. Lindbergh, fresh from his solo flight across the Atlantic. These gestures helped ease the way to a face-saving arrangement reviving the previous Bucareli agreement. It proved to be only a temporary solution to the oil problem, but at least it silenced talk of intervention and restored a degree of harmony to Mexican-American relations.

President Hoover made such notable contributions to Pan Americanism that some historians credit him with originating the Good Neighbor policy. While President-elect, Hoover undertook a good will tour of Latin America in 1928 during which he tried to dispel distrust and several times used the phrase "good neighbor" in his speeches. In office he refrained from further armed interventions, despite revolutionary disturbances in Panama, removed American troops from Nicaragua in 1933, and promised withdrawal in Haiti. He also abandoned the moralistic Wilson recognition policy for a return to the traditional practice of recognizing *de facto* regimes regardless of how they came to power. Yet like his predecessors, Hoover refused to pledge that armed intervention would never again be used. Treaty arrangements with several Caribbean states sanctioned the right of intervention and he and his advisers felt the United States could not be certain that it might not again be necessary to intervene to protect foreign lives and property.

President Roosevelt in his inaugural address pledged a policy of the Good Neighbor toward all the world, but the phrase soon came to be applied exclusively to his policies in Latin America. His contributions to hemispheric harmony constituted virtually a new policy and entitled his administration to primary credit as the originator of the Good Neighbor policy. The policy paid handsome dividends in promoting the security and unity of the Western Hemisphere as the danger of another world war increased. Latin Americans hailed FDR as "el gran demócrata," and many viewed his New Deal as a model for reform in their own countries. His accomplishments in Latin America and his role as leader of the western world during the Second World War, the spokesman for the aspirations of the common man everywhere, earned Roosevelt near deification in Latin America. Whatever the historical debate about the authorship of the Good Neighbor Policy, Latin Americans almost unanimously gave the credit to FDR.

The Good Neighbor policy is best defined as non-interventionism and the multi-lateralization of the Monroe Doctrine from a US doctrine into a hemispheric defense responsibility. Further, it supplanted the high protectionism of the Republican era with reciprocal trade agreements and was prepared to sacrifice when necessary private American economic interests in Latin America for the national interests of the United States. Cordell Hull delighted apprehensive Latin Americans at the Seventh Pan American Conference at Montevideo in 1933 when he voted for a resolution of non-intervention by armed force in the internal affairs of any Western Hemisphere state, except as sanctioned by international law. He reiterated this pledge without any reservation at the special Pan American Conference convened at Buenos Aires in 1936 that was personally opened by President Roosevelt. Latin Americans cheered these renunciations by the United States. A Mexican delegate at the Montevideo Conference expressed the conviction that "there is in the White House an admirable, noble, and good man—a courageous man who knows the errors of the past but who feels that the errors really belong to the past."

In the interval between these two conferences, the marines left Haiti as Hoover had promised and in 1934 the State Department agreed to abrogate the so-called Platt Amendment with Cuba, a treaty that had given the United States the right to intervene in the island. The latter action came only after the United States twice perilously neared armed intervention during the overthrow of the Gerardo Machado dictatorship and its successor. Sumner Welles, U.S. Ambassador to Cuba, had encouraged Machado's fall but he was great distressed when the next regime also was toppled and threatened armed intervention. Rejecting Welles' recommendation, an alarmed FDR and Hull perceived the danger that diplomatic interference might culminate in armed intervention. These experiences made Roosevelt willing to renounce forceful measures unconditionally.

Alarmed at the threat of war in Europe and by fascist activities in Latin America, the United States sought to multilateralize the Monroe Doctrine from a US unilateral policy into a collective defense system for the Western Hemisphere. Argentina, traditionally a rival of the United States for leadership in the Western Hemisphere and a country increasingly under strong fascist influences itself, repeatedly blocked Washington's proposals for a binding commitment for mutual measures to repel outside aggression. Hull finally managed to obtain a loose declaration at the Eighth Pan American Conference held at Lima in 1938 for consultation and cooperation against subversion or external threats to the peace of the hemisphere.

Canada, a fully self-governing dominion within the British Commonwealth, remained apart from the Pan American movement in order to preserve its nationality and its ties to England. In effect, however, Roosevelt brought Canada under the scope of the inter-American system when at Kingston, Ontario, in 1938 he declared that the United States could not see Canada threatened by conquest. After the outbreak of the Second World War, Canada and the United States concluded joint defensive arrangements. The U.S. prepared the way for close hemispheric collaboration during World War II and the creation of the Organization of American States after the war.

The Roosevelt administration revealed during these years that while it continued to be concerned with the legitimate economic interests of American citizens in Latin America, it would no longer act as a bond collector for Wall Street. In fact, when necessary, the administration was prepared to sacrifice substantial private interests for the sake of better political relations with Latin America. When Bolivia expropriated Standard Oil Company holdings and Venezuela demanded increased royalties from American oil companies operating in that country, the State Department refrained from threats or retaliation and sought to arrange equitable settlements. Mexico proved more difficult, but there too the State Department successfully applied the new tactics. President Lázaro Cárdenas, a leftist reformer, expropriated foreign-owned lands and oil properties in 1938. Although an exasperated Hull inclined toward retaliation, Roosevelt, at the inspiration of Ambassador Josephus Daniels, arranged settlements that left American investors highly displeased but avoided a serious crisis between the two countries. American oil companies had to accept compensation of $24 million for holdings they valued at half a billion dollars. A subsequent Import-Export Bank loan from the United States helped Cárdenas' successor pay for these reduced compensations.

ISOLATIONISM AT HIGH TIDE

Isolationist sentiment became stronger and more pervasive in America in the mid-1930s. Economic distress at home, disillusionment with the 1917-1918 Great Crusade, and war clouds abroad, generated a growing conviction that the United States should shun foreign entanglements that might lead to war. As Senator Borah said in 1934, America was not and would not be isolated economically, "But in all matters political, in all commitments of any nature or kind, which may encroach in the slightest upon the free and unembarrassed action of our people, or which circumscribe their discretion and judgment, we have been free, we have been independent, we have been isolationist." Isolationism seemed particularly strong in the mid-West, though it was not limited to that region. The midwestern reaction was a reflection of the large number of German- and Scandinavian-

Americans and geographical remoteness, but above all of agrarian radicalism. Farmers looked with distrust upon eastern big business and financial firms as exploiters of rural folk. Many agrarian isolationists believed that big businessmen and financiers had brought about intervention in the recent World War, from which they had profited at the farmers' expense. Of course isolationism appealed to other than agricultural groups. It drew support as well from urban reformers and idealists and cut across political lines. Isolationism gradually became more conservative as liberals swung toward internationalism in the last years of the decade.

Anti-war novels, articles, movies, and revisionist histories reflected and contributed to the popular mood of pacifism, disillusionment, and withdrawal. Peace movements proliferated and flourished, and college students, like their counterparts in the late 1960s, demonstrated against war and demanded the expulsion of ROTC units from campuses. Novels by writers such as Erich Remarque—his *All Quiet on the Western Front* became a popular movie—Ernest Hemingway, and John Dos Passos depicted war as senseless and barbaric. Muckraking books by Helmuth C. Englebrecht, *Merchants of Death*, and George Seldes, *Iron, Blood and Profits*, strengthened the popular conviction that the common man fought so that bankers and munitions manufacturers might prosper.

Some historians revised the previously accepted version that Germany had been solely responsible for the war in 1914 and for American involvement in 1917. Revisionist scholars sought not merely to find the truth about events in 1914-1917 but to influence current public discussions on foreign policy and to prevent intervention in another war injurious to liberal reform at home. Harry Elmer Barnes pioneered in revisionist studies during the mid-1920s. Barnes had been an ardent supporter of Wilsonian internationalism until disillusioned by the postwar settlement. His *Genesis of the World War* (1935), a Book-of-the-Month Club selection, and C.C. Tansill's *America Goes to War* (1938) also indicted the one-sided nature of American neutrality in 1914-1917. To a very large degree, the revisionists won the intellectual community to their views and helped create that climate of public opinion that explains passage of the neutrality laws in the 1930s. A

Gallup poll in April 1937, for example, revealed that 64 percent of the public regarded American intervention in the World War I as a mistake. In that same year the emergency Peace Crusade observed the 29th anniversary of the 1917 war entry with a "no foreign war crusade," and those senators and representatives who had voted against war in 1917 were lavishly praised.

The Nye Committee hearings were symptomatic of the popular disillusionment. Responding to demands for federal regulation of the arms industry, from groups such as the Women's International League for Peace and Freedom, the Senate in 1934 authorized a special inquiry into the munitions industry. The administration, caught off-guard, failed to block the selection of Republican Senator Gerald P. Nye of North Dakota, a rough-hewn arch-isolationist, to head the inquiry. FDR probably could have made a greater effort to remind the nation that the country had fought for more serious reasons than profits in the recent war, but he failed to do so. Apparently Roosevelt shared popular aversion to arms profiteers, and he hoped to obtain controls over them.

Nye's committee, heavily over-representative of rural isolationist viewpoints but also backed by urban pacifists and anti-big business liberals, staged a public circus in uncovering the huge profits made by eastern financiers and the munitions industry during the neutrality years. The committee's sensational releases helped convince many citizens that profit-hungry capitalists had dragged the United States into the World War. As Nye summed it up, "When Americans went into the fray, they little thought that they were there and fighting to save the skins of American bankers who...had two billions of dollars of loans to the Allies in jeopardy." The investigation seemed almost as much anti-big business in bias as anti-war, and it reflected the widespread view that greedy bankers and industrialists encouraged international strife. Americans seemed periodically susceptible to "devil theories" of history, as the "military-industrial complex" stereotype of the late 1960s again indicated.

Ironically, Roosevelt himself suggested neutrality legislation to the Nye Committee in 1935 to bar American citizens from travelling on belligerent ships. A threatened conflict between Italy and Ethiopia offered the occasion. FDR apparently hoped to avoid the risks of being involved in a future war by issues of neutral rights; American policy, freed of the burden that had plagued President Wilson, then could be based on more fundamental national interests. Roosevelt hoped that any ban against the arms trade would permit him to discriminate between aggressive and defensive nations, but he encountered a threatened filibuster by the pacifist and isolationist bloc in Congress. He accepted a substitute measure, prepared by Senators Key Pittman and Borah, that provided for a mandatory arms embargo. Upon a presidential proclamation of the existence of a foreign war, the sale or transportation of munitions to belligerent countries would be prohibited, and at the executive's discretion citizens could be warned not take passage on belligerent vessels. FDR, to Hull's disappointment, signed the measure because it was due to expire in six months and he hoped at that time to obtain a more satisfactory law. Apparently he also thought that application of the 1935 Neutrality Act would hurt Italy in case of war with Ethiopia.

When Congress passed the Neutrality Act, Europe seemed once more on the threshold of a major war. As noted earlier, fascism, a peculiar blend of idealism, romantic nationalism, conservatism, and militarism, had come to power in Italy in 1922. Led by their "Duce," Benito Mussolini, the Fascists achieved some worthwhile reforms and social stability but at the price of a totalitarian dictatorship. Mussolini in general remained pacific in foreign policy until the Great Depression and the rise of Adolf Hitler in Germany began to undermine the Versailles settlement. Hitler adeptly exploited popular resentment of the Versailles Treaty, mass unemployment and economic distress, and the weaknesses of the postwar democracy in Germany. His National Socialist or Nazi Party espoused policies similar to Italian Fascism and took power in early 1933, only a few weeks before Roosevelt's inauguration in the United States. Using violence and intimidation, Hitler fastened a brutal dictatorship on the German people. He began to rearm Germany, threatened to use force to rectify the 1919 settlement, and launched violently anti-Jewish persecutions within the Third Reich.

The American Ambassador, William E. Dodd, warned the President and the State Department about Hitler's plans for conquest, while the anti-Semitic Nuremberg Laws fully revealed the vile nature of the Nazi regime. Several German Jews fled to the U.S., among them the noted physicist Albert Einstein. (It should be noted, however, that the administration and Congress, owing to apathy and prejudice, failed to relax the immigration laws to permit large numbers of Jews to seek haven in United States.) Yet until Mussolini's Ethiopian venture revealed the supineness of Great Britain and France, Hitler acted fairly cautiously in foreign affairs.

When Mussolini invaded Ethiopia in the fall of 1935, the League Council condemned the attack and invoked economic sanctions prohibiting loans and the export of arms and war materials to Italy. However, the alarmed British and French governments, anxious not to drive Italy into Hitler's arms, carefully left oil—vital to Mussolini's war machine—off the list of sanctions. This appeasement of dictatorship also led to a still-born attempt at compromise, the Hoare-Laval plan for giving Mussolini two-thirds of Ethiopia, but public wrath in Britain and France caused its repudiation. Meanwhile, Mussolini's legions, armed with advanced weapons and using poison gas, completed the conquest of primitive Ethiopia, the first victim to appeasement.

Roosevelt and Hull deemed it politically unwise to cooperate openly with League sanctions, but they invoked the Neutrality Law even though Mussolini had not formally declared war. Unfortunately this action had little effect on Italy, which did not need to import arms, while hurting Ethiopia which did. The administration then called for a moral embargo against oil shipments to Italy, urging American firms not to increase supplies to Mussolini's war machine. It was difficult to enforce the moral embargo, however, and U.S. actions failed to encourage the League to adopt sterner sanctions. Britain and France thereby missed a promising opportunity to involve the American government more closely with League efforts to defend the peace. Their timidity encouraged Hitler to reoccupy and fortify the Rhineland, to restore conscription, and to launch a large naval and military aviation program in defiance of the Versailles Treaty. Conclusion of the Rome-Berlin Axis in 1936 solidified the new alignment of fascist powers against the western democracies, supplemented in the same year by German and Italian anti-Comintern pacts with Japan.

Congress approved the second Neutrality Act in February, 1936, while Mussolini digested his Ethiopian conquest. The act prohibited loans a well as sales of arms to belligerents and directed the President to extend the ban to new belligerents entering a war, an obvious warning of non-cooperation with League members that might be drawn into hostilities through sanctions against aggressors. The isolationist tenor of American sentiment and policy became even clearer when the Spanish Civil War broke out in the summer of 1936. Despite a non-intervention agreement among the major European powers, Germany and Italy actively supported the arch-conservative and Fascist-tinged rebel forces of General Francisco Franco against the Spanish Republican (Loyalist) armies. Many American liberals and intellectuals sympathized deeply with Republican Spain and several hundred American volunteers fought for the Republic in the Abraham Lincoln Battalion and other units. Although the communists and other leftists were active in organizing pro-Loyalist committees in America, most American sympathizers simply admired the heroic resistance of the Republicans and viewed the civil war as a crucial struggle between democracy and fascism. Conversely, some American conservatives and Roman Catholic spokesmen saw Franco as a bulwark against atheism, socialism, and communism in spain. The majority of Americans, however, tended to be apathetic or neutral about the civil war—one poll classified 12 percent of the public pro-Franco, 22 per cent pro-Loyalists, and the remainder either neutral or without an opinion.

The Roosevelt administration gave full support to Anglo-French efforts to isolate the Spanish Civil War. Although normally a recognized government is permitted to import arms despite internal disturbances, Roosevelt and Hull treated the conflict virtually as one between two sovereign states. They proclaimed a moral embargo against shipment of war material to either the rebels or the legal government in Spain. Subsequently Congress formally extended the neutrality law to apply to the civil war. The Loyalists alone suffered from the Anglo-French and American attempts to isolate the conflict, for Germany and especially Italy cynically violated their non-intervention pledges to supply Franco with arms and "volunteer" troops. President Roosevelt was to contemplate raising the embargo against the Loyalists, but he desisted because of domestic opposition and the obvious hopelessness of the Republican cause.

The third Neutrality Act, enacted in 1937, marked the final stage in the effort to immunize America from war. Although FDR still desired more flexible provisions to permit him to discriminate between aggressors and their victims, he was deeply involved in the court-packing fight and left the responsibility primarily to Senator Pittman of Nevada, Chairman of the Senate Committee on Foreign Relations. Pittman, not an ardent internationalist and anxious to preserve the independent role of his committee, repeatedly advised the administration to move cautiously in seeking modifications in the neutrality laws. The 1937 act renewed the ban on arms sales and loans to belligerents and prohibited travel on belligerent passenger and merchant vessels whenever the President should proclaim the existence of a foreign war. At the executive's discretion, the export of non-military goods to belligerents could also be prohibited during any war in the following two years unless done on a "cash and carry" basis. In a sense the new measure represented a compromise, benefitting the Axis powers in case of war with an arms embargo and yet offering the western democracies, who would control the seas, the opportunity to purchase vital raw materials for cash and to transport them away in their own ships. "Cash and carry" also reflected an agrarian bias against eastern industrialists and financiers and a determination to keep open profitable markets for farm products in Europe.

The President found his freedom of maneuver sharply restricted by the neutrality law. Arms and loan bans would have to be applied to aggressive and peaceful states alike. Underlying this act and the earlier neutrality laws were highly debatable assumptions that no basic moral issues were involved in the struggles taking place abroad, no fundamental American national interests were at stake, and that the nation could be secure in its hemisphere regardless of external developments. For the sake of isolation and peace, Congress had abandoned the nation's traditional policy of defending neutral trading rights on the high seas. As several commentators quipped, the neutrality acts appeared to be an attempt by Congress to legislate the United States *post facto* out of World War I. The whole episode seemed to reveal not that people do not learn from history but that too often they learn the wrong lessons.

ROOSEVELT AND COLLECTIVE SECURITY

Events moved inexorably toward a second world war. In July 1937, in the "China Incident," Japan launched a campaign to bend China to her will, an effort that bogged down her armies in China, drenched the country in blood, and eventually culminated in war with the United States. In March 1938 Hitler entered Vienna and annexed Austria to the new Third Reich, in violation of the Versailles Treaty. Flushed with easy triumphs, the Fuehrer next turned his attention to the Sudeten Germans living in Czechoslovakia and threatened war if these people were not returned to the Reich. The British and French governments lacked the will to defend the Versailles settlement, and the Italo-Ethiopian War had discredited the League. British Prime Minister Neville Chamberlain, under the delusion that he was dealing with rational men, still hoped to appease the dictators. Politicians in England and France, unnerved by memories of the staggering casualties of World War I and apologetic for the "harsh" Versailles Treaty, deluded themselves that concessions to the "legitimate" grievances of Germany would appease the Nazis and avert a new war.

Chamberlain and the French Premier, Edouard Daladier, journeyed to Munich in the fall of 1938 and bought "peace in our time" by sacrificing Czechoslovakia. The Nazi dictator quickly broke his promises. After digesting the Sudetenland, he seized the remainder of Czechoslovakia early in 1939. Not to be outdone, Mussolini invaded tiny Albania in April 1939. Only then, as Hitler turned his attention to the German population in the Polish Corridor and Danzig, did Britain and France resolve to resist even if meant war.

Prior to 1937, Roosevelt and Hull had not followed a consistent foreign policy. Not only had the administration accepted crippling neutrality legislation without putting up prolonged resistance, but

FDR himself sometimes sounded an isolationist note in public. The Democratic platform in 1936 reassured the electorate that the country would not be pulled into war by political or commercial entanglements. During the campaign, Roosevelt declared his resolve to insulate America from foreign conflicts and remarked, "I hate war. I have passed unnumbered hours, I shall pass unnumbered hours, thinking and planning how war may be kept from the Nation."

The China war and the crises in Europe caused Roosevelt to take a more decided internationalist course. He hoped somehow to prevent a general war but, if that failed, to strengthen peace-loving states against their assailants. When Japan launched the "China Incident" in 1937, his concern involved more than sympathy with China; it seemed to him that the forces of order and security everywhere stood on the defensive. Japan's aggressions comprised only one aspect of this assault against world peace and decency. FDR did not invoke the neutrality laws in Japan's undeclared war, because he wanted to give China whatever aid possible.

In his "Quarantine Speech" in Chicago, on October 5, 1937, President Roosevelt tried to alert the American people and to prepare them for a more responsible foreign policy. Speaking in the heartland of isolationist America, he indicated that the nation's security depended on cooperation with other peaceful states: "Let no one imagine that America will escape, that America may expect mercy, that this hemisphere will not be attacked." After proclaiming the principle that international gangsters should be segregated as society quarantines the carriers of dangerous diseases, Roosevelt declared, "We are determined to stay out of war...but we cannot *insure* ourselves against the disastrous effects of war and the danger of involvement; we cannot have complete protection in a world of disorder in which confidence and security have broken down."

The Chicago address aroused favorable response across the country, but it also ignited isolationist criticism and charges of war-mongering. Some alarmed isolationists even muttered threats of impeachment. It soon became apparent, however, that the president had no clear policy changes in mind. He may have contemplated some kind of collective neutrality whereby, without adopting economic or military sanctions, peaceful states would morally condemn aggressive powers. In subsequent remarks to reporters, however, he beat a hasty retreat and denied even the intention of passing moral condemnation on the aggressors. In retrospect it seems clear that FDR burnt his fingers at Chicago and thereafter felt more apprehensive than probably he should have about the strength of isolationism in America.

The League of Nations condemned Japan's aggression in China as a violation of the Kellogg-Briand and Nine Power pacts and suggested a conference of signatories of the Nine Power agreeemt. Shortly before the United States and the other signers, plus the Soviet Union, met at Brussels in November 1937, Roosevelt made it clear that he did not favor vigorous measures against Japan; apparently he saw the role of the Conference simply as bringing moral pressure to bear. Japan declined to attend and only USSR advocated strong measures. Britain and France left the initiative to the U.S., however Roosevelt and Hull recoiled from economic sanctions against Japan. Consequently the Conference achieved nothing beyond a pious reaffirmation of treaty principles. The Brussels Conference was not only a fiasco but a disaster. The fact that it met encouraged China to continue resistance in the hope of substantial aid, while its failure emboldened Japan's leaders to persist in their course.

The *Panay* incident in December, 1937, further revealed the reluctance of the United States to risk conflict with Japan. Japanese warplanes deliberately attacked the American gunboat *Panay* and three Standard Oil Company tankers on the Yangtze River and strafed survivors in the water. Yet unlike the *Maine* incident in 1898, most Americans reacted mildly and wanted to withdraw all U.S. ships and men from the area to avoid future incidents. The government accepted Japanese apologies and reparations. The incident also quickened congressional support for the so-called Ludlow Amendment to the Constitution, prohibiting war except in case of actual invasion or with majority approval in a national referendum. The administration had to exert strong pressure, including a letter from the President that was read in the House of Representatives, to block the bill from coming to the floor for formal debate and action.

Encouraged by slowly increasing public support for a stronger course, the State Department began to deal more firmly with Japan. The Two-Ocean Naval Act of 1938 vastly increased naval construction—even isolationists accepted the need for greater hemispheric defense. Meanwhile Japan, heretofore apologetic for many of her acts, openly proclaimed in 1938 a "New Order" for East Asia; no longer would she give even lip-service to the principles of the Open Door in China. Hull strongly objected to the "New Order" and reasserted American rights in China and the Far East. The administration gave Chiang Kai-shek a small loan in 1938 to bolster China's currency and its morale and proclaimed a moral embargo against the sale and shipment of aircraft to Japan. FDR ordered the Pacific fleet moved temporarily to Pearl Harbor as graphic reminder to Tokyo of American power and will to resist. Finally, the State Department opened the way for economic retaliation on July 26, 1939, when it gave notice terminating the Japanese-American commercial treaty of 1911.

War between the United States and Japan was not yet inevitable, although clearly the two countries followed sharply diverging courses. From the standpoint of practical interests, American policy has been viewed as highly unrealistic. The American economic stake in China, as noted before, fell far short of its trade with Japan. Moreover, Japan clearly ranked as the strongest power in East Asia. Would Washington have been wiser merely to lodge formal protests against the aggressions in China while patiently working for greater moderation by Japan? Or, if that failed, to have acquiesced in fact to Japanese control of China as inevitable?

From the later perspective of the Cold War and the Japanese-American Security Treaty, U.S. policy in the 1930s has seemed questionable to some scholars. Roosevelt and Hull, however, not able to read the future, believed that aggression must be opposed lest it spread everywhere. In short, they saw Japan's attack upon China as part of the general breakdown in world security and peace. Moreover, the American leaders thought that a greater display of firmness offered a chance of restraining Japan. Even after the European war erupted in 1939, FDR and Hull continued to hope that hostilities could be avoided with Japan, while they concentrated American attention upon Hitler's conquest of Europe. They did not view Japan as an immediate threat to American security until Tokyo concluded the Tripartite Alliance with the Axis powers in September 1940.

THE WANING OF ISOLATIONISM

Public opinion splintered under the impact of foreign events. Isolationists and non-interventionists feared involvement in war and were increasingly suspicious of FDR's leadership, as the Ludlow Amendment indicated. The internationalists, however, felt a growing apprehension about the Axis threat in Europe and Japanese militarism in Asia, and they supported the administration's movement toward collective security. Many previously pacifist or isolationist liberals began to shift into the internationalist camp. Some professed to fear the dangers of fascism at home, where anti-Semites rallied behind fascist organizations such as William Dudley Pelley's Silver Shirts, the German-American Bund, and the Christian Front. The formation of the House Committee on Un-American Activities in 1938 also disturbed thoughtful citizens. Headed by Representative Martin Dies of Texas, the Committee tended to ignore right-wing activities and concentrated on ferreting out Communist infiltration and front organizations. The Dies Committee permitted witnesses at its hearings to make unsubstantiated and reckless charges of communism against individuals who often had no opportunity for rebuttal. Some 640 organizations were denounced as controlled or infiltrated by the Communists.

Communism became more respectable during periods when the Soviet Union joined the Western democracies in opposition to fascist aggression. Earl Browder, who replaced William Z. Foster as General Secretary of the American Communist Party, pursued the Popular Front strategy, playing down revolutionary jargon and urging a coalition of all democratic forces to oppose fascism. A number of organizations, such as the American League Against Fascism, apparently had been founded by the Communists as front organizations to rally intellectuals and other groups. Browder boasted of his Revolutionary War ancestry and described communism as merely twentieth-century Americanism. The

Communist Party successfully penetrated various peace and youth groups and provided hard-working organizers for CIO labor unions. A few also found places in the federal government, but none in key policy-making positions and their importance often has been grossly exaggerated.

Roosevelt played only a small and indirect role in the Czechoslovakian crisis. He cabled Hitler twice on behalf of peace and approved Prime Minister Chamberlain's request that Mussolini use his influence to avert hostilities. Americans greeted the Munich settlement with profound relief that war had been avoided. Thus the American government and people at this time obviously favored appeasement of the Nazi Fuehrer. As Hitler violated his pledges and anti-Jewish outrages multiplied in Germany Roosevelt publicly voiced disapproval. He recalled the American Ambassador after the violent *Kristallnacht* in Germany—a wave of anti-Jewish riots and stringent repressive measures that followed the assassination of a German diplomat in Paris by a Jew.

Hitler fully reciprocated American dislike and recalled his ambassador. He viewed the U.S. as a racially mongrelized society that could not even cope with the Depression. America need not be taken seriously, he told his intimates in 1938, because it was too impotent to fight and would not go beyond meaningless moral gestures in international affairs. The German military shared his opinion. Using "racial arithmetic," Hitler concluded that the polyglot United States was held together only by the glue of 20 million superior Anglo-Saxons or 60 million of valuable racial stock; therefore, Germany with its larger population of Aryans was far more powerful. The neutrality laws strengthened his contempt; yet after war broke out, he wisely concentrated on Europe leaving the U.S. to deal with Japan's East Asian ambitions.

In the light of Hitler's "restraint" toward the United States prior to December 1941, how seriously did he menace American interests? Some revisionist historians have argued that a Nazi conquest of most of Europe would not have endangered the United States. In an immediate sense, such criticisms may be sound— probably Hitler would have been too exhausted to have turned upon the Western Hemisphere for many years. Yet he did contemplate expansion into Latin America, and obviously if triumphant in Europe he would have increased German penetration. American leaders feared that successful aggression spawned more aggression and that it would be potentially dangerous to live isolated within an Axis-dominated world.

By 1939 President Roosevelt clearly recognized the bankruptcy of isolationism. He warned Congress and the nation of the serious crisis facing the world and advocated measures short of war to restrain aggression. In mid-April 1939, he appealed to Hitler and Mussolini to reassure thirty-one countries that they would not be attacked. Hitler rebuffed him in a satirical speech to the Reichstag, his puppet legislature, while Mussolini failed to respond. FDR and Hull attempted without success to persuade Congress to repeal the Neutrality Law or at least to modify it so that the president would not have to apply an arms embargo against countries attacked by the dictators. Although unstated, the administration implied that in case of war between the western democracies and the totalitarian states, America's own interests required a victory by the democracies. The isolationists refused to relent, however, and Senator Borah confidently predicted that there would be no war in Europe in 1939.

Contrary to Senator Borah's prediction, Hitler was about to unleash the *Wehrmacht* against Poland and the western democracies. On August 23, 1939, the world was shocked at news of the signing of the Nazi-Soviet Pact in Moscow. With the danger of a major two-front war eliminated, Hitler felt free to pursue his Polish venture despite Anglo-French opposition. On September 1 the *Luftwaffe* rained destruction on Poland; two days later, Great Britain and France fulfilled their pledge to the Poles and declared war on Nazi Germany.

The twenty-year armistice had expired; World War II had begun. But while isolationism remained powerful in America, the shock of the recent events had weakened it badly. Various polls after 1937 had indicated that most Americans viewed Nazi Germany as morally wrong and that in case of a major war they favored supplying arms to the western democracies despite the neutrality laws. Now as war raged in Poland, another Gallup poll indicated that 84 percent of the American people desired an Allied victory and 76 percent, despite an overwhelming desire to remain at peace, expected America to become involved sooner or later. Although over two years more elapsed before the United States entered the war, public opinion had begun to adjust to that prospect by the fall of 1939.

SUGGESTED READINGS

Borg, Dorothy. *The United States and the Far Eastern Crisis of 1933-1938* (1964).

Burns, Richard Dean and Bennett, Edward M., eds. *Diplomats in Crisis: United States-Chinese-Japanese Relations, 1919-1941* (1974).

Dallek, Robert. *Franklin D. Roosevelt and American Foreign Policy* (1979).

Divine, Robert A. *The Illusion of Neutrality* (1962).

Feis, Herbert. *The Road to Pearl Harbor* (1950).

Ferrell, Robert H. *American Diplomacy in the Great Depression* (1957).

Heinrich, Waldo H., Jr. *American Ambassador: Joseph C. Grew and the Development of the United States Diplomatic Tradition* (1966).

Hull, Cordell. *Memoirs,* 2 vols. (1948).

Iriye, Akira. *The Origins of the Second World War in Asia and the Pacific* (1988).

Kimball, Warren. *The Most Unsordid Act: Lend Lease, 1939-1941* (1965).

Langer, William L., and Gleason, S.E. *The Challenge to Isolation* (1952).

__. *The Undeclared War* (1953).

Chapter Eight

AMERICA AND WORLD WAR II

On September 1, 1939, German armies, led by mechanized divisions and supported by devastating air power, invaded Poland. On September 3, making good their pledge, Great Britain and France declared war against Hitler's Germany. On that same day President Roosevelt proclaimed that America would preserve its neutrality in the great war breaking out in Europe, though unlike Woodrow Wilson before him the President did not ask the public to avoid moral judgment about the origins and meaning of this conflict. Then in mid-September Roosevelt called Congress into special session to repeal the arms embargo and thereby to return to the rules of what he misleadingly labelled "true neutrality."

The majority of Americans, believing that their country should do at least this much to aid the democracies resisting Nazism, recognized that repeal in fact would favor Britain and France. Opponents of repeal, however, attacked it as a measure inevitably leading toward involvement in the war. After bitter debate which lasted six weeks Congress finally passed the so-called fourth Neutrality Act that became law on November 4, 1939. As a consequence belligerents were permitted to purchase arms and related war materials in the United States provided they paid cash for such purchases and transported the goods in their own vessels. To be sure, the new law continued to prohibit loans to belligerents and still forbade American ships from entering war zones. "Cash and Carry," as the legislation became known obviously favored the Allies and, seemingly, gave the American people a profitable market without the accompanying risk of involvement in the fighting. Apparently most Americans shared the private view of the Roosevelt administration that England and France, assured thereby of access to the nation's war supplies, could survive and ultimately triumph over Hitler without the necessity of direct American intervention.

After the fall of Poland in late September—with the bulk of that nation divided between Germany and the Soviet Union based on their secret August agreement—the war in Europe entered a protracted lull. In the interval Roosevelt sought to tighten hemispheric security. To this end, a conference of foreign ministers met at Panama in October 1939, and proclaimed that the warring parties should not carry on combat operations within a zone or "hemispheric safety belt" drawn around the Western Hemisphere but excluding Canada. Needless to say the belligerents understandably ignored the novel prohibition. Subsequently, after Nazi forces overwhelmed the Lowlands and France, another conference of foreign ministers assembled at Havana, Cuba, in July 1940 and declared that an outside attack upon one hemispheric state would be construed as an attack upon all, in effect multilateralizing the prohibitions of the traditional Monroe doctrine.

The conclusion of the "phony war" in Europe ended abruptly in the spring of 1940. Without warning and principally to outflank France's heavily fortified Maginot Line, German armies invaded and overran the Netherlands, Belgium, and Luxemburg. Allied forces were consequently trapped in Belgium and forced to evacuate the continent at Dunkirk, an accomplishment that witnessed the rescue of some 200,000 British and 140,000 French troops. Nazi forces had eliminated France from the war on June 22, 1940, when a new French government under the direction of Marshall Henri-Philippe Petain agreed to an armistice. Among other things, the armistice provided for disarming French forces and handing over control of three-fifths of the French nation to the Germans. A stunned America began to fear that Britain also might soon fall, removing the last bulwark between the victorious Nazis and an unprepared United States.

President Roosevelt soon set out to alert his fellow citizens. At Charlottesville, Virginia, on June 10, 1940, the same day that Italy declared war against France and Britain. FDR warned Americans that both democratic institutions and the safety of the Western

Hemisphere stood in immediate peril. Therefore, he called for the strengthening of America's defenses and providing aid to nations resisting aggression. Clearly Roosevelt recognized that neutrality was no longer a meaningful national policy and, while still hoping to avoid *direct* involvement in the war, that the ultimate defeat of the aggressors required more than merely opening American markets to their opponents. FDR also decided during this crisis to seek an unprecedented third term as president, and he took steps to broaden the base of his support by appointing two prominent Republican internationalists, Frank Knox and Henry L. Stimson, respectively, as Secretary of the Navy and Secretary of War. Congress, under the lash of these events, appropriated over $10 billion for defense and adopted the first peacetime selective service act in U.S. history.

Great Britain, now led by the indefatigable Winston Churchill, pleaded for more arms, especially for some old World War I-vintage American destroyers needed desperately to counter the Nazi underseas war upon British and Allied shipping. Roosevelt, fully aware of the British mood of desperation, eagerly sought ways to aid her survival. Yet he feared, with some reason, that isolationist sentiment was still too strong to be directly challenged. In these circumstances his advisors formulated what became known as the destroyer-bases swap, whereby the president would trade Britain over-aged destroyers for the use of defense bases located upon British territory within the Western Hemisphere. Thus on September 2, FDR formally approved the exchange of 50 American destroyers for long-term leases to British bases, in addition to an outright British gift of two more bases and a London pledge that the British fleet would never be allowed to fall into German hands. The eight bases, ranging from Newfoundland to British Guiana, contributed immensely to American security and defenses.

Although Roosevelt publicly defended the swap as the most important action in the reinforcement of the national defense since the Louisiana Purchase, it aroused a furore of criticism by domestic isolationists, especially as the president had acted on his own initiative without the consent of Congress. Nonetheless, polls revealed that 70 percent of the public approved his bold move. In any event, the destroyer-bases swap marked the end of meaningful neutrality for the United States. Thereafter the nation, unlike the neutrality period of World War I, simply assumed the role of a non-belligerent openly aiding the Allies.

Understandably, the war fragmented public opinion in the United States. William Allen White, Republican editor of the Emporia (Kansas) *Gazette*, formed the Committee to Defend America by Aiding the Allies in May 1940. Through more than 600 local chapters, the White Committee mounted a massive campaign to persuade Americans that the nation must enhance its security while remaining formally at peace and that the only way to achieve that goal was by providing massive aid to the Allies. Public opinion polls attested to the success of the White Committee, indicating that four of every five Americans favored all out aid to Britain, while 82 percent opposed entry into the war. To counter the White group, opponents of interventionism, led by General Robert E. Wood, a middle western business executive, organized the American First Committee in July. America First orators, including the Charles A. Lindbergh and Senator Gerald P. Nye, contended that Hitler posed no real danger to America and that aid to Britain would pull the nation into the war. America First not unexpectedly drew much of its financial backing from wealthy conservative Republicans, particularly those in the Midwest. Increasingly, as most liberals rallied to the side of the administration's course, America Firsters became more and more identified with anti-New Deal reactionaries.

Republicans by-passed a number of well-known conservatives to nominate Wendell L. Willkie for the presidency in 1940. Willkie, a wealthy liberal businessman, approved of aid short of war to the Allies and initially sought to mute foreign policy issues in the campaign. By late September, however, fearful that Democrats were profiting unfairly politically from the sentiment of most Americans for peace and aid to the Allies, Willkie began to query the sincerity of the Roosevelt administration's profession of peaceful policies. If FDR's promise to keep American boys out of foreign wars were no better than his promise to balance the budget in 1932, declared Willkie, Americans were already "almost on the [troop] transports for Europe." In reply, FDR assured Americans that "Your boys are not going to be sent into any foreign wars," meaning except in the case of attack. But the President's failure to declare his meaning fully left him open to charges of deliberately deceiving the American people. Roosevelt was nevertheless elected to a third term of office, though by a closer margin than in 1932 and 1936, defeating the challenger by 27 million to 22 million popular votes. The electoral vote, 38 states to 10, was more conclusive.

INTO A SHOOTING WAR IN THE ATLANTIC

With the election safely behind him, Roosevelt finally agreed with his advisers who had urged that piecemeal aid to Britain would not suffice to ensure her survival much less the defeat of the Axis powers. Prime Minister Churchill had apprised the President that Great Britain was already hard-pressed to pay for goods on order and that "ten times as much" would be required to carry on the war. FDR responded to the British plight in the affirmative. In a fireside radio chat to the nation, late in December 1940, the President declared that the United States must become the "arsenal of democracy." The nation, he maintained, must make vast quantities of aid available to those nations fighting aggressors. To avoid the painful experience of World War I loans and debts, Roosevelt ingeniously proposed that he be authorized to transfer or to lease defense materials to those countries resisting aggression, for payment in kind or any other direct or indirect benefits of value to American security.

Again another great public debate erupted. Critics charged that lend-lease was the path most likely to involve the nation directly in war, while proponents counter-charged that it offered the only realistic hope of protection so long as the U.S. remained a nonbelligerent. Although the subject of much controversy among scholars, there can be little doubt that FDR earnestly hoped that lend-lease would enable the nation to remain at peace while ensuring the defeat of the aggressor nations, a wish shared by most of his countrymen. Congress after spirited debate passed the Lend-Lease Act by decisive majorities; on March 11, 1941, FDR signed the Lend-Lease Act into law.

The new measure, in every sense a negation of the nation's traditional concept of neutrality, marked a major turning point in America's involvement in World War II. Clearly, Hitler could have seized upon it as an excuse for declaring war but he chose to follow a different policy. Additionally, the passage of lend-lease indicated the waning of isolationism in America. To be certain, most citizens would still prefer to stay out of the war but they were prepared to risk involvement in order to secure Hitler's defeat. Congress appropriated $7 billion to launch lend-lease and ultimately the country expended around $50 billion under the act.

Hitler's invasion of the Soviet Union, on June 22, 1941, dramatically altered the context of the war though it failed at first to alter America's deep-seated hostility to the dictatorial regime of Joseph Stalin. The events of the past several years—the Nazi-Soviet pact, the partition of Poland, and the neutrality pact with Japan—had caused Americans to question whether the USSR would be a suitable ally. On the eve of the Nazi invasion the State Department suggested that in the event of hostilities "We should steadfastly adhere to the line that the fact that the Soviet Union is fighting Germany does not mean that it is defending, struggling for, or adhering to, the principles in international relations which we are supporting."

When the attack did occur the State Department was loath to more than lift trade restrictions with the Soviets. Churchill, on the other hand, urged that aid be extended to Russia in the belief that her survival, which according to some was not expected to be long, meant the defeat of Hitler. Roosevelt concurred with Churchill that Soviet entry into the war at least promised a breathing spell for the West and, if the USSR survived, its enormous territory and population would ensure ultimately an Axis defeat. FDR had never been very inclined to take ideology seriously, and apparently he expected that the passage of time would harmonize the two systems, capitalist and communist, by democratizing the latter. As a consequence he decided to extend aid to the Soviet Union, a decision approved by most Americans. Those who at first suggested otherwise included Senator Harry S. Truman, who in an off-the-cuff remark to a newspaperman asuggested that the U.S. should alternately assist the Germans and the Russians in killing as many of each other as possible, soon changed their opinion as the Red Army proved to be a match for the *Wehrmacht*.

Events rapidly swept the United States into an undeclared shooting war with Germany in the Atlantic. The president, to the dismay of his critics, acted upon his own authority in adopting measures that led to this undeclared war. Apparently Roosevelt felt that the dangers facing the nation were too immediate to await approval by an isolationist-influenced Congress, particularly as the House of Representatives had only recently extended the length of service of draftees by a slim one-vote margin. He seems to have decided by mid-1941, that the U.S. probably would have to enter the war to assure its interests.

FDR acted decisively. The United States seized Axis ships in American ports, the navy patrolled the Atlantic shipping routes, and American forces occupied Greenland and Iceland in April-July 1941 on the grounds of forestalling a possible Axis invasion. Using this latter measure to cover his action with a cloak of legitimacy, Roosevelt finally ordered the U.S. Navy to convoy American and Allied shipping, including vital lend-lease goods, through U-boat infested waters as far as Iceland. Isolationist fears now seemed to have become true.

In early August 1941, in Argentia Harbor of Placentia Bay in Newfoundland, Roosevelt and Prime Minister Churchill met to discuss, among other things, ways of deterring the Japanese from attacking British or Dutch positions in the Far East and the coordination of their war effort against Germany. At this time, they issued a joint statement of principles on which they hoped the postwar world might be built. The impact of the message, mainly from the pen of the Prime Minister, was at once profound and far-reaching. For despite the subsequent controversy over whether or not FDR or Churchill actually signed the document, and despite the well-known British and Soviet reservations, the Atlantic Charter, as it came to be called, captured the public's imagination and went a long way in conditioning and influencing policymakers' opinions about the future role of American policy. Among the Charter's idealistic objectives, not unlike those of Wilson's Fourteen Points, were the destruction of Nazi tyranny, the principles of self-determination, equality of states, and, most significantly, the promise of a postwar "establishment of a wider and permanent system of general security."

In any case, American clashes with German U-boats inevitably resulted in an undeclared war in the Atlantic. The United States destroyer *Greer*, engaged in trailing a German submarine and signalling its position to a British plane, was fired upon in September 1941; in October the destroyer *Kearny* was torpedoed with the loss of eleven men on convoy duty while the *Reuben James* suffered the loss of 96 men in a similar incident. President Roosevelt, apparently less than candid with the American people, announced these as unprovoked attacks and issued commands to the Navy to shoot on sight at such "rattlesnakes on the sea." Flowing from the events an outraged American public caused Congress to revise the Neutrality Acts to permit the arming of the nation's merchant vessels and their sailing into previously forbidden war zones.

WAR VIA THE "BACKDOOR"

The Roosevelt administration's policy of putting Japan on her good behavior, signalled by the abrogation of the commercial treaty in mid-1939, seemed initially to be effectively curbing Japanese expansionism until Hitler's dazzling victory in Europe shifted the scales within Japan toward the more extremist elements. The militarists, emboldened by such signs, determined to exploit the conflict in Europe to obtain long-held objectives in Asia. Reflective of the attitude a new ministry came to power, headed by Prince Konoye and General Hidiki Tojo as War Minister. Yosuke Matsuoko a violent Yankee-phobe, whom Secretary of State Cordell Hull once described "as crooked as a basket of fishhooks," took charge of foreign affairs committed to a course of expansionism. Early in September 1940, the Japanese proceeded to force a weakened France to agree to Japanese occupation of northern Indochina, a maneuver aimed mainly at cutting off Chiang Kai-shek's supply routes. Later in that month Japan signed the Tripartite Alliance or so-called Axis Pact with Germany and Italy, while in April 1941 it concluded a neutrality pact with Moscow.

Although Washington officially dismissed the Axis Pact as a formality, ratifying what had, in fact, been a de facto alliance with the European fascist aggressor, it doubtless contributed to hardening American opinion and policy toward Tokyo. Japan, consequently, seemed a fit partner for the league of dictators seeking world hegemony. In turn, the Roosevelt administration adopted increasingly tougher measures in the thinly-held hope that it could stop Japan without recourse to war. In July 1940, FDR prohibited without license, the export of petroleum or its products and scrap metal to Japan, followed shortly by an embargo upon the export of aviation gasoline. In late September, in response to Japanese incursions into Indochina and news of the Axis Pact, the President banned the export of scrap iron and steel as well. Other signals to Tokyo included a $25 million loan to Chiang Kai-shek under auspices of the Export-Import Bank and the permanent removal of the Pacific fleet to Pearl Harbor, the latter amounting to a graphic reminder to Japan of American power and will to resist further expansion. Yet the administration carefully refrained from embargoing crude petroleum exports altogether to Japan, reserving that as the last desperate weapon in view of that nation's dependence upon western-controlled sources for 80 percent of its vital oil needs.

Thus by mid-1940 American-Japanese relations had reached an impasse. Neither, it seems fair to conclude, though for different reasons, wanted war but neither could or would retreat. The majority of Americans viewed both morality and security as dictating that Japanese imperialism be halted. Nevertheless, they perceived Hitler's Germany as the principal threat to the national security and still hoped to avoid war with Japan. Conversely, Japanese leaders also hoped to avoid war with America, but they refused to abandon their conquests in China. Moreover, Japan's military leaders—nationalistic, proud, and largely ignorant of the western world—were determined to end, once and for all, what they viewed as a dangerous economic dependence upon the United States. In this sense, then, the stage was set for war between two proud and unyielding powers.

Unceasing rounds of negotiations of course continued. Admiral Kichiasaburo Namura was dispatched to Washington as ambassador early in 1941 for another round of talks. Again, the Americans demanded that Japan withdraw its forces from China and give reassurance against further, presumably, aggressive moves; for their part, the Japanese sought to have trade barriers removed and American encouragement of Chiang Kai-shek's resistance halted. When in late July 1941, subsequent to Hitler's invasion of Soviet Union, Tokyo sent troops into southern Indochina in an obvious preparatory maneuver to gain control of oil supplies in the Dutch East Indies, Washington felt itself compelled to place a complete freeze upon oil shipments to Japan. American public opinion grew more and more hostile toward Japan. At this point, it came to be believed that not only must future Japanese expansion be resisted but that Japan be forced out of China. Any lesser course, it was feared, would only weaken Chinese resistance and encourage additional Japanese conquests.

Japan's military rulers chose to fight rather than to submit to what they regarded as a humiliating surrender. Prince Konoye proposed a last-ditch personal conference with Roosevelt, but the latter, although at first intrigued by the idea, was dissuaded by his advisers, mainly Secretary Hull, who doubted the ability of the Premier to agree to anything that would be acceptable to the military. Meanwhile the Japanese military prepared to seize the Dutch East Indies and to attack the Anglo-Americans by late November if an agreement or *modus vivendi* could not be reached by then. The Japanese navy was ordered to practice a surprise attack upon the Pacific fleet at Pearl Harbor. Doubtless, many Japanese recognized full well that a war with America carried grave peril for Japan, but the militarists ignored such considerations. They were confident that the ideological superiority of Shintoism would prevail over America, and they hoped Americans would fight only half-heatedly before capitulating to Japan's successes. In short, even the most pessimistic concurred that Japan was taking a calculated risk and that national suicide, if it should come to that, would be preferable to ignoble surrender.

In the final series of talks at Washington, Tokyo submitted what the Americans knew from cracking the Japanese secret codes was her final offer before the outbreak of hostilities. Essentially, the Japanese repeated their demands for the revoking of trade restrictions and for a cessation of American encouragement of continued resistance by Chiang Kai-shek in China, promising in exchange the recall of troops from southern Indochina and pledges that Japan would not launch new military ventures elsewhere. But this so-called final offer proved unacceptable to Roosevelt, inasmuch as it would continue to give Tokyo a free hand in China. When consultations with the British and the Chinese Nationalists revealed that those two powers also opposed any conciliation of Japan, FDR and Hull decided, too, to reject this final offer. Subsequently, Secretary of State Hull presented Japan with a note fully restating the American position for a complete Japanese withdrawal from China and Indochina. Although Hull's note has been termed an "ultimatum" by some historical critics, it was merely a formal summary of the American case for the historical record.

The Roosevelt administration anxiously awaited Japan's next move, for it was certain that Tokyo would strike without warning somewhere in the Pacific. The consensus among officials was that British and Dutch territories would be the targets; some even suggested the Soviet Union's maritime provinces. Would they also attack American possessions? The uncertainty ended soon. Early on the morning of Sunday, December 7, the Japanese navy executed a daring surprise aerial assault upon the United States Pacific fleet at the Pearl Harbor naval base in Hawaii. On the same day other Japanese forces attacked the Philippines, Guam and Midway Island, as well as British forces at Hong Kong and Malaya. The aftermath of the attack on Pearl Harbor was awesome. Five battleships, three cruisers, and lesser American warcraft were sent to the bottom, with about 3,000 men killed. Fortunately for the U.S., their aircraft carriers were absent from Pearl Harbor and these escaped destruction. Yet the suprise attack had severely damaged American naval power in the Pacific and allowed Japanese forces to overrun their targets in Southeast Asia.

The surprise attack aroused great controversy in the United States at the time and later. Some revisionist writers—in contrast to FDR's defenders who are usually referred to as "internationalists"—subsequently charged that the administration deliberately plotted the Pearl Harbor disaster in order to get America into the European war via the "backdoor," that is, by provoking the Japanese into attacking. The evidence simply does not support such an interpretation. FDR and his associates did not want war with Japan, because they recognized American weaknesses in the Pacific and, in any case, perceived Hitler as the primary threat to U.S. security. Yet they rejected purchasing peace with Japan at the expense of abandoning China. As for Pearl Harbor itself, the evidence suggests that there was no single or simple cause. The government and the military, not unlike the public, were unprepared for war. Even the breaking their secret codes failed to reveal, with any degree of clarity, Japanese intentions.

Yet while the Pearl Harbor attack represented a daring, though qualified, tactical success for Japan, in the long-term it proved to be her own undoing. For Americans were outraged by the attack— an act of perfidy in President Roosevelt's words—and they launched an all-out effort to crush Japan. Congress, with only one dissenting vote, declared war against Japan on December 8. Three days later, on December 11, Germany and Italy removed the last doubts by declaring war against the United States. A united America stood ready to battle for democracy and national survival.

THE HOME FRONT

Pearl Harbor, in many ways the mid-wife of modern American internationalism, silenced the isolationist versus internationalist debate within the United States. It created a unified public sentiment that the nation had no choice but to win the war as soon as possible. Public support of the war, unlike in World War I, was complete and there was relatively little hysteria this time about so-called disloyal elements, except for the disgraceful treatment accorded to thousands of Japanese-Americans, an episode, that most historians agree, constituted a blatant violation of civil liberties.

Anti-Japanese sentiment had of course long existed in the United States. And because of geography, those resentments tended to be concentrated within the western states, particularly in California, long the center of Japanese migration to America. Since the turn of the century, as Japan underwent modernization of its economy, its surplus rural population had caused a significant migration of Japanese workers to the west coast of the United States, as well as Hawaii, Australia and Canada. This migration triggered adverse, at times violent reactions, by so-called "native" Americans especially n California. At the heart of anti-Japanese sentiment, not unlike the earlier experience of the Irish in Boston, lay fear of these recent arrivals as serious economic competition.

Pearl Harbor presented the anti-Japanese elements with an opportunity to brand indiscriminately all Japanese, whether natural born citizens or not—there were 80,000 in the former category and 47,000 in the latter—as traitors and disloyal. They were accused of deliberately living near military and naval installations for purposes of future espionage and sabotage. Various agricultural, labor and business groups, led by American Legionnaires and members of the Daughters and Sons of the Golden West, welcomed the chance to denounce the hated alien and to demand in the name of national security their mass evacuation from the west coast. More moderate citizens, especially members of the clergy and educators, opposed such a demand in vain. Even such civil libertarians as California's Attorney-General Earl Warren and journalist Walter Lippmann joined the chorus in arguing for evacuation.

At this point the United States Army joined in. Lieutenant General John L. De Witt, commander of the Fourth Army and the Western Defense Command, who was originally opposed to drastic action on the ground of race, became increasingly convinced that deportation of Japanese-Americans was essential and urged a tough course in the name of national security upon the War Department. By early 1942 De Witt reached the conclusion that "A Jap's a Jap...It makes no difference whether he is an American citizen or not...I don't want any of them."

Although the Justice Department sought to act with the utmost caution, distinguishing carefully between Japanese and American citizens, heavy pressure from the West Coast and the War Department, led by Secretary of War Stimson, persuaded it to capitulate. On February 19, 1942, the War Department, at the direction of FDR, drew up Executive Order 9066, authorizing

Stimson to designate military areas and to exclude from them all those thought necessary. The forced evacuation of Japanese Americans from west coast states commenced in March, culminating shortly in a full-scale program of internment under the direction of the newly-created War Relocation Authority headed by Milton Eisenhower. Thousands of Japanese-Americans, without regard to whether they were citizens or not or any other factors, soon were rounded up and transported to ten so-called "relocation centers" in seven western states. Of the 110,000 evacuees approximately 17,000 were able to obtain leaves of one kind or another, the most notable of these being those who enlisted in the 442 Regimental Combat Team and distinguished themselves in battle in Italy. The episode has rightly been termed outrageous and the Supreme Court upheld the policy of relocation in 1944 but did order the release of loyal citizens.

The United States, under the Selective Service Act of 1940, raised mammoth armies in a short time. All males between the ages of 18 and 45 were required to register with their local draft boards; of these 40 percent were rejected for physical and mental disabilities or other deferrable causes. Altogether, the U.S. raised wartime forces totalling fifteen million men and women, the latter serving as volunteer corps adjuncts to the Army (WACs), Navy (WAVES), Coast Guard (SPARS), Army Air Force (WASPs), and Marines. Conscientious objectors also performed special war-related work.

A vast increase in economic production was necessitated by the war effort. Only then under the lash of mobilization did the huge unemployment of the Great Depression disappear, moving from 8,000,000 unemployed persons in 1940 to an increase of the civilian work force by nearly 7,000,000 in 1945. Of these, millions were women who poured into defense plants to take up duties as welders and riveters, with profound social consequences for the postwar era. As early as August 1939, President Roosevelt set up the War Resources Board—in 1941 the Office of Production Management—to manage the conversion of civilian industry to war production.

By early 1943, the Office of War Mobilization, under the direction of James F. Byrnes, assumed control over the economic side of the war effort. Recognizing the important role of technology, FDR established the Office of Scientific Research and Development in June 1941, with Vannevar Bush as chairman. Directed to coordinate the nation's scientific efforts, this agency assisted in the development of such innovations as radar, the proximity fuse, sonar, and the atomic bomb. Production reached prodigious heights. The nation produced a total of 296,000 aircraft and 5,400 merchant vessels, in addition to 71,000 naval craft of various sizes. The latter included, by 1945,. 28 aircraft carriers, 70 escort carriers, 72 cruisers, 373 destroyers, 365 destroyer escorts, 240 submarines, and 23 battleships.

To curb wartime inflation, prices, wages, and rents came under the control of the Office of Price Administration in 1942. By then, general prices had already risen by 25 percent, but the line was held thereafter. A system of rationing, which was comparatively mild in relation to the other wartime powers, controlled supplies of scarce commodities such as sugar, coffee, gasoline, and automotive tyres. Since Japan had cut off the nation's accustomed source of raw rubber, American industry began to develop synthetic rubber for tires and other needs. Agriculture boomed under the war stimulus, further encouraged by very high parity prices and supports. Industrial production, too, reached new heights despite less manpower, as machinery and fertilizers were utilized in unprecedented ways. Between 1939 and 1945 manufacturing output doubled while agriculture rose 22 percent.

During the course of the war, labor was allocated by a War Manpower Commission. The National War Labor Relations Board, at first, preserved industrial peace and kept the number of strikes below normal. Even so, 1943 witnessed an increase in strikes as labor felt squeezed by wartime inflation. Although most of these labor disruptions were unauthorized "wild-cat strikes"—with some notable exceptions such as when John L. Lewis led the United Mine workers out of the coal mines in 1943—labor's record on the whole was good and disruptions did not seriously impair war productivity.

War finance posed another great challenge. By mid-1943, War costs ran at $8 billion per month—as much as the yearly New Deal budgets of the past. By the end of the war, the national debt had risen to $247 billion, from $48 billion in 1941. Increased taxes raised an estimated 40 percent of the total costs, a greater proportion than in any previous war; the remainder was met by the time-honored method of borrowing. Millions of Americans were encouraged—even coerced by public pressure—into investing in war bonds. The 1942 War Revenue Act instituted a novelty to Americans—the payroll deduction system—and sharply increased tax rates. The introduction of the payroll income tax deduction, proposed by Beardsley Ruml, Chairman of the Federal Reserve Bank of New York, produced a veritable tax revolution as the number of people paying income taxes increased from four million in 1939 to nearly 50 million by 1945. Naturally rates were raised most sharply on the upper income brackets and corporate earnings. The total war costs of $350 billion surpassed the record World War I costs by at least ten times the 1917-1920 totals.

Voluntary censorship of the press, radio and motion picture industry worked well on balance. Borrowing again from World War I experiences, FDR established the Office of War Information in June 1942 with the following mandate:

> ...to coordinate the dissemination of war information by all federal agencies and to formulate and carry out, by means of the press, radio and motion pictures, programs designed to facilitate an understanding in the United States and abroad of the progress of the war effort and the policies, activities, and aims of the Government.

OWI, like Creel's CPI earlier, performed excellently as a propaganda machine to arouse the war spirit at home and broadcast American goals abroad. In these years Hollywood contributed to Allied unity with a sympathetic portrayal of the Soviet Union in such movies as the *Song of Russia* and in *Mission to Moscow*, the latter based on former Ambassador Joseph Davie's best-selling book. Meanwhile *Life* magazine observed that Russians were much like Americans in the way they thought and *Time* selected Stalin as its "Man of the Year" in 1943. Even the popular comic strips did their part with such characters as Joe Palooka reminding Americans what the War was all about.

RACE PROBLEMS, POLITICS, AND THE WAR

World War II witnessed growing unrest in racial relations within the United States. Negroes were determined both to attain full equality and to share in the wartime prosperity. During the course of the War over a million black Americans migrated from the Deep South in search of new opportunities, figures reaching 60,000 in Detroit, 100,000 in Chicago, and 250,000 on the West Coast. Wherever blacks went, it seemed, they encountered discrimination, much of it of the most ugly variety. Tensions, fed by a number of factors including critical housing shortages, erupted into violence in such places as Beaumont and Port Arthur, Texas, Mobile, Alabama, and in the barracks at Fort Dix, New Jersey. The worst incident of the war years occurred in Detroit in June 1943, as white-black tensions exploded into a race riot that required federal troops to suppress it and restore order. Before it was over, twenty-five blacks and nine whites had been killed. At the same time, Mexican-Americans in Los Angeles, the so-called "zoot suiters"—the Spanish-speaking youths who dressed in zoot suits that emanated from Harlem—became the targets of white servicemen while the local and military police turned the other way.

In other respects the war saw marked advances for black Americans. Lynchings declined, Georgia repealed the poll tax, and the white primary in Texas was outlawed by the United States Supreme Court. In these and in other ways liberals of both races united in campaigns against Jim Crowism and on behalf of civil rights for black people. But perhaps black Americans made their greatest advances on the economic level. Under pressure of a threatened protest march on Washington, organized by A. Philip Randolph, President of the Brotherhood of Sleeping Car Porters, Roosevelt issued Executive Order 8802 declaring it to be the policy of the United States "that there should be no discrimination in the employment of workers in defense industries or government because of race, creed, color, or national origins." To enforce this policy, the President established a Fair Employment Practices Committee to investigate any complaints of discrimination and to take the necessary measures to redress grievances. The FEPC worked effectively after 1943, and as the war ended approximately two million blacks had found employment in war industries, though it is no doubt true that the critical labor shortage played the large role in this development.

Politics continued as usual during the War. Making a determined bid to recapture Congress in the 1942 election, Republicans gained 46 seats in the House and nine in the Senate. Moreover, Republican Thomas E. Dewey won the governorship of New York, the first member of that party to head the Empire State since 1920; altogether, Republicans controlled the governorship in 26 states by 1944. This resulted in increasing presidential-congressional struggles over domestic issues, though both parties continued to support the war effort.

Although Wendell Willkie was theoretically the titular head of the Republican Party, his star faded rapidly due to his lack of rank and file support and to his close identification with the Roosevelt administration's foreign policies. After suffering a defeat in the Wisconsin primary, Willkie early in 1944 withdrew from the campaign. Thus the way was left open to Dewey, who brought strong assets to his quest for the GOP nomination—youthful vigor, moderate liberalism, and a proved vote-getting ability. Not unexpectedly, he easily defeated his principal rivals, including Governor John W. Bricker of Ohio, to gain the nomination at the Republican convention at Chicago in June 1944.

Having already flouted the third-term tradition, Roosevelt announced in July that "as a good soldier" he would accept a fourth nomination to the presidency. Despite the lack of enthusiasm on the part of the party's leaders to his decision, none dared to challenge him as he still enjoyed a vast popularity at the grassroots' level across the nation. Accordingly, the Democratic National Convention renominated FDR on July 20 at Chicago. The only matter in doubt was the struggle over the vice-presidential nomination. Henry A. Wallace, the incumbent, had the support of organized labor and the more liberal New Deal elements, but was strongly opposed by the professional politicians and party bosses. And although Roosevelt publicly endorsed Wallace, he refused to fight for his nomination. In fact, FDR had apparently decided upon South Carolina's James "Jimmy" Byrnes. However, Byrnes met growing opposition from liberal democrats and organized labor.

Sidney Hillman of the CIO had organized the Political Action Committee (PAC) in 1943 to gain an increased voice for labor, and he warned the president that the former Senator from South Carolina was unacceptable to organized labor. At this point FDR shifted to Senator Harry S. Truman of Missouri who had headed a well-publicized congressional probe into war contract abuses. Truman was chosen on the third ballot.

In the campaign that followed Dewey fought hard but could not overcome certain severe handicaps. As Allied forces won victories in Europe and the Far East, he faced an electorate reluctant to change leadership in the midst of the greatest foreign war ever fought by the United States. Moreover, suspicions about Roosevelt's ill health were overcome by his vigorous campaigning. FDR promised voters a full continuation of progressive New Deal programs and policies after the war. The PAC performed ably in mobilizing the nation's workers on his behalf. Hence on election day President Roosevelt scored a sweeping victory, defeating the challenger by 25.5 to 22 million popular votes and an overwhelming electoral college victory (36 to 12 states). In Congress, the Democrats lost one Senate seat while gaining 20 in the House.

THE DIPLOMACY OF VICTORY

America's first year in the war, 1942, had witnessed several military defeats. The United States continued lend-lease to its allies, including the Soviet Union, while Tokyo turned the Pacific into a Japanese lake and Berlin drove upon Moscow. Allied representatives assembled in Washington and in a brave show of unity and purpose they signed on January 1, 1942, the Declaration of the United Nations, pledging pursuit of the Atlantic Charter ideals. No questions were asked at that time as to whether or not the Soviet Union really meant such pledges, for the general ruin and peril of 1942 seemed hardly the moment to raise potentially embarrassing issues.

Besides, the USSR seemed to be changing; after all, Moscow had signed the Declaration of the United Nations and spoke of the need to liberate Europe. In 1942, its government concluded an alliance with Great Britain, as a further assurance, and, in the following year, it formally dissolved the much-feared Comintern. Presumably the Soviet Union under Stalin's rule seemed to abandon the goals of world revolution and to be prepared to peacefully coexistence with a postwar capitalist world. Public opinion in the United States reflected this changed attitude. According to one poll, 46 percent of the American people viewed theUSSR's government as simply mirroring Russian conditions, while 30 percent believed they were improving. As noted, popular journals and Hollywood motion pictures promoted the Soviet Union in a more favorable light than before. The cumulative effect was that most Americans seemed to share the optimism of their leaders that cooperation with the Soviets was both possible and desirable.

Even prior to the Japanese attack upon Pearl Harbor, the Roosevelt administration had agreed with Britain that the defeat of Nazi Germany must have priority. Pearl Harbor catapulted the U.S. formally into the War, it reaffirmed that Germany was the most formidable opponent. Consequently the Pacific theater of operations received less emphasis. Within this Europe-first strategy, which had its share of critics in the United States, certain differences emerged between the British on the one side and the Americans on the other. British leaders preferred to contest Hitler through a peripheral strategy of invasions—first through the Mediterranean Sea or the so-called "soft underbelly" of the Axis. Churchill, the author of the ill-fated Gallipoli invasion of a previous era, feared that a premature cross-channel invasion might culminate in trench butcheries resembling the horrors of World War I; the Prime Minister wanted to weaken Hitler by cautious peripheral campaigns preparatory to a direct invasion of Western Europe. American military planners, conversely, advocated a swift military decision in the War via a cross-channel campaign and as soon as possible. Due mainly to Aemrican power and the rapid build-up of its armed forces to comprise the bulk of Western forces, the Americans finally forced Britain to accept their strategy.

But this was not to be realized before important operations began in the Mediterranean areas. In early November 1942, a combined Anglo-American force launched *Torch*, an offensive against German troops in North Africa. Coordinating the invasions with an offensive launched from Egypt by Field Marshal Sir Bernard Montgomery, the British and American forces quickly closed the trap upon the Germans commanded by the "Desert Fox," the dashing Field Marshall Erwin Rommel. The operation cost the Axis heavily, with some 349,000 men killed or captured, 250 tanks destroyed, and over 2,300 aircraft lost. The Allies, on the other side of the ledger, suffered far fewer losses (70,000 casualties) and acquired invaluable experience for future campaigns.

"UNCONDITIONAL SURRENDER"

Roosevelt joined Churchill for the Casablanca Conference in January 1943. There the American delegates reluctantly acceded to British plans to follow up North Africa with an invasion of Sicily and Italy, again deferring a cross-channel operation, this time until 1944. On January 24, 1943, in the course of a press conference at this meeting, FDR released his "unconditional surrender" policy statement after, apparently, previous consultation with Churchill. The President's message to the Axis was plain and simple: "The elimination of German, Japanese and Italian war power means the unconditional surrender by Germany, Italy, and Japan."

This particular policy sought to reassure the Soviet Union, which did not officially subscribe to it until June 1944, that despite Western failures to establish an early "Second Front" on the European continent, as the Soviets had repeatedly urged, the war would be fought to a decisive conclusion. Any dealing with the enemy seemed unthinkable to most Americans and British, though there were vague fears in certain western quarters of a separate German-Soviet peace. A number of scholars have judged the policy of unconditional surrender to be a great mistake, allegedly undercutting resistance to the war within the Axis powers; although evidence points to little or no serious resistance to Hitler. Even after the war clearly turned against the Axis, German military leaders bungled an attempt upon Hitler's life in mid-1944, paying with their own lives.

The Allies invaded Sicily in July 1943, and later that month Mussolini was removed from office and placed under arrest. In early September, as Allied forces invaded southern Italy, the newly-formed Italian government sued for peace and concluded an armistice. Fighting on the peninsula continued, however, as Hitler ordered German forces into Italy and set up Mussolini as head of a puppet Italian republic. Meanwhile, the Allies, without consulting the Soviet Uions to any meaningful degree, established occupation policies for Italy on their own.

FROM THE MOSCOW CONFERENCE TO YALTA

A Conference of Foreign Ministers at Moscow in October 1943 seemed to have resolved the roadblocks to greater Allied coordination in the War and to herald a cooperative postwar world. Armed with congressional resolutions—the Fulbright Resolution from the House and the Connally Resolution from the Senate—that the U.S. intended to take advantage of a "second chance" in establishing postwar machinery aimed at building a collective security system, Cordell Hull flew to Moscow to join British Foreign Secretary Anthony Eden in conferences with Soviet leaders. Anxious to avoid disruptive debate over postwar settlement details, Hull obtained a Big Three consent to establish future United Nations Organization. The Secretary of State assured his hosts that plans for an imminent cross-channel invasion were well advanced, while Stalin, for his part, promised to throw his strength against Japan after the war in Europe had ended. The conference, which also created the European Advisory Commission and the Advisory Council for Italy, concluded on a promising note of cordiality and cooperation.

The way was now clear for the meeting with Stalin long sought by Roosevelt. FDR and Churchill met the Soviet dictator at Teheran, the capital of Iran, in late November 1943. Stalin repeated his promise to enter the war against Japan after Germany had finally been crushed. Roosevelt and Churchill both listened attentively and, presumably, favorably when Stalin sketched his postwar demands. Stalin spoke at length of Russia's historic quest for a ice-free port in Manchuria and the return of the southern half of Sakhalin Island, lost to Japan in the Russo-Japanese War of 1904. It was also agreed that the USSR should obtain pre-war Poland east of the so-called Curzon Line, with Poland being compensated with German territory up to the Oder River. The Big Three further concurred that they should jointly occupy Germany with an inter-allied zone to be established in Berlin. Thus Teheran foreshadowed the Yalta decisions. On the balance, FDR was pleased at the progress made at Teheran and was impressed by Stalin's realism. Upon his return home, the president announced that continuing cooperation had been assured among the members of the Grand Alliance.

Sweeping Allied military victories set the stage for the next summit meeting. On June 6, 1944, Anglo-American forces, under the command of General Dwight David Eisenhower, landed at Normandy in the single greatest amphibious operation in history. The invasion forces broke through the Nazi defenses and swiftly liberated France. Meanwhile, Anglo-American airpower pounded fortress Europe, aided by radar guidance and long-range aircraft. Between 8,000 and 9,000 Allied aircraft took part in a campaign that paralyzed the German transportation system by early 1945. The German economy was near collapse by March 1945. On the Eastern Front, the Soviet Union opened a grand offensive in the spring of 1944 that coincided with Allied thrusts in the West. By early February 1945, the Soviet army had driven to within 45 miles of Berlin.

As victory neared, strains appeared within the Grand Alliance. This was no less true for the West and the Soviets than it was for the British and the Americans. Various difficulties emerged involving the structure of the new world organization, the United Nations, while the Anglo-American partners quarrelled over the organization of a new Italian government, and differences with the Soviets threatened to arise over Poland. Accordingly the Big Three agreed to meet at Yalta in the Crimea for further consultation.

Roosevelt, recently victorious over the Republican nominee Thomas E. Dewey in the 1944 presidential elections, had just entered his fourth term in office. Despite his age and a tendency to tire more quickly than before, the president appeared as mentally alert as ever. The atmosphere of the Yalta Conference, which took place February 4-11, 1945, was, again, amiable. As at Teheren, President Roosevelt once again employed his personal charm, attempting to perpetuate the good relations earlier established with the Soviet dictator. And despite subsequent criticism that he was a very sick man at the time and made unnecessary and unwise concessions to "good old Uncle Joe" Stalin, available evidence indicates that FDR followed both a pragmatic and realistic course. Common sense and practical politics required recognition of the enormous gains in Soviet power and influence that the defeat of the Axis had ensured and that had in fact been conceded at Teheran.

The most pressing issues at Yalta involved the disposition of Germany and the future of postwar Europe. With regard to the former the question remained: should Germany be left a unified state or partitioned into several weaker ones? Related to this was how much in reparations for the wartime destruction should the successor to the Third Reich be forced to pay to its victims? Within the Roosevelt administration debate over such questions had produced deep divisions between the State and War Departments on the one side and the Treasury Department on the other. State Department planners together with Secretary of War Stimson believed that while Germany should be dealt with drastically, it should not be reduced to a level of semi-starvation, incapable of providing the basis for the anticipated postwar economic revival of Europe. This group was mainly concerned with preventing a revival of militarism with its attendant aggressive tendencies.

The Secretary of the Treasury, Henry Morgenthau, Jr., who as a Jew had especially deep misgivings about the German character that tried to systematically annihilation of Europe's Jewry, had developed a plan for drastic the deindustrialization and the outright partition into several states of Hitler's Germany. Such a Germany, deprived of the sinews of war, would no longer be a threat to world peace. Moreover, according to Morgenthau, Germany ought not escape the payment of heavy reparations, both in kind and in forced labor. FDR was initially attracted to the so-called Morgenthau Plan, remarking in 1944 that "every person in Germany should realize that this time Germany is a defeated nation...collectively and individually." But before long, the president was dissuaded from such a drastic approach and adopted to a more moderate one. Hence while at Yalta he still spoke of Germany in harsh terms, he actually followed a more reasoned course.

Not unlike Morgenthau, but for different reasons, Stalin too favored a drastic policy toward the defeated Nazi state. The Soviet

Union wanted large reparations to rebuild its war-shattered economy, and its leaders suggested a sum of $20 billion with half going to Moscow. As it turned out, the Big Three leaders finally agreed at Yalta to leave the amount of reparations to a special commission, with $20 billion as a discussion point and with payments to be made in capital goods and from annual production. They also left the question of German dismemberment for future discussion. In the meanwhile, it was agreed that Germany would be dividied into zones occupied by the victors, with Berlin coming under joint occupation, and a joint control commission to set policies for the whole of Germany. France joined the occupation, primarily at British insistence. Unfortunately for the West, the Conference failed to provide clearly defined access routes between the western zones and their areas of Berlin. Neither side, as yet, foresaw the rivalry that would follow the war.

As for Poland, an issue that absorbed more time than any other single topic at Yalta, Stalin insisted upon transfer to Russia of that part of prewar Poland east of the Curzon Line. The line had been drawn by the Paris Peace Conference after World War I as the most suitable demarcation between ethnic Poland and other nationalities, but the new Poland gained areas east of it as a consequence of the 1921 Soviet-Polish War. Both Western leaders saw justice in Stalin's demand and had, as indicated, already recorded their approval at Teheran. At Yalta they concentrated instead upon obtaining variations in favor of Poland's government-in-exile, but Stalin resisted all such pressures. All agreed that the new Poland deserved compensation at Germany's expense, although Churchill questioned the wisdom of Soviet proposals that would extend Polish boundaries to the Western Neisse River. The result was that Yalta set no definitive western boundary for postwar Poland.

Roosevelt and Churchill also made a great effort on behalf of a free democratic Poland, despite their acknowledge appreciation of Stalin's interest in "friendly countries" along his borders and the simple truth that Poland was being liberated solely by the Red Army. Stalin refused a supervised "free" election in the Western sense and supported the Communist-dominated Lublin government that he had already established within Poland. Churchill and FDR thereupon decided to compromise rather than endanger Allied unity. The compromise essentially involved the reorganization of the Lublin government "on a broader democratic basis, so as to include democratic leaders now in Poland." Accordingly, elections were to take place as soon as possible. Although the Polish aspect of the Yalta Agreement would come under heavy criticism in later years, it is doubtful that either Roosevelt or Churchill could have extracted more out of a determined Stalin.

Turning his attention to the war in the Pacific, the Soviet dictator reiterated his earlier promise to enter the War against Japan within two to three months after the defeat of Germany. He then asked and obtained secret concessions in the Far East in exchange. The Western leaders agreed that the Soviets should recover the Kurile Islands, southern Sakhalin, and obtain a naval base at Port Authur in Manchuria; that Darien should become an internationalized port, that the USSR should have joint control with China of the Manchurian railways, and Outer Mongolia's status as a Soviet-dominated state was recognized. Roosevelt, desirous of Soviet aid in ending the Japanese War, took the lead in making these concessions, though Churchill concurred. FDR believed that Soviet entry into the final stages of the Pacific War would further weaken the Japanese will to resist, as well as strengthening Chiang Kai-shek's regime in China presumably at the expense of communist forces. On this latter point, Stalin indicated that he would support only the Chinese Nationalists and not the communists led by Mao Tse-tung.

All in all, President Roosevelt seemed pleased with the outcome of the Conference and gave the nation, in retrospect, probably a false sense of Allied unity. In his report to Congress, FDR offered no hint of differences within the Grand Alliance. As he observed on March 1, 1945: "I think the Crimean Conference was a successful effort by the three leading nations to find a common ground for peace. It spells—and it ought to spell—the end of the system of unilateral action, exclusive alliances, and spheres of influence, and balances of power, and all the other expedients which have been tried for centuries and have always failed."

By the spring of 1945, Western forces had liberated France and pushed across the Rhine in a final drive into the heart of the

German Third Reich. In a parallel development, the Soviet Red Army began a last offensive within 30 miles of Berlin. Anticipating the political value accruing to the conqueror of the Nazi capital, the British led by Prime Minister Winston Churchill sought to launch a quick drive to reach Berlin first but were overruled on military grounds by General Dwight Eisenhower and the American government. Guided by the more calculating hand of Soviet leader Marshal Joseph Stalin, the Red Army liberated all the ancient capitals of central Europe, including Prague, Vienna and Budapest. The decision to hold back was probably a mistake, the full implications of which became clear only after the war. In any case, by the second week of April the Americans had reached the Elbe River just 63 miles from Berlin, while the Soviets prepared for the final assault.

The sudden death of President Franklin Roosevelt, of a massive cerebral hemorrhage on April 12, 1945, came at this fateful moment in the war. The feeling of loss was immense. The British *Economist* summed it up this way: "It would be difficult to find hyperbole strong enough to exaggerate the sense of loss felt all over the free world at the sudden news of President Roosevelt's death. Never before in a statesman of another country and rarely for one of our own leaders have the outward pomp of ceremonial mourning and also the inward and personal lamentation of the public been more universal and heartfelt." Much the same was said in the Soviet Union where, according to the Moscow correspondent of *The Times* of London, "President Roosevelt has been the personification of enlightened American liberalism."

When he died the United States armed forces magazine, *Yank*, observed without exaggeration that FDR had been commander-in-chief not only of the armed forces but also of a whole generation. He was the only president younger Americans had ever known; his New Deal legislation, with its humanitarian spirit of the government, was the only political program they had experienced. In World War I the federal government was still comparatively a small enterprise; by the death of Roosevelt it touched in one way or another almost every facet of American life. The question of government intervention in the American economy to promote the welfare of the people—the hallmark of the New Deal—left a lasting legacy. Equally significant, FDR gradually broke down the nation's interwar isolationist psychology and prepared for the nation's participation in World War II. Pearl Harbor together with the President's diplomacy made certain things would never be the same again.

The mantle of American leadership fell upon the shoulders of Harry S. Truman, the seventh vice-president to succeed to the presidency upon the death of the chief executive. President Truman rose to his position from humble beginnings. Born in Lamar, Missouri, on May 8, 1884, the 33rd President of the United States was educated in the public school system, operated the family farm near Independence, Missouri, and served in World War I, seeing action in France. Studying law nights for two years in the early 1920s, Truman became involved in county government and worked with Kansas City political "Boss" Tom Pendergast. Though elected to the U.S. Senate in 1934, it was not until America entered World War II that he truly distinguished himself, reaching national prominence as chairman of the Senate Committee to Investigate the National Defense Program. During his chairmanship, Truman was voted by Washington correspondents "the civilian who, next to President Roosevelt, 'knew most about the war'."

In sharp contrast to this contemporary image of Truman as a man with a strong capacity for national leadership, scholars of all political persuasions have usually portrayed him as generally uninformed about his predecessor's foreign policies who was forced to rely heavily on Roosevelt's political and military advisers. To some extent this was so for FDR had failed to bring him into the larger picture of the internal workings of the Grand Alliance, as well as knowledge of the atomic bomb project.

Still, for all these limitations, Truman was a man of his times, an avowed internationalist and an accomplished politician. Though acutely aware that, in his own words, "No man could possibly fill the tremendous void left by the passing of that noble soul [FDR]," the new occupant of the White House soon showed he was fully determined to be President in his own right, responsible for the decisions that would have to be made. Like Roosevelt, he, too, would learn the art of managing the unmanageable.

During the transition of power in Washington, Germany collapsed. As Soviet shells fell onto Berlin and exploded over his beleaguered bunker beneath the Reichschancellery, Adolph Hitler, committed suicide on April 30, 1945, his body cremated in the garden by loyal followers. Facing the inevitable, German armies surrendered unconditionally at Reims on May 7-8. The Third Reich, which was supposed to last a thousand years, was finished.

President Truman initially adhered to Roosevelt's policy of collaboration with the Soviet Union, though evidence today suggests that FDR was having second thoughts about how best to deal with Stalin. Truman, like his advisers, came to recognize that Moscow viewed conciliatory gestures as a sign of weakness. The composition of the government of the re-emerging Polish state continued to remain the great stumbling block, symbolizing in Western eyes Stalin's determination to have his own way throughout Eastern Europe and opportunity presented itself.

By the time Vyacheslav Molotov, the People's Commissar for Foreign Affairs, arrived for talks in Washington in April 1945 en route to the founding of the United Nations in San Francisco, Truman served notice, to cite an account of the shift in mood, "that our agreements with the Soviet Union so far had been a one way street and that could not continue: it was now or never." In their celebrated meeting of April 23, the president rebuked Molotov for Soviet behavior, in the roughest Missouri language. The Soviet Foreign Minister defended his nation's interpretation of the Polish accord worked out at Yalta in February, adding that he had never been spoken to in such terms. According to Truman's interpreter, Charles Bohlan, these were "probably the first sharp words uttered during the war by an American president to a high Soviet official."

On May 11, 1945, 30 days following the Nazi collapse, Truman ordered a sharp cutback in lend-lease shipments, including those to the Soviet Union; unfortunately, subordinates enforced the directive even more narrowly than the president probably intended, recalling Russian-bound ships at sea. Lend-lease to the USSR had previously been on a special—no information requested, no conditions of any kind—basis and apparently the president meant to send a signal to the Kremlin indicating a change in attitude.

Stalin professed to be deeply pained and offended by the order, though the episode was soon smoothed over.

THE POTSDAM CONFERENCE

The way was then cleared for the last of the wartime summit conferences—code-named "Terminal"—held at Potsdam, near Berlin, from July 17 to August 2, 1945. Churchill was replaced midway through the Conference by Clement Atlee whose Labor Party had won the recent general election. The Allies (excluding the USSR on Japanese matters) agreed to issue a last warning to surrender to Tokyo, and to establish a Council of Foreign Ministers to prepare treaties for Italy and the lesser Axis states, ie, Rumania, Hungary, Bulgaria and Finland. Moreover, the Big Three reaffirmed the policy of a joint occupation of vanquished Germany with fixed zonal boundaries. The vexing problem of reparations was also settled.

According to the compromise reached, each occupying force would obtain its share of reparations from its own zone, with the Soviet Union to be compensated for its greater losses by 25 percent of the capital goods located within the western industrialized zones, a part of which would in turn be exchanged for food shipments from the largely agricultural areas occupied by the Soviet element. Moreover, the occupying forces were to embark on an overall program designed to denazify, decentralize, disarm, and democratize Germany until such time as it was deemed fit to rejoin the family of nations. Finally, Stalin, who was still technically at peace with Tokyo, agreed to enter into the war against Japan on August 15, making good a pledge given earlier.

Potsdam, not unlike the Yalta Conference before it, ended on a note of apparent friendship and continued cooperation. Truman's diary makes it clear that Stalin greatly impressed the president: "He [Stalin] is honest—but smart as hell." Still, Truman and the American planners were much less optimistic than their public remarks indicated. Soviet leaders had all too clearly revealed the unilateralness of their concept of cooperation and their own plans for the future of eastern Europe. Many years later Truman recalled:

I hardly ever look back for the purpose of contemplating 'what might have been:' Potsdam brings to mind 'what might have been.' ...Certainly...Russia had no program except to take over the free part of Europe, kill as many Germans as possible, and fool the Western Alliance. Britain only wanted to control the Eastern Mediterranean, keep India, oil in Persia, the Suez Canal, and whatever else was floating loose.

There was an innocent idealist at one corner that Round Table who wanted free waterways—Danube-Rhine-Kiel Canal, Suez, Black Sea Straits, Panama—a restoration of Germany, France, Italy, Poland, Czechoslovakia, Rumania, and the Balkans, and a proper treatment of Latvia, Lithuania, Finland, free Philippines, Indonesia, Indo-China, a Chinese Republic, and a free Japan.

What a show that was! But a large number of agreements were reached in spite of the set up—only to be broken as soon as the unconscionable Russian dictator returned to Moscow! And I liked the little son of a bitch....

The shape of the Cold War loomed ahead by the closing days of World War II.

JAPAN COLLAPSES IN THE PACIFIC

Long-range B-29 bombers from Guam and other island bases had begun to rain destruction upon Japan by the close of 1944, culminating the next year in an even larger air offensive. In all, approximately 160,000 tons of bombs were dropped upon Japan toward the end of the war, including firebomb raids that destroyed the center of Tokyo and other large Japanese cities. These raids alone killed some 333,000 Japanese and wounded an additional one-half million. Air raids by July 1945 had, then, all but smashed the Japanese war economy.

Although elements within Japan long recognized they had lost the war and were prepared to sue for peace, the American government, still committed to a policy of unconditional surrender, was not inclined to bargain with them. Truman's warning to the Japanese issued at Potsdam to surrender or face total destruction still stood. The Japanese government and the Emperor favored making peace, but the militarists, led by the Army resisted. No less than one million American and Allied casualties were estimated by the Joint Chiefs of Staff to be the cost of invading the home islands.

Faced with this prospect, Truman and his advisers determined to use the atomic bomb against Japan, in order to conclude the war as quickly as possible. On the morning of August 6, 1945 shortly after 8.00 am, a lone B-29 bomber dropped the first atomic bomb on Hiroshima (population 350,000), the second most important military center in Japan, killing 140,000 people on the day of the attack and in the weeks immediately after it. The first atomic bomb to be used possessed the equivalent of only 12,500 tons of TNT— puny and primitive by current thermonuclear standards. Still, sixty per cent of Hiroshima, an area equal to one-eighth of Manhattan, was destroyed. Three days later a second, slightly larger, atomic bomb was dropped on the city of Nagasaki, an important industrial and shipping area with a population of 253,000 of whom 70,000 were ultimately killed. The second atomic bomb possessed more power than 20,000 tons of TNT, a destructive force equivalent to the collective load of 4,000 B-29 bombers.

Though it was not admitted at the time, many residents of both cities would subsequently succumb to radiation illness; there were patients who had not been wounded but were wasting away. Japanese doctors were at a loss to explain it. In the U.S. there was a mixed reaction: "There was," according to one account, "an element of elation in the realization that we had perfected this devastating weapon for employment against an enemy who started the war and has told us he would rather be destroyed than surrender...[yet] there was sobering awareness of the tremendous responsibility involved." A turning point in the history of the world had been reached.

Meanwhile, reluctant to miss out on the kill, the Soviet Union declared war on Japan on August 8, a week sooner than the pledge Stalin gave to Truman at Potsdam. Nine minutes after its declaration, the Soviet Union's Far Eastern Army and Air Force attacked Japanese troops along the eastern Soviet-Manchuria borderlands. Yielding to the reality of the situation, the Emperor, supported by civilian advisers, finally overcame the Japanese militarists and ordered a surrender on August 14. For its part, the U.S. agreed to retain the institution of the Emperor system, stripped of pretension to divinity and subject to American occupation headed by General Douglas MacArthur.

On September 2, a great Allied fleet sailed into Tokyo Bay for the formal surrender ceremony which took place on board the USS Missouri. World War II was thus brought to a close.

SUGGESTED READINGS

Ambrose, Stephen. *Eisenhower* (1983).

Barilek, Richard E. *A Loyal Opposition in Time of War* (1976).

Beard, Charles A. *President Roosevelt and the Coming of War, 1941*(1948).

Beitzell, Robert. *The Uneasy Alliance* (1977).

Blum, John Morton. *V Was for Victory* (1976).

Buchanan, A. Russell. *The United States and World War II*, 2 vols. (1965).

Campbell, D'Ann. *Women at War with America* (1984).

Dalfuime, Richard M. *Desegregation of the US Armed Forces* (1975).

Daniels, Roger. *Concentration Camp USA* (1971).

Divine, Robert A. *A Second Chance* (1967).

Greenfield, Kent R. *American Strategy in World War II: A Reconsideration* (1963).

Hartman, Susan M. *The Home Front and Beyond* (1987).

Leckie, Robert. *Delivered from Evil* (1987).

Leigh, Michael. *Mobilizing Consent: Public Opinion and American Foreign Policy, 1937-1947* (1976).

Morison, Samuel Eliot. *Strategy and Compromise* (1958).

O'Connor, Raymond G. *Diplomacy for Victory: FDR and Unconditional Surrender* (1971).

Prange, Gordon W. *At Dawn We Slept: The Untold Story of Pearl Harbor* (1981).

Rose, Lisle A. *Dubious Victory: The United States and the End of World War II* (1974).

Sherwin, Martin J. *A World Destroyed* (1975).

Shogan, Robert and Craig, Tom. *The Detroit Race Riot* (1964).

Siracusa, Joseph M. *The American Diplomatic Revolution: A Documentary History of the Cold War, 1941-1947* (1976).

___. *New Left Diplomatic Histories and Historians: The American Revisionists* , 2d ed. (1993).

___. "The Night Stalin and Churchill Divided Europe," *Review of Politics* 43 (1981): 381-409.

Smith, Gaddis. *Diplomacy During the Second World War* (1965).

Theoharis, Athan G. *The Yalta Myths* (1971).

Waller, Geroge M., ed. *Pearl Harbor: Roosevelt and the Coming of War* (1976).

Weglyn, Michi. *Years of Infancy: The Untold Story of America's Concentration Camps* (1976).

Weigley, Russell F. *The American Way of War* (1973).

Winkler, Allan M. *The Politics of Propaganda: The Office of War Information, 1942-1945* (1978).

Wohlsetter, Roberta. *Pearl Harbor: Warning and Decision* (1967).

Yergin, Daniel. *Shattered Peace* (1977).

Young, Roland. *Congressional Politics in the Second World War* (1956).